First World War
and Army of Occupation
War Diary
France, Belgium and Germany

4 DIVISION
10 Infantry Brigade
Royal Dublin Fusiliers
2nd Battalion
22 August 1914 - 31 October 1916

WO95/1481/4

The Naval & Military Press Ltd
www.nmarchive.com
Published in association with The National Archives

Published by

The Naval & Military Press Ltd

Unit 10 Ridgewood Industrial Park,

Uckfield, East Sussex,

TN22 5QE England

Tel: +44 (0) 1825 749494

www.naval-military-press.com

www.nmarchive.com

This diary has been reprinted in facsimile from the original. Any imperfections are inevitably reproduced and the quality may fall short of modern type and cartographic standards.

Contents

Document type	Place/Title	Date From	Date To
Heading	4th Division 10th Inf Bde 2nd Battalion Royal Dublin Fusiliers Aug-Dec 1914		
Heading	10th Brigade 4th Division Disembarked Boulogne 23.814 2nd Battalion Royal Dublin Fusiliers August 1914		
War Diary	Harrow	22/08/1914	22/08/1914
War Diary	Boulogne	23/08/1914	24/08/1914
War Diary	Beaumont	25/08/1914	25/08/1914
War Diary	Haucourt	26/08/1914	26/08/1914
War Diary	Le Catelet	27/08/1914	27/08/1914
War Diary	Voyennes	28/08/1914	28/08/1914
War Diary	Bussy	29/08/1914	29/08/1914
War Diary	Beaurains	29/08/1914	29/08/1914
War Diary	Noyon	30/08/1914	30/08/1914
War Diary	Berneuil-Aux-Line	31/08/1914	31/08/1914
Heading	Appendix I Battle Of Haucourt Aug 26/1914 Casualties		
Miscellaneous	Appendix I	24/09/1914	24/09/1914
Heading	Appendix II Battle of Haucourt 26 Aug 1914 Distribution Of Battalion After Battle		
Miscellaneous	Appendix II Distribution of Battn. after Battle of Haucourt	26/08/1914	26/08/1914
Heading	Appendix III Battle of Haucourt 26 Aug 1914 General Remarks-Equipment		
Miscellaneous	Appendix III General Remarks Equipment	24/09/1914	24/09/1914
Heading	Battle of Haucourt 26 Aug 1914 Account By Capt Watson (Adjt)		
Miscellaneous	Account By Capt Watson Ajt 2nd Royal Dublin Fusiliers Haucourt	20/09/1914	20/09/1914
Heading	10th Brigade 4th Division 2nd Battalion Royal Dublin Fusiliers September 1914		
War Diary	Nery	01/09/1914	01/09/1914
War Diary	Baron	02/09/1914	02/09/1914
War Diary	Dammartin	03/09/1914	03/09/1914
War Diary	Lussigny	04/09/1914	04/09/1914
War Diary	Magny-Le-Hongres	05/09/1914	05/09/1914
War Diary	Chevry	05/09/1914	06/09/1914
War Diary	Voulangis (near)	07/09/1914	07/09/1914
War Diary	Le Fermiere Fm	08/09/1914	08/09/1914
War Diary	Jouarre	09/09/1914	09/09/1914
War Diary	Popelain	10/09/1914	10/09/1914
War Diary	Coulombs	11/09/1914	11/09/1914
War Diary	Villers Le Petit	12/09/1914	12/09/1914
War Diary	Septmonts	13/09/1914	13/09/1914
War Diary	La Montagne	14/09/1914	30/09/1914
Heading	Sketch "A"		
Diagram etc	Diagram		
Heading	Sketch "B"		
Diagram etc	Trenches		
Heading	Appendix I & Sketch "C"		
Miscellaneous	Appendix I		

Diagram etc	Rough Sketch Of Protected Latrine		
Heading	4th Div. 10th Bde. War Diary 2nd Batt. Royal Dublin Fusiliers October 1914		
War Diary	Bucy Le Long	01/10/1914	01/10/1914
War Diary	St Marguerite	02/10/1914	06/10/1914
War Diary	Hartenns	07/10/1914	07/10/1914
War Diary	Oulchy La Ville	08/10/1914	08/10/1914
War Diary	Pisseleux	08/10/1914	11/10/1914
War Diary	St Omer	12/10/1914	12/10/1914
War Diary	Hazebrouck	13/10/1914	13/10/1914
War Diary	Fletre	13/10/1914	13/10/1914
War Diary	Fontaine	14/10/1914	14/10/1914
War Diary	Meteren	15/10/1914	15/10/1914
War Diary	Bailleul	16/10/1914	16/10/1914
War Diary	Armentieres	17/10/1914	28/10/1914
War Diary	Houplines	29/10/1914	31/10/1914
Heading	Appendix I.		
Miscellaneous	Appendix I	02/11/1914	02/11/1914
Heading	Order Received From The Brigade On 13th Oct 1914		
Miscellaneous			
Heading	Rough Sketch Of Trenches Of R.Dub Fus: Oct 23rd 1914		
Diagram etc	Diagram		
Heading	4th Div. 10th Bde. War Diary 2nd Batt. Royal Dublin Fusiliers November 1914		
War Diary		01/11/1914	30/11/1914
Miscellaneous			
Heading	4th Div. 10th Bde. War Diary 2nd Batt. Royal Dublin Fusiliers December 1914		
War Diary	St Yves	01/12/1914	01/12/1914
War Diary	Nieppe	02/12/1914	04/12/1914
War Diary	St Yves	05/12/1914	08/12/1914
War Diary	Saint L3	09/12/1914	09/12/1914
War Diary	La. Creche	10/12/1914	11/12/1914
War Diary	63	12/12/1914	12/12/1914
War Diary	St.Yves	13/12/1914	24/12/1914
War Diary	Point 63	25/12/1914	28/12/1914
War Diary	St. Yves	29/12/1914	31/12/1914
Heading	Appendix I		
Miscellaneous	Appendix I	02/01/1915	02/01/1915
Heading	4th Division 10th Infantry Bde 2nd Battn Royal Dublin Fus January To 20th June 1915		
Heading	10th Inf. Bde. 4th Div. 2nd Battn. The Royal Dublin Fusiliers January 1915		
War Diary	St. Yves	01/01/1915	01/01/1915
War Diary	La. Creche	02/01/1915	05/01/1915
War Diary	St. Yves	06/01/1915	09/01/1915
War Diary	La Courte Dreve	10/01/1915	12/01/1915
War Diary	St. Yves	13/01/1915	16/01/1915
War Diary	La. Creche	17/01/1915	20/01/1915
War Diary	St. Yves	21/01/1915	24/01/1915
War Diary	La. Courte Dreve	25/01/1915	28/01/1915
War Diary	St. Yves	29/01/1915	31/01/1915
Heading	Appendices 1 & 2		
Miscellaneous	Appendix I		

Miscellaneous	Appendix 2. 2nd Bn Royal Dublin Fusiliers List of Re-Inforcements January 1915		
Heading	10th Inf. Bde. 4th Div. 2nd Battn. The Royal Dublin Fusiliers February 1915		
War Diary	St Yves	01/02/1915	01/02/1915
War Diary	La Creche	02/02/1915	05/02/1915
War Diary	St Yves	06/02/1915	09/02/1915
War Diary	.63	10/02/1915	13/02/1915
War Diary	St. Yves	14/02/1915	17/02/1915
War Diary	La Creche	18/02/1915	21/02/1915
War Diary	St. Yves	22/02/1915	25/02/1915
War Diary	.63	26/02/1915	28/02/1915
Heading	Appendix 1		
Miscellaneous	2nd Bn Dub. Fus. Casualties In Action During February 1915		
Heading	10th Inf. Bde. 4th. Div 2nd Battn. The Royal Dublin Fusiliers March 1915		
War Diary	Pt. 63	01/03/1915	01/03/1915
War Diary	St. Yves	02/03/1915	05/03/1915
War Diary	La. Creche	06/03/1915	09/03/1915
War Diary	St. Yves	10/03/1915	13/03/1915
War Diary	Pt. 63	14/03/1915	14/03/1915
War Diary	Pont. Nieppe	15/03/1915	17/03/1915
War Diary	St. Yves	18/03/1915	21/03/1915
War Diary	La. Creche	22/03/1915	24/03/1915
War Diary	Steenbeque	25/03/1915	29/03/1915
War Diary	Pt. 63	30/03/1915	31/03/1915
Heading	Appendices 1 & 2		
War Diary	Appendix No.1 2nd Bn Royal Dublin Fusiliers		
Miscellaneous	Appendix No.2 2nd Bn Royal Dublin Fusilier		
Heading	10th Inf. Bde. 4th Div. 2nd Battn. The Royal Dublin Fusiliers April 1915		
War Diary	Billets at La Hutte (pt.63)	01/04/1915	01/04/1915
War Diary	Trenches	02/04/1915	06/04/1915
War Diary	Billets at La Creche	07/04/1915	09/04/1915
War Diary	Billets at La Creche	10/04/1915	10/04/1915
War Diary	Trenches (Douvre)	11/04/1915	11/04/1915
War Diary	Trenches	12/04/1915	12/04/1915
War Diary	Bailleul	13/04/1915	23/04/1915
War Diary	On Line of March	24/04/1915	24/04/1915
War Diary	(Attack On) St. Julien	25/04/1915	30/04/1915
Heading	10th Inf. Bde. 4th Div. 2nd Battn. The Royal Dublin Fusiliers May 1915		
War Diary	Trenches (Faliny St. Julien)	01/05/1915	04/05/1915
War Diary	Bivouac (E. Bank of Canal)	05/05/1915	05/05/1915
War Diary	Bivouac (Chateau Des Trois Tours)	06/05/1915	08/05/1915
War Diary	Trenches (Wieltje)	09/05/1915	12/05/1915
War Diary	Bivouac Vlamertinghe Chateau	13/05/1915	16/05/1915
War Diary	Trenches (Div. Support Line)	17/05/1915	19/05/1915
War Diary	Trenches (Front Line)	20/05/1915	24/05/1915
War Diary	Bivouac (Canal Bank)	25/05/1915	25/05/1915
War Diary	Bivouac (Vlamertinghe Chateau)	26/05/1915	26/05/1915
War Diary	Bivouac (with 1st L of Transpt.)	27/05/1915	31/05/1915
Heading	Casualty List		
Miscellaneous	Remarks And References To Appendices Casualties & Drafts	12/08/1915	12/08/1915

Heading	Report On Action Of 24th May		
Miscellaneous	2nd Royal Dublin Fusiliers Report on Action	24/05/1915	24/05/1915
Heading	10th Inf. Bde 4th Div. 2nd Battn. The Royal Dublin Fusiliers June 1915		
War Diary	Canal Bank Wood La Bridge	01/06/1915	04/06/1915
War Diary	Bivouac in Woods Vlamertinghe Chateau	05/06/1915	06/06/1915
War Diary	Canal West Bank Zwaanhoff Bridge	07/06/1915	15/06/1915
War Diary	Reserve Trenches Canal Bank	16/06/1915	22/06/1915
War Diary	C.19.13 (Sheet 27)	23/06/1915	28/06/1915
War Diary	Billets A16A	29/06/1915	30/06/1915
Heading	Casualty & Reinforcement List		
Miscellaneous	Remarks And References To Appendices		
Heading	4th Divisions 10th Infantry Bde 2nd Battn Royal Dublin Fles July To 31st December 1915		
Heading	10th Inf. Bde. 4th Div. 2nd Battn. The Royal Dublin Fusiliers July 1915		
War Diary	A.16.A	01/07/1915	09/07/1915
War Diary	Houtkerque	10/07/1915	22/07/1915
War Diary	Line Of March	23/07/1915	23/07/1915
War Diary	Vauchelles-Les-Authie	24/07/1915	25/07/1915
War Diary	Bertrancourt	26/07/1915	26/07/1915
War Diary	Trenches	27/07/1915	30/07/1915
War Diary	Bertrancourt	31/07/1915	31/07/1915
Heading	Casualty & Reinforcement List		
Miscellaneous	Appendix to War Diary		
Heading	10th Inf. Bde. 4th Div. 2nd Battn. The Royal Dublin Fusiliers August 1915		
War Diary	Bertrancourt	01/08/1915	02/08/1915
War Diary	Lealvillers	03/08/1915	08/08/1915
War Diary	Trenches	09/08/1915	22/08/1915
War Diary	Mailly, Maillet	23/08/1915	31/08/1915
Heading	Casualty & Reinforcement List		
Miscellaneous	Remarks And References To Appendices		
Heading	10th Inf. Bde. 4th Div. 2nd Battn. The Royal Dublin Fusiliers September 1915		
War Diary	Mailly-Maillet	01/09/1915	01/09/1915
War Diary	Auchonvillers	02/09/1915	09/09/1915
War Diary	Forceville	10/09/1915	15/09/1915
War Diary	Trenches	16/09/1915	22/09/1915
War Diary	Varennes	24/09/1915	24/09/1915
War Diary	Courcelles	25/09/1915	29/09/1915
War Diary	Trenches	30/09/1915	30/09/1915
Heading	Casualty & Reinforcement List		
Miscellaneous	Appendix to War Diary Sept 1915		
Heading	10th Inf. Bde. 4th Div. 2nd Battn. The Royal Dublin Fusiliers October 1915		
War Diary	Trenches	01/10/1915	06/10/1915
War Diary	Acheux	07/10/1915	13/10/1915
War Diary	In The Trenches	14/10/1915	20/10/1915
War Diary	Mailley-Maillet	21/10/1915	30/10/1915
War Diary	Trenches	30/10/1915	31/10/1915
Heading	Casualty & Reinforcement List		
Miscellaneous	Appendices to War Diary		
Heading	10th Inf. Bde. 4th Div. 2nd Battn. The Royal Dublin Fusiliers November 1915		
War Diary	In The Trenches	01/11/1915	07/11/1915

War Diary	Forcevillle	08/11/1915	14/11/1915
War Diary	In The Trenches	14/11/1915	20/11/1915
War Diary	Varennes	20/11/1915	30/11/1915
Heading	Casualty & Reinforcement List		
Miscellaneous	Appendices to War Diary		
Heading	10th Inf. Bde. 4th Div. 2nd Battn. The Royal Dublin Fusiliers December 1915		
War Diary		01/12/1915	30/12/1915
Heading	Casualty & Reinforcement List		
Miscellaneous	Appendices to War Diary for December 1915		
Heading	4th Division 10th Bde 2nd Battn Royal Dublin Fus February To June 1916		
Heading	2nd R.Dublin January 1916 Missing		
Miscellaneous			
Heading	10th Brigade 4th Division 2nd Battalion Royal Dublin Fusiliers February 1916		
Miscellaneous	Acknowledge		
War Diary	Forceville	01/02/1916	02/02/1916
War Diary	Trenches	03/02/1916	05/02/1916
War Diary	Colincamps	06/02/1916	07/02/1916
War Diary	Orville	08/02/1916	29/02/1916
Miscellaneous	2nd Bn Royal Dublin Fusiliers Appendix To War Diary February 1916		
Miscellaneous	2nd Bn Royal Dublin Fusiliers Appendix No.2 To War Diary February 1916		
Miscellaneous	2nd Bn Royal Dublin Fusiliers In The Field	05/02/1916	05/02/1916
Miscellaneous	Perforated Sheet Giving detail of Personnel and Horses Wanting to Complete shown on Army Form B 213	05/02/1916	05/02/1916
Miscellaneous	2nd Bn Royal Dublin Fusiliers In The Field	12/02/1916	12/02/1916
Miscellaneous	In The Field	18/02/1916	18/02/1916
Miscellaneous	Perforated Sheet Giving detail of Personnel and Horses Wanting to Complete shown on Army Form B 213	12/02/1916	12/02/1916
Miscellaneous	2nd Battalion Royal Dublin Trenches In The Field	19/02/1916	19/02/1916
Miscellaneous	In The Field	19/02/1916	19/02/1916
Miscellaneous	Perforated Sheet Giving detail of Personnel and Horses Wanting to Complete shown on Army Form B 213	19/02/1916	19/02/1916
Miscellaneous	2nd Bn Royal Dublin Fusiliers In The Field	26/02/1916	26/02/1916
Miscellaneous	In The Field	26/02/1916	26/02/1916
Miscellaneous	Perforated Sheet Giving detail of Personnel and Horses Wanting to Complete shown on Army Form B 213	26/02/1916	26/02/1916
Miscellaneous	Special Order Of The Day By His Majesty The King	01/11/1915	01/11/1915
Heading	10th Brigade 4th Division 2nd Battalion Royal Dublin Fusiliers March 1916		
Heading	2 R Dublin Fus Vol XIX		
War Diary	Orville	01/03/1916	02/03/1916
War Diary	St Amand	03/03/1916	17/03/1916
War Diary	Trenches	18/03/1916	21/03/1916
War Diary	Bienvillers	22/03/1916	25/03/1916
War Diary	Trenches	26/03/1916	31/03/1916
Heading	Appendices to War Diary March 1916		
Heading	10th Brigade 4th Division 2nd Battalion Royal Dublin Fusiliers April 1916		
Heading	2 R. Dublin Fus Vol XX		
War Diary	Bienvillers	01/04/1916	05/04/1916
War Diary	Trenches	06/04/1916	12/04/1916
War Diary	Bienvillers	13/04/1916	18/04/1916

War Diary	Trenches	19/04/1916	24/04/1916
War Diary	Bienvillers	25/04/1916	30/04/1916
Miscellaneous	2nd Bn Royal Dublin Fusiliers Appendix To War Diary Month Of April 1916		
Heading	10th Brigade 4th Division 2nd Battalion Royal Dublin Fusiliers May 1916		
War Diary	St. Amand	01/05/1916	01/05/1916
War Diary	Halloy	02/05/1916	02/05/1916
War Diary	Mezerolles	03/05/1916	05/05/1916
War Diary	Cramont	06/05/1916	15/05/1916
War Diary	Longvillers	16/05/1916	21/05/1916
War Diary	Argenvillers	22/05/1916	31/05/1916
Miscellaneous	Appendix to War Diary 2nd Bn Royal Dublin Fusiliers Month of May 1916		
Heading	10th Brigade 4th Division 2nd Battalion Royal Dublin Fusiliers June 1916		
War Diary	Agenvillers	01/06/1916	01/06/1916
War Diary	Bernaville	04/06/1916	04/06/1916
War Diary	Authie	05/06/1916	10/06/1916
War Diary	Bertrancourt	11/06/1916	14/06/1916
War Diary	In The Trenches	14/06/1916	14/06/1916
War Diary	Tenderloin Street	14/06/1916	17/06/1916
War Diary	Mailly-Maillet	18/06/1916	26/06/1916
War Diary	Beaussart	26/06/1916	29/06/1916
War Diary	In The Trenches	30/06/1916	30/06/1916
Miscellaneous	2nd Bn Royal Dublin Fusiliers Appendix To War Diary Month Of June 1916		
Miscellaneous	In The Field	03/06/1916	03/06/1916
Miscellaneous	2nd Bn Royal Dublin Fusiliers In The Field	10/06/1916	10/06/1916
Miscellaneous	2nd Bn Royal Dublin Fusiliers In The Field	17/06/1916	17/06/1916
Miscellaneous	2nd Bn Royal Dublin Fusiliers In The Field	24/06/1916	24/06/1916
Miscellaneous	2nd Bn Royal Dublin Fusiliers In The Field	30/06/1916	30/06/1916
Miscellaneous	2nd Bn Royal Dublin Fusiliers In The Field	04/06/1916	04/06/1916
Miscellaneous	In The Field	04/06/1916	04/06/1916
Miscellaneous	2nd Bn Royal Dublin Fusiliers In The Field	10/06/1916	10/06/1916
Miscellaneous	In The Field	10/06/1916	10/06/1916
Miscellaneous	2nd Bn Royal Dublin Fus In The Field	17/06/1916	17/06/1916
Miscellaneous	In The Field	17/06/1916	17/06/1916
Miscellaneous	2nd Bn Royal Dublin Fusiliers In The Field	24/06/1916	24/06/1916
Miscellaneous	In The Field	24/06/1916	24/06/1916
Miscellaneous	Field Return	30/06/1916	30/06/1916
Miscellaneous	In The Field	30/06/1916	30/06/1916
Miscellaneous		30/06/1916	30/06/1916
Miscellaneous	Perforated Sheet Giving detail of Personnel and Horses Wanting to Complete shown on Army Form B 213	24/06/1916	24/06/1916
Miscellaneous	Perforated Sheet Giving detail of Personnel and Horses Wanting to Complete shown on Army Form B 213	17/06/1916	17/06/1916
Miscellaneous	Perforated Sheet Giving detail of Personnel and Horses Wanting to Complete shown on Army Form B 213	16/06/1916	16/06/1916
Miscellaneous	Perforated Sheet detail of Personnel and Horses Wanting to Complete, Shown on Army Form B 213	03/06/1916	03/06/1916
Heading	4th Division 10th Bde 2nd Battn Royal Dublin Fus July To October		
Heading	10th Brigade 4th Division 2nd Battalion Royal Dublin Fusiliers July 1916		
War Diary	Trenches H.Q. Tenderloin St	01/07/1916	02/07/1916

War Diary	Mailly-Maillet	03/07/1916	06/07/1916
War Diary	Bn H.Q. Tenderloin	07/07/1916	14/07/1916
War Diary	Forceville Road	15/07/1916	17/07/1916
War Diary	Bertrancourt	17/07/1916	19/07/1916
War Diary	Beauval	20/07/1916	22/07/1916
War Diary	Proven	23/07/1916	26/07/1916
War Diary	Yser Canal Bank	27/07/1916	27/07/1916
Miscellaneous	In The Field	01/07/1916	01/07/1916
Miscellaneous	2nd Bn Royal Dublin Fusiliers Appendix To War Diary Month Of July 1916	31/07/1916	31/07/1916
Miscellaneous	2nd Royal Dublin Fus In The Field	08/07/1916	08/07/1916
Miscellaneous	In The Field	08/07/1916	08/07/1916
Miscellaneous	Perforated Sheet Giving detail of Personnel and Horses Wanting to Complete shown on Army Form B 213	08/07/1916	08/07/1916
Miscellaneous	2nd Bn Roy Dublin Fus In The Field	16/07/1916	16/07/1916
Miscellaneous	Perforated Sheet Giving detail of Personnel and Horses Wanting to Complete shown on Army Form B 213	15/07/1916	15/07/1916
Miscellaneous	2nd Bn Royal Dublin Fus In The Field	23/07/1916	23/07/1916
Miscellaneous	In The Field	23/07/1916	23/07/1916
Miscellaneous	Perforated Sheet Giving detail of Personnel and Horses Wanting to Complete shown on Army Form B 213	25/07/1916	25/07/1916
Miscellaneous	2nd Bn Royal Dublin Fus In The Field	30/07/1916	30/07/1916
Miscellaneous	In The Field	30/07/1916	30/07/1916
Miscellaneous	Perforated Sheet Giving detail of Personnel and Horses Wanting to Complete shown on Army Form B 213	29/07/1916	29/07/1916
Miscellaneous	1 Second In Command Urgently Required		
Miscellaneous	In The Field	08/07/1916	08/07/1916
Miscellaneous	In The Field	16/07/1916	16/07/1916
Miscellaneous	In The Field	25/07/1916	25/07/1916
Miscellaneous	In The Field	30/07/1916	30/07/1916
Heading	10th Brigade 4th Division 2nd Battalion Royal Dublin Fusiliers August 1916		
War Diary	Trenches Camp "P"	01/08/1916	11/08/1916
War Diary	H.Q. Elverdinghe Chateau	12/08/1916	13/08/1916
War Diary	H.Q. Trois Tours Chateau	14/08/1916	15/08/1916
War Diary	H.Q. Canal Bank	16/08/1916	20/08/1916
War Diary	M Camp	21/08/1916	24/08/1916
War Diary	E Camp	24/08/1916	24/08/1916
War Diary	Winnipeg Camp	24/08/1916	24/08/1916
War Diary	Dickebush Area 19.b.3.5	24/08/1916	24/08/1916
War Diary	Winnipeg Camp	25/08/1916	28/08/1916
War Diary	Trenches Opposite Hill 60	29/08/1916	31/08/1916
Miscellaneous	2nd Bn Royal Dublin Fusiliers Appendix To War Diary Month Of August 1916	03/09/1916	03/09/1916
Miscellaneous	In The Field	06/08/1916	06/08/1916
Miscellaneous	In The Field	13/08/1916	13/08/1916
Miscellaneous	In The Field	19/08/1916	19/08/1916
Miscellaneous	In The Field	27/08/1916	27/08/1916
Miscellaneous	2nd Bn Royal Dublin Fus At In The Field	06/08/1916	06/08/1916
Miscellaneous	In The Field	06/08/1916	06/08/1916
Miscellaneous	In The Field	13/08/1916	13/08/1916
Miscellaneous	2nd Bn Royal Dublin Fus At In The Field	19/08/1916	19/08/1916
Miscellaneous	In The Field	19/08/1916	19/08/1916
Miscellaneous	No of Report 50	27/08/1916	27/08/1916
Miscellaneous	In The Field	27/08/1916	27/08/1916

Miscellaneous	Perforated Sheet Giving detail of Personnel and Horses Wanting to Complete shown on Army Form B 213	27/08/1916	27/08/1916
Miscellaneous	A Second in Command Urgently Required		
Miscellaneous	1 Second In Command Urgently Required		
Miscellaneous		19/08/1916	19/08/1916
Miscellaneous	1 Second In Command Urgently Required		
Miscellaneous	Perforated Sheet Giving detail of Personnel and Horses Wanting to Complete shown on Army Form B 213	13/08/1916	13/08/1916
Miscellaneous	Perforated Sheet Giving detail of Personnel and Horses Wanting to Complete shown on Army Form B 213	06/08/1916	06/08/1916
Miscellaneous	1 Second-In-Command Urgently Required		
Miscellaneous	Nominal Roll of Officers For Week Ending 4-8-16	04/08/1916	04/08/1916
Heading	10th Brigade 4th Division 2nd Battalion Royal Dublin Fusiliers September 1916		
War Diary	Trenches H.Q Opposite "The Dump"	01/09/1916	01/09/1916
War Diary	Erie Camp G.11.c.7.4	02/09/1916	03/09/1916
War Diary	Poperinghe	04/09/1916	04/09/1916
War Diary	Rue De Furnes	05/09/1916	09/09/1916
War Diary	En Route	09/09/1916	09/09/1916
War Diary	Tatinghem	10/09/1916	16/09/1916
War Diary	En Route	17/09/1916	17/09/1916
War Diary	Rainneville	17/09/1916	23/09/1916
War Diary	Cordie	24/09/1916	24/09/1916
War Diary	Sailly-Le-Sec	25/09/1916	28/09/1916
War Diary	Daours	29/09/1916	30/09/1916
Miscellaneous	2nd Bn Royal Dublin Fusrs Appendix To War Diary Month Of September 1916		
Miscellaneous	In The Field	02/09/1916	02/09/1916
Miscellaneous	In The Field	09/09/1916	09/09/1916
Miscellaneous	In The Field	16/09/1916	16/09/1916
Miscellaneous	In The Field	24/09/1916	24/09/1916
Miscellaneous	In The Field	30/09/1916	30/09/1916
Miscellaneous	No of Report 50	02/09/1916	02/09/1916
Miscellaneous	In The Field	02/09/1916	02/09/1916
Miscellaneous	No of Report 51	09/09/1916	09/09/1916
Miscellaneous	In The Field	08/09/1916	08/09/1916
Miscellaneous	No of Report 52	16/09/1916	16/09/1916
Miscellaneous	In The Field	16/09/1916	16/09/1916
Miscellaneous	No of Report 53	24/09/1916	24/09/1916
Miscellaneous	In The Field	24/09/1916	24/09/1916
Miscellaneous	No of Report 54	30/09/1916	30/09/1916
Miscellaneous	In The Field	30/09/1916	30/09/1916
Miscellaneous	Perforated Sheet Giving detail of Personnel and Horses Wanting to Complete shown on Army Form B 213	30/09/1916	30/09/1916
Miscellaneous	1 Sergt Shoemaker to replace Sgt Hayes Due from Discharge November		
Miscellaneous	Perforated Sheet Giving detail of Personnel and Horses Wanting to Complete shown on Army Form B 213	24/09/1916	24/09/1916
Miscellaneous	Perforated Sheet Giving detail of Personnel and Horses Wanting to Complete shown on Army Form B 213	16/09/1916	16/09/1916
Miscellaneous	1 Sergt Shoemaker to replace Sgt Hayes Due from Discharge November		
Miscellaneous	Perforated Sheet Giving detail of Personnel and Horses Wanting to Complete shown on Army Form B 213	08/09/1916	08/09/1916
Miscellaneous	1 Sergt Shoemaker to replace Sgt Hayes Due from Discharge November		

Miscellaneous	Perforated Sheet Giving detail of Personnel and Horses Wanting to Complete shown on Army Form B 213	03/09/1916	03/09/1916
Miscellaneous	1 Second in Command urgently required		
Heading	10th Brigade 4th Division Battalion Transferred To 48th Bde 16th Division 15th Nov. 1916 2nd Battalion Royal Dublin Fusiliers October 1916		
War Diary	Daours	01/10/1916	12/10/1916
War Diary	Front Line Trenches	13/10/1916	17/10/1916
War Diary	A.3.c.4.0	18/10/1916	22/10/1916
Miscellaneous	Appendix	03/12/1916	03/12/1916
War Diary	Gun Pits	23/10/1916	24/10/1916
War Diary	Mansel Camp	25/10/1916	26/10/1916
War Diary	Corbie	27/10/1916	31/10/1916
Miscellaneous	2nd Bn Royal Dublin Fusiliers Appendix To War Diary Month Of October 1916		
Miscellaneous	2nd Bn Royal Dublin Fusiliers In The Field	06/10/1916	06/10/1916
Miscellaneous	In The Field	07/10/1916	07/10/1916
Miscellaneous	Perforated Sheet Giving detail of Personnel and Horses Wanting to Complete shown on Army Form B 213	06/10/1916	06/10/1916
Miscellaneous	No. of Report 56	14/10/1916	14/10/1916
Miscellaneous	In The Field	14/10/1916	14/10/1916
Miscellaneous	In The Field		
Miscellaneous	In The Field	29/10/1916	29/10/1916
Miscellaneous	Perforated Sheet Giving detail of Personnel and Horses Wanting to Complete shown on Army Form B 213	29/10/1916	29/10/1916
Miscellaneous	Perforated Sheet Giving detail of Personnel and Horses Wanting to Complete shown on Army Form B 213	22/10/1916	22/10/1916
Miscellaneous	Perforated Sheet Giving detail of Personnel and Horses Wanting to Complete shown on Army Form B 213	14/10/1916	14/10/1916

4TH DIVISION
10TH INF BDE

2ND BATTALION

ROYAL DUBLIN FUSILIERS.

AUG - DEC 1914.

—

Oct 1916

10th Brigade.
4th Division.

Disembarked Boulogne 23.8.14

2nd BATTALION

ROYAL DUBLIN FUSILIERS

AUGUST 1 9 1 4

WAR DIARY 2/R. Dub. Fus.

or

~~INTELLIGENCE SUMMARY~~

(Erase heading not required.)

Army Form C. 2118.

Instructions regarding War Diaries and Intelligence Summaries are contained in F. S. Regs., Part II. and the Staff Manual respectively. Title pages will be prepared in manuscript.

Hour, Date, Place	Summary of Events and Information	Remarks and References to Appendices
Harrow, Aug. 22nd 3.5am left in trains	Left in two trains. Each party entrained in 45 minutes. Arrived SOUTHAMPTON 7 and 8 am. Embarked in S.S. CALEDONIA. Arrived BOULOGNE about 9pm. Disembarked some wagons; Troops slept on board.	
Boulogne. Aug. 23rd 5am.	Disembarked about 5am & marched to camp.	
9pm.	Marched down and entrained in one train in two hours. All vehicles side-loaded.	
Boulogne. Aug. 24th 12.15am.	Left BOULOGNE. Arrived LA CATEAU about 10am: marched to BEAUMONT.	
Beaumont. Aug. 25th 2am.	Marched to about one mile S. of ST. PYTHON.	
6am.	Gun-fire heard in distance. Moved E. & took up position N. of FONTAINE. a TERTRE Fm.	
4.30pm.	Withdrew to position nearer Farm. 6pm. Shelled from N.E.	
9.pm.	Two Uhlans seen in front of line and shot	
11.pm.	Marched to HAUCOURT.	
Haucourt. Aug. 26th. 5am.	Arrived at HAUCOURT.	
6.15am.	Enemy opened fire from N. Battn deployed "A" "D" and one platoon of "B" Coy. under Major Shewan in the firing line. First line transport and horses went round by road. Owing to officers being dismounted, "B" & "C" Coys. went a long way to the rear before they were told to halt. They then took up a position N. of CAULLERY as supports. Guns were in position just to their North. Positions reported to 4th Divn. Communication could not be established with 10th Bde H.Q.	App: I. Casualties – " – II. Distribution of Battn during retirement.
12.30pm.	Verbal order to hold on at all costs received from H.Q. 4th Divn.	Owing to two nights strenuous work men were extremely tired and many of them discarded part of their equipment on coming under fire.
2.pm.	Supports were shelled from 2pm. At 5pm. the Adjutant was sent to H.Q. 4th Divn. to ask for orders as guns were retiring. He was informed that all the guns were being withdrawn and that nothing was known of Battn, and that it had better retire. Did so in small parties. No orders had been issued as to direction in case of retirement and Battn therefore became split up.	
6pm.	Headquarters, less Lt Col. Mainwaring marched to LE CATELET, being escort to guns part of the way, arriving there at 11.30.pm.	
LE CATELET. Aug. 27th 5am	Marched to ROISEL. Position taken up on East of town with Seaforths on our left. The Brigade at this time consisted of a Staff Captain, about two Coys Seaforths & 100 Dublins.	Great confusion was caused by men being put in carts. The Battn was split up into small parties and many men lost their equipment through being sent on different carts from those they rode in. This also gave men the idea that whenever they fell out they would be brought along in conveyances.
12.noon	Withdrew about two miles & took up fresh position. Battn left of line, Seaforths on our right. Artillery in line behind. French Cavalry on our left. Enemy did not appear. Withdrew at 7pm. Men put in carts and proceeded to VOYENNES.	

(9 26 6) W 257 976 100,000 4/12 H W V 79 3298

Army Form C. 2118.

Instructions regarding War Diaries and Intelligence Summaries are contained in F. S. Regs., Part II. and the Staff Manual respectively. Title pages will be prepared in manuscript.

WAR DIARY
or
~~INTELLIGENCE SUMMARY~~
(Erase heading not required.)

Hour, Date, Place	Summary of Events and Information	Remarks and References to Appendices
Aug 28th. Voyennes. 4.0am	Reached VOYENNES	The Bn had been marching & fighting for four days with practically no rest. The men were completely exhausted & badly in want of sleep. Many of them fell asleep while marching.
9.0am	Marched off. Battalion detailed to guard bridges over canal North East of OFFOY	
1.0pm	Withdrew to BUSSY	
Aug 29th Bussy. 11.0am	Battalion took up outpost position at MURANCOURT to cover retirement of Division.	App: III – General remarks Equipment & Boots
Beaurains 9.0pm	Brigade took up outpost position. Battalion & R. War. R. in reserve at BEAURAINS.	
Aug 30th. Noyon 9.0am.	Crossed R. OISE at NOYON. Bridges destroyed. Bivouaced at BERNEUIL-SUR-AINE. Cold night. Bivouacs made of straw which kept men warm.	
Aug 31st. Berneuil-sur-Aine. 8 oam	Marched through FORET de COMPEIGNE. Bivouaced beyond VALERIE. Men very done up.	

24/9/14 — [signature] Capt
Comdg 2/R Dub. Fus

(9 26 6) W 257—976 100,000 4/12 H W V 79/3298

APPENDIX I.

[illegible]. [illegible]/1914.

[illegible].

Appendix I

Casualties of 2nd Royal Dublin Fus. Battle of HAUCOURT

August 26th 1914

The Battn had 16 men wounded & 16 taken prisoners on above date. The latter included Captain Davy R.A.M.C.

531 men were missing after this battle & up to the present date it is not known what happened to them or what casualties they suffered.

[illegible] Captain

24/9/14 —— Comdg 2nd R. Dub. Fus.

APPENDIX II.

BATTLE OF LE CATEAU 26 Aug 1914.

Distribution of Battalion after Battle.

Appendix II.

Distribution of Battn after Battle of HAUCOURT.
Aug. 26th 1914

Officer Commanding	Strength	Remarks.
Hd. Qrs. Capt & Adjt. R.M. Watson	50.	Marched with Divisional troops. Lt Col Mainwaring became separated from Hd. Qrs. about 6.30 pm. 26/8/14.
Capt S.G. de C. Wheeler.	50.	Rejoined Battn 5. am 27th at LE CATELET.
Major H.M. Shewan DSO	about 450.	This party formed the firing line on the 26th & retired independently. No information as to their whereabouts has since been received.
Coy Sgt Major R Hall	100.	Joined details of other Regts 10th Infantry Bde & rejoined Battn Sept 5th 1914.
Sergt. Major F. Treacher	50	This party with 1st line transport rejoined the Battn. on 30th Aug. near CARLEPONT.

[signature] Capt
24-9-14 — Comdg 2/R. Dr. G. Lrs

APPENDIX III.

[illegible] 26 [illegible] 1914.

General Remarks - Equipment.

Appendix III

General Remarks – Equipment.

The weight of the web equipment together with the contents of pack, haversack, & 120 rounds ammunition was found to be so great that many men were physically incapable of carrying it. After a long march the weight tells, especially on the shoulders.
Great difficulty was experienced in impressing on reservists the necessity of the equipment fitting correctly, and many of them afterwards suffered from this.

Boots

Many reservists boots were badly fitted & had to be cut before they could get them on. This was, I think due to the measurements which were taken when they went to the reserve being incorrect.

T H C Frankland Capt
Comdg 2/R Dub. Fus

24-9-14

<u>BATTLE OF LE CATEAU. 26 Aug 1914.</u>

Account by Capt Watson (Adjt).

Account by Capt Watson , Ajt. 2nd Royal Dublin Fusiliers.

H A U C O U R T.

On August 26th 1914 the Battalion deployed at about 6.15 a.m. I was with Colonel Mainwaring and we remained for a short time with A & D Coys whilst he gave instructions to the Officers. The other two Companies had in the meanwhile gone towards CAULLERY. I ran after them and finally they took up positions about 800 x to 1,000 x North of the village. We got into communication with 4th Division but, although we made repeated efforts to get 10th D.Bde, failed to do so. The 4th Division informed us that under no circumstances would anyone retire.

We were under shell fire from 2.0 p.m. onwards and about 4.45 p.m the guns began to go. I was sent back to try and find 4th Division, met a Staff Officer who said that he knew nothing about us, but as all the guns had gone, we should retire.

I went back and told Colonel Mainwaring this and we retired. We had completely lost touch with the two companies in the firing line and I understood that the other Companies in support had already gone.

As we were passing through the village we met Capt Frankland and accompanied him in the direction of ELINCOURT and were then diverted to MALINCOURT. Colonel Mainwaring took Capt Frankland's horse and went off with about 40 men. I had about 30 with me, and lost touch with the other parts.

At MALINCOURT we were ordered to act as escort to the guns by a Staff Officer. The men got on the limbers and I rode beside.

On arrival at LE CATELET I was told that I was no longer required and accordingly halted and collected as many men as possible off the limbers.

I met the 10th D.Bde train in this village with Capt Burke, stopped there till 5 a.m. when I met Capt Wheeler and also a party of Seaforths. I reported to Capt Wheeler and joined his party.

(Signed) R.M.Watson. Capt & Ajt.
2nd R.Dublin Fusiliers.

20.[illegible].14.

10th Brigade.

4th Division.

2nd BATTALION

ROYAL DUBLIN FUSILIERS

SEPTEMBER 1 9 1 4

Instructions regarding War Diaries and Intelligence Summaries are contained in F. S. Regs., Part II. and the Staff Manual respectively. Title pages will be prepared in manuscript.

WAR DIARY 2/R. Dub. Fus.

~~or~~

~~INTELLIGENCE SUMMARY~~

(Erase heading not required.)

Army Form C. 2118.

Hour, Date, Place	Summary of Events and Information	Remarks and References to Appendices
6am. 1st Sept 1914. NERY.	On the night 31st Aug/1st Sept the Battn & detachment 1/R War: Regt were bivouaced about 1 mile S. of VERBIERIE as protection for Divnl: Artillery. At about 6am a message was received asking for assistance for guns ("L" Batt:) at NERY who were in difficulties. A detachment 1/R. War. R. followed by the Battn. moved out at once towards NERY. On approaching NERY a sound of firing was heard & Warwicks deployed on right, 2/R Dub Fus. on left, and moved to ridge overlooking NIRI. The action which had been proceeding there was dying down. The 19th Bde & Cav: were in occupation of town. The remaining Battns of 10th Inf. Bde came up about 9am and the Bde took up a position as rearguard, subsequently the Bde retired leisurely in line of Battns. moving on to road at . Marched on to BARON arriving 10.30 pm & the Divn bivouacked there for the night. Owing to bodies of Uhlans being in rear of Divn in neighbouring woods a perimeter of outposts was formed.	
2am BARON. 2nd Sept.	Little rest. At 12 m.n. the Divn moved South. The Bde marched off at 2am. the Battn being in rear of Bde. Uneventful march to DAMMARTIN where Battn billeted in a small street, finding outpost at	
3am. 3rd Sept DAMMARTIN	Paraded 3am, passed Bde starting point 4am. Bde being rearguard Battn with rearguard. After long march, Bde crossed R. MARNE at LAGNY and marched into bivouacs near LUSSIGNY.	
5pm. 4th Sept LUSSIGNY	Expected a rest and hoped to refit, but at 5pm. Bde moved 5 miles to MAGNY-LE-HONGRES with a view to taking up a position.	
3am. 5th Sept MAGNY-LE-HONGRES.	At 3am. the rearward movement was resumed, much to the disappointment of all ranks and Bde marched in main body to CHEVRY, arriving 12.30pm. First reinforcement, Lt. Campbell 40th Pathans (attached) & 36 other	

(9 26 6) W 257—976 100,000 4/12 H W V 79/3298

Instructions regarding War Diaries and Intelligence Summaries are contained in F. S. Regs., Part II. and the Staff Manual respectively. Title pages will be prepared in manuscript.

WAR DIARY ~~or INTELLIGENCE SUMMARY~~

2/R. [illegible]

(Erase heading not required.)

Army Form C. 2118.

Hour, Date, Place	Summary of Events and Information	Remarks and References to Appendices
5pm. 5th Sept. CHEVRY (continued)	ranks arrived. They had done long marches [illegible] to the main body the Battn. Coy Sgt Major Hall also arrived with 103 of the Battn who had got lost on 26th August. These men had travelled and kept together in difficult circumstances. The party had been sent to LE MANS where large bodies of stragglers had been collected & had returned from there with a large detachment of the R. War. Regt.	
3.30am 6th Sept. CHEVRY.	The British Army was ordered to advance against the Rt. Flank of the German Army, which, ignoring PARIS had moved S.E. and was now starting to retire. Leisurely advanced to [illegible] was made. At about 2pm. heavy firing heard [illegible] Bde moved [illegible] to a position near [illegible] to support of First Corps which [illegible] attacked. All quiet however and bivouacked on [illegible].	
10.15am 7th Sept. VILLENEUVE (Mon?)	Captain [illegible] Captain [illegible] The Battn [illegible] 10.15. we moved in the direction of [illegible] where the Battn bivouacked [illegible] from 3rd [illegible] Coy.	
[illegible] 8th Sept. [illegible]	The general move of the Army was to be [illegible] but the 3rd Army Corps was to [illegible] with the [illegible] The Battn. Moved off at 6am. [illegible]	

9-26 6. W 257-976 100,000 4/12 H W V. Forms/C. 2118/ 3298

Army Form C. 2118.

Instructions regarding War Diaries and Intelligence Summaries are contained in F. S. Regs., Part II. and the Staff Manual respectively. Title pages will be prepared in manuscript.

WAR DIARY

~~or~~

~~INTELLIGENCE SUMMARY~~

(Erase heading not required.)

Hour, Date, Place	Summary of Events and Information	Remarks and References to Appendices
	Corps reserve. Expected fighting but soon saw we should have little chance. Heavy firing N.E. by E. and N. both dying away later. Men looking much better. There is a great difference in pursuing to retiring: one is less bustled and less anxious. Moved by LE Gd LOU FERME and slowly moved from place to place till we finally bivouacked near L'HOTEL DES BOIS. Heavy shower just before we went into bivouac. 7pm. The Revd W. Forrest came round & held a short service with the men. A rumour that 6,000 Germans are cut off in the valley of the MARNE & that 2000 surrendered. Heavy firing till nightfall. 2nd reinforcement, 2Lt French & 71 other ranks arrived. Third Coy (A) formed under Lt Campbell. Battn now composed of three Coys "A" "B" & "C".	
2.30am. 9 Sept M/16 JOUARRE	Battn was ordered to take up a position N of JOUARRE, which had been strengthened by the RE as a point d'appui behind the other two brigades. The Divn was to attack TATEREL E. of LA FERTE. Held up at bridge defended by maxims. Much shelling both of village to find maxims & of high ground behind to search for retreating columns. In the evening the Bde marched to POPELAIN and bivouacked.	
5.30am. 10 Sept. POPELAIN	Marched at 5.30am. to cross by pontoon bridge at LA FERTE but orders were changed and we crossed by railway bridge at LE SAUSSOI. Here the Battn was left to help the transport & guns over. Bivouacked for night at COULOMBS, not arriving there till 11.30pm. Men very tired.	
3.30am. 11 Sept. COULOMBS	Marched off 3.30am. therefore had very short rest. A very weary day. Long halts owing to bad roads. Heavy rain about midday. Everyone soaked. Fortunately billeted at VILLERS LE PETIT. Certainly if you can get good billets it is more comfortable than bivouacking. The Germans had only just left and had not done any damage. Appear to have behaved well.	

Army Form C. 2118.

WAR DIARY
or
~~INTELLIGENCE SUMMARY~~

(*Erase heading not required.*)

Instructions regarding War Diaries and Intelligence Summaries are contained in F. S. Regs., Part II. and the Staff Manual respectively. Title pages will be prepared in manuscript.

Hour, Date, Place	Summary of Events and Information	Remarks and References to Appendices
6am 12 Sept. VILLERS LE PETIT.	Marched at 6am. [illegible] 9.50am heavy [illegible] to left [illegible]. Thought French [illegible] [illegible] [illegible] LA CARRIERE L'EVEQUE where [illegible] [illegible] French [illegible] [illegible] [illegible]	
7am 13 Sept. [illegible]	Bde marched 7am and [illegible] an easy day. [illegible] LA CARRIERE L'EVEQUE then marched to [illegible] [illegible] [illegible] [illegible] LA MONTAGNE [illegible] [illegible] to support 11th & 12th Bdes. Crossed R. AISNE by [illegible] [illegible] bridge had been partially [illegible] [illegible] [illegible] [illegible] [illegible] connect line of Somersets with [illegible] [illegible]	
[illegible] Sept. [illegible]	[illegible] [illegible] [illegible]	See [illegible]

9 26 6 W 257-976 100,000 1/12 H W V (P 779) 3298

Instructions regarding War Diaries and Intelligence Summaries are contained in F. S. Regs., Part II. and the Staff Manual respectively. Title pages will be prepared in manuscript.

WAR DIARY ~~or INTELLIGENCE~~ SUMMARY

(*Erase heading not required.*)

2/R Dub Fus.

Army Form C. 2118.

Hour, Date, Place	Summary of Events and Information	Remarks and References to Appendices
14 Sept.	decided to hold our trench and to rely on a counter attack for the defence of the [illegible]. Shelling started 7.30 am. One man killed almost at once. Rest of the Coy fairly safe under cover though fire was very searching. Meanwhile instructions were received to be ready to advance. Got into communication with Somersets and agreed that the Hampshires would have to go forward first. All preparations made for an advance. Later fresh instructions came, that as the 5th Div on right & French 45 Div on left had not made material progress the rôle of the 4th Divn was to be passive for the present.	
12 noon	About 12 noon the Germans seemed to be making a strong attack by fire on Hampshire's ridge. It was clear that were this taken the position of the whole of the left would be almost untenable. Consequently one Coy ("B") was sent to the Ridge & A Co under Lt Campbell was sent to counter-attack to N. of ridge. This counter-attack went forward very steadily. About 800 yds off they engaged hostile infantry in a root-field & completely subdued their fire at about 400 yds range. Retiring afterwards on my instructions. Meanwhile B Co led by Captains Supple & Watson had pushed up on to the ridge under heavy shell fire. Meanwhile heavy shelling round my post & 2Lt McGuire & 2 men were killed; 10 men wounded. I now learnt that there had been no attack on Hampshires but I consider that the reconnaissance by A Co was not wasted, it bucked up the men & is the way, I think, to carry out the defence. Men behaved very well indeed. Lt Campbell showed himself to be a first-class officer & leader & 2Lt French showed great promise. In the evening we buried the killed in one grave.	

(9 26 6) W 257—976 100,000 4/12 H W V 70 / 3298

15 Sept 1914. LA MONTAGNE.

Present [illegible] very [illegible] situation appears to be as follows:— 1st [illegible] have got over R. AISNE. 1st Corps [illegible] French 45th Divn in front of SOISSONS. Genl Maunoury with [illegible] army [illegible] German right. [illegible] Brussels reported to be [illegible] Ostend. [illegible] a large [illegible]

Heavy shelling all day and [illegible] enemy's [illegible] and did considerable damage. Both suffered [illegible] casualties.

In evening [illegible] under Gen. Hunter-Weston, 'B' & 'C' Coys put in [illegible] line [illegible]

At 7 [illegible] heavy shell & rifle fire broke out all along the line. [illegible] and an attack was expected but all quieted down.

16th Sept 1914. LA MONTAGNE

A very wet night clearing up later. Humphries & Somersets shelled. Enemy's artillery otherwise much quieter: our artillery in action again. In afternoon enemy appeared to be retiring [to] their trenches about 600 yds off [illegible] were [illegible] & shelled by our guns. Enemy's artillery gradually [illegible] 6th Divn. close behind at [illegible]. One man killed by sniper.

17 Sept. LA MONTAGNE.
Very wet. Trenches very sloppy & greasy. Fear we shall get a lot of sick. Germans renewed their activity in shelling. 'B' Co. shelled about midday when making obstacles. One man wounded. Later heavy howitzers shelled BUCY LE LONG.

18 Sept. LA MONTAGNE.
Heavy firing during morning. Some alarm. Hampshires came to relieve Batt., who were to take over the trenches temporarily occupied by various [illegible] to get the different Brigades together. [illegible] & Batt. placed in good cover in rear of LA MONTAGNE FARM. After dark took over trenches which were situated below the crest line but exposed to & receive much attention from enemy's artillery. 'C' & 'A' in trenches 'B' Co in support. Trenches bad as by day we must be very quiet & can only communicate with them safely by night. Every evening half the troops in trenches are relieved by those in reserve. Hot tea & rations sent out in evening.

Important [illegible] Trenches sheet 'B'

11

19[illegible] Sept. (Saturday) [illegible]

Raining wet last night [illegible]

[illegible]

[illegible]

[illegible] 35 [illegible] England.

20 Sept (Sunday) [illegible]

[illegible]

[illegible]

[illegible]

[illegible]

[illegible]

[illegible]

[illegible]

[illegible]

[illegible]

[illegible]

given.

[illegible]

[illegible] 32nd Div [illegible]

[illegible]

[illegible]

[illegible]

[illegible] was wounded.

21st Sept. (Monday) [illegible]

[illegible]. It appears that the [illegible]

[illegible] YPRES [illegible]

22nd Sept. (Tues.) [illegible]

Last night heavy battle [illegible]

On the right the direction of 5th Div[illegible]

[illegible] & shelling [illegible]

A German aeroplane [illegible]

a row of [illegible] trenches,

result [illegible] field [illegible].

[illegible] trenches during it.

23rd Sept (~~Thurs~~ Wed.) LA MONTAGNE.
French 6th Div. was to have attacked, but does not appear to have done so. Our own & enemy's artillery did some shooting. Three men wounded in the trenches. Fourth re-inforcement 2nd Lts Tarleton & Moffit & 163. Section D arrived. Fourth Coy (D) formed. Lt Leahy in command.

24th Sept (Thurs). – Quiet day.

25th Sept (Friday). LA MONTAGNE.
Firing at aeroplanes. Otherwise quiet.

26th Sept (Sat) LA MONTAGNE.
Everything seems to be going on all right. The Divn. has informed us that we are to expect an attack from the Germans who will probably try to relieve pressure on their flank.

27th Sept (Sunday). LA MONTAGNE.
Quiet day. French envelopment progressing. 1st Bavarian Corps said to be reinforcing. German right flank is said to have had to face N. to meet turning movement. Strong rumours of some enterprise from DUNKIRK or OSTEND. Rev. W. Forrest came round at lunch time & field service. Sniping began at 10.30 pm & lasted for about an hour.

28th Sept (Mon) [illegible]
Rather [illegible]. The heavy guns did [illegible] with the [illegible] in Vermandovillers [illegible] did [illegible]
[illegible]
[illegible] between [illegible] and PERONNE. The [illegible] movement against Mt. Kemmel [illegible] has [illegible] Corps. [illegible]
Gen Rawlinson [illegible]
4th Div, [illegible]
[illegible]
Communication trench [illegible]
[illegible]
29th Sept (Tues) [illegible]
Great [illegible] came [illegible] 4th Div reported [illegible] German withdrawal. Later message that [illegible] located three strong German companies deployed in front [illegible] 77 Bde. No German attack [illegible] Germans still in trenches.
57 reinforcement, 2nd [illegible] & 50 [illegible] these were men & [illegible] who were cut off on 26th Aug & had escaped to BOULOGNE. [illegible] 43 [illegible] Regiment.
Sept 30th (Wed) [illegible]
Posted forward communication trench [illegible]

[illegible]
Capt
Comdg 2/R [illegible]

S K E T C H " A ".

A

S.L.I

Corn

Trench

C Coy

A Coy

B Coy

14 Sept 1914

60

S K E T C H " B ".

"B

36

A P P E N D I X. I

&

S K E T C H " C "

Appendix I

[illegible] Shay Council [illegible]

[illegible] should be [illegible] could be [illegible] nature.

[illegible] experience [illegible]

[illegible]

Capt.
[illegible]

"C"

Rough Sketch of

Protected Latrine

for use with ordinary fire trench

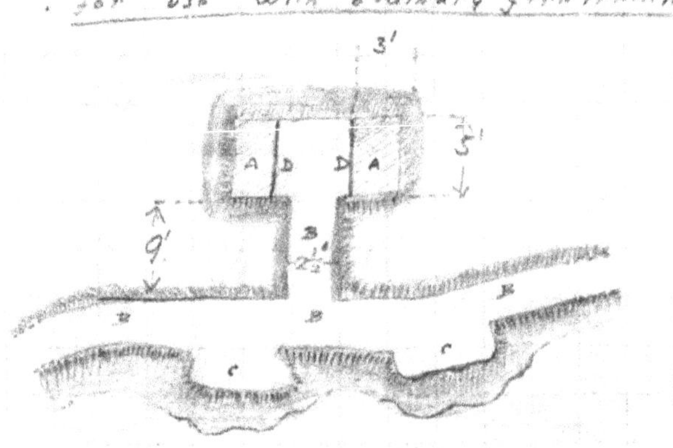

A = Latrine (depth 4' below bottom of trench)

B = communicating trench

C = fire recesses

D = strong branch of tree for use as seat, fixed ~~[illegible]~~ at each end into wall of trench & supported with biscuit box if necessary.

At night empty biscuit tins are placed in recesses specially cut in rear wall of fire trench ~~for~~ to serve as urinals.

97

4th Div.

10th Bde.

WAR DIARY.

2nd BN. ROYAL DUBLIN FUSILIERS.

[illegible]

1914.

Instructions regarding War Diaries and Intelligence Summaries are contained in F. S. Regs., Part II. and the Staff Manual respectively. Title pages will be prepared in manuscript.

WAR DIARY
or
INTELLIGENCE SUMMARY
(Erase heading not required.)

Army Form C. 2118.

Hour, Date, Place		Summary of Events and Information	Remarks and References to Appendices
5p.m, Bucy de Long	1st October 1914	This afternoon at 5pm received orders to move to relieve Lancashire Fusiliers opposite CHIVRES. This move with others allows 2nd Corps to be withdrawn. Rifle Brigade relieved us. New line somewhat intricate on wooded spur mostly facing east towards CHIVRES.	
ST MARGUERITE	2nd October 1914	Very misty. Not a bad position though apt to be sniped.	
	3rd October 1914	Quiet day. Some sniping and a few shells in the evening.	
	4th October 1914	Good deal of accurate sniping in morning and some shelling but no damage. 11a.m. R.C. Service. Capt H.O. Clarke took over command of the Battalion.	
	5th October 1914	Quiet day. In the afternoon received orders to be ready to move that or following night. Four S.A.A Carts went at 9pm.	
	6th October 1914	Relieved by French Troops. Transport moved 6.30pm. B & C Companies 7.40pm remainder of the Battalion relieved by Chasseurs Alpin 12.30am.	
12.30AM. HARTENNS.	7th October 1914	marched to HARTENNS – 13 miles. Bivouaced in trees. 10.40pm marched off	
1.40AM. OULCHY LA VILLE	8th October 1914	Arrived 1.40AM. Very comfortable Billets. 35 Stragglers & sick rejoined Battalion.	
4.40pm. PISSELEUX	—"—	marched off 4.40pm to PISSELEUX. Halted for two hours half way.	
2.AM.	—"— 9th October 1914	Arrived PISSELEUX. 2.30pm, marched to RULLY. 2Lt Webb. Gregg & Elsworthy joined	
2pm	—"— 10th October 1914	marched to Point POINT. Entrained 7.30pm. POINT ST MAXCENCE. Moved off mid-night. men were in trucks which had been previously used for horses and they were thoroughly filthy	
	11th October 1914	Travelled at a snails pace reached HESDINAULD at 11AM. One hours halt. Arrived WEZENNES at 4pm where we detrained & marched to STOMER. Billeted in Military Barracks.	
STOMER	12th October 1914	Received orders to send off Transport at 9.30 am. and that we were to go by motor lorries at 1pm. accordingly the whole Brigade paraded on the Square. About 4pm a German aeroplane dropped two bombs apparently aimed at us. They killed two women and injured two children. 6pm Warwicks started to leave in motor lorries. We started at 11pm not a very comfortable journey. Reached HAZEBROOCK 4AM.	
4AM. HAZEBROOCK.	13th October 1914	marched 4 miles to SYLVESTRE and we had breakfasts. marched off 9.30am eastwards to FLETRE against the enemy holding a line BERTHEN — METREN. The 4th Division was to attack this line. 12th Brigade on right, 10th on left. 11th in Reserve. Cavalry Brigade on left flank. 6th Division on right flank. a lot of waiting about but at last attack launched: Seaforths & Irish Fusiliers in firing line. Warwick [illegible] holding [illegible] on right. [illegible] in [illegible]	

103

Army Form C. 2118.

Instructions regarding War Diaries and Intelligence Summaries are contained in F. S. Regs., Part II. and the Staff Manual respectively. Title pages will be prepared in manuscript.

WAR DIARY
or
INTELLIGENCE SUMMARY
(Erase heading not required.)

Hour, Date, Place	Summary of Events and Information	Remarks and References to Appendices
FLETRE October 13th 1914	Battalion moved accordingly to point 31. On reaching this point Cavalry who were holding ridge north of that being attacked by Irish Fusiliers reported heavy counter attack advancing and asked for help. C & D Coys were hurriedly sent forward. They deployed very quickly considering the thick hedges and moved up the ridge expecting to come under heavy fire on top, but the Germans seeing the mass of Infantry [illegible] had cleared off. It was now getting dark. Firing line was ordered to push out to the right to try [illegible] in touch with the Irish Fusiliers. The remainder of the Battn were sent to fill up gaps. Head Qrs A & B Coys finally closing on LA BESACE farm where Irish Fusiliers were also assembled	
FONTAINE October 14th 1914	A & B Coys moved off to farm house NTH of FONTAINE where C & D Coys had [illegible] a position during the night. 3.0 pm moved to METEREN where we [illegible]	Order received from [illegible]
METEREN October 15th 1914	6am marched to BAILLEUL	
BAILLEUL October 16th 1914	11am moved off and billeted in [illegible] along the NIEPPE road.	
ARMENTIERES October 17th 1914	6AM marched off to ERQUINGHEM bridge. [illegible] by Irish Fusiliers and Cyclists who move forward through ARMENTIERES. Battalion followed [illegible] Inhabitants wild with joy at our entry surrounded the Troops [illegible] the Irish Fusiliers up against snipers at east end of Town. Battalion detailed to [illegible] house to house search for Germans. At nightfall the Battalion moved [illegible] of Town and had to send two Companies to furnish outposts in continuation of a line held by Irish Fusiliers. A & B outposts C & D billeting in the ASILE D' ETRANGERS	one man killed
October 18th 1914	Last night we were somewhat disturbed by heavy firing on the left flank. 7 am orders received 10th Brigade was to take FRELINGHEIN. Seaforths supported by Irish Fusiliers were to do this. The Battalion to act as right flank guard. D Coy advance Guard to Battalion pushed on to PONT BALLOT. Enemy suddenly opened a regular raffale with his guns. Battalion [illegible] the leading Company being within 500x of enemy's trenches & about 300 yds from a German Battery. Towards nightfall the Battalion pushed further north for about 200x and dug themselves in. Seaforths on left. Warwicks on our Right. Col. Clarke wounded Capt. Franklin took over command of the Battalion. 2 men killed 3 wounded.	

9-26-6 W 257-976 100,000 1-12 H W V 79 / 3298

Army Form C. 2118.

Instructions regarding War Diaries and Intelligence Summaries are contained in F. S. Regs., Part II. and the Staff Manual respectively. Title pages will be prepared in manuscript.

WAR DIARY
or
INTELLIGENCE SUMMARY
(Erase heading not required.)

Hour, Date, Place	Summary of Events and Information	Remarks and References to Appendices
October 19th 1914	Fairly quiet day although we had a good deal of shelling. Brigade to attack FRELINGHEIN tomorrow by gaining ground by river bank rest of line assisting by fire	
October 20th 1914.	Hd Qrs heavily shelled for 3 hours. In afternoon orders were received to link up with right of Irish Fusiliers. [Seaforths took one German Trench by assault and captured a good many prisoners.] 2 men killed 5 wounded during the day.	
Wednesday October 21st 14	Things have come rather to a standstill Seaforths not pushing any further as our line is getting very extended. 12th Brigade has been attacked on West of River. 11th Brigade counterattacked with success. Royal Fusiliers on our Right were attacked at night but only a few snipers opposite us.	
October 22nd 1914	Hd Qrs moved to brick field near Convent. Quiet day.	
October 23rd 1914	Late Hd Qrs heavily shelled. Had to extend right of Brigade (10th) to allow 6th Division to form a reserve. 'C' had to take over the lines of the Warwicks. —	Plan of Trenches attached.
October 24th 1914	Some heavy firing broke out on the right. More ammunition sent to A & C Coys. Some sniping against right Platoon but most of the firing in front of the Warwicks. B Coy lost 1 killed 4 wounded from reverse fire. Bullets aimed at the Warwicks. One Platoon under Lt Maffett which had been sent on 23rd to guard approach to ARMENTIES returned. General attack by 6th Army expected all day but never came.	
October 25th 1914	Colonel Loveland took over Command. A very quiet day.	
October 26th 1914	Captains Trigona & Weir and 179 other ranks (6th Reinforcement) arrived. [1st & 4th Divs are fighting hard to day and doing very good work. Seaforths shelled out of some houses at FRELINGHEIN which they were holding as an advanced post.] The Battalion had 2 men wounded	
October 27th 1914	Seaforths attacked during night bullets whistled over Bn Hd Qrs. At Dawn machine guns fired at 'C' Coy. Our guns got on to them and silenced them. Germans have suffered heavily lately during night attacks. Our Trenches are being improved & wire fences strengthened. 3 men wounded by snipers	
October 28th 1914	Quiet night. German heavy Howitzer shelled observation Station 39th Battery and knocked it out. It ranged on Hd Qrs to commence with.	

(9 26 6) W 257—976 100,000 4/12 H W V 79 / 3298

Instructions regarding War Diaries and Intelligence Summaries are contained in F. S. Regs., Part II. and the Staff Manual respectively. Title pages will be prepared in manuscript.

WAR DIARY
or
INTELLIGENCE SUMMARY

(*Erase heading not required.*)

Army Form C. 2118.

Hour, Date, Place	Summary of Events and Information	Remarks and References to Appendices
Thursday October 29th [illegible]	Quiet day. Fairly [illegible] [illegible] evening. Our lives are getting [illegible] daily as we get up more wire. Arrangements made for digging another trench between our right flank and the [illegible] at present there is a gap. One man killed [illegible] [illegible]	
Friday October 30th	Cleared up at midnight. Rifle Brigade on our left attacked. 12.30 pm a curiously shaped captive balloon arose from the German lines somewhere N.EAST of FRELINGHEIN with five balls hanging underneath [illegible] [illegible]	
Saturday October 31st	Some firing last night [illegible] [illegible] [illegible] otherwise all quiet. [The Brigade office got [illegible] in the morning that the Cavalry [illegible] were retiring WEST from MESSINES. Later [illegible] news came of a [illegible] [illegible] attack on MESSINES] As result of the advance [illegible] [illegible] 2/Lt [illegible] went off to A.S.C. [illegible] [illegible] [illegible] [illegible] [illegible] [illegible] [illegible] [illegible] [illegible] [illegible] up [illegible] all day	

A. [illegible]

Commanding [illegible]

3/11/14.

APPENDIX I.

D I S E A S E.

Objection I [illegible]

[illegible]

2/11/14 [illegible]

ORDER received from the Brigade on 13th Oct 1914.

The following is a message received from the Brigade on the 13th

" The B G C congratulates all units of the Brigade on the successful result of [illegible] being the first time the Brigade has been faced with a combined attack. Considering that the attack took place in thick weather and in the dark he is much pleased with the manner in which touch was maintained and post combat arrangements made re adjustment of Units, occupation of ground, collection of wounded."

(2)

O.C.
"A" Coy.

This message is to be read to the Company on parade this morning.

(Sd) R.W. Watson Capt & Adjutant.

Rough Sketch of Trenches of R.Dub Fus:

Oct 23rd 1914.

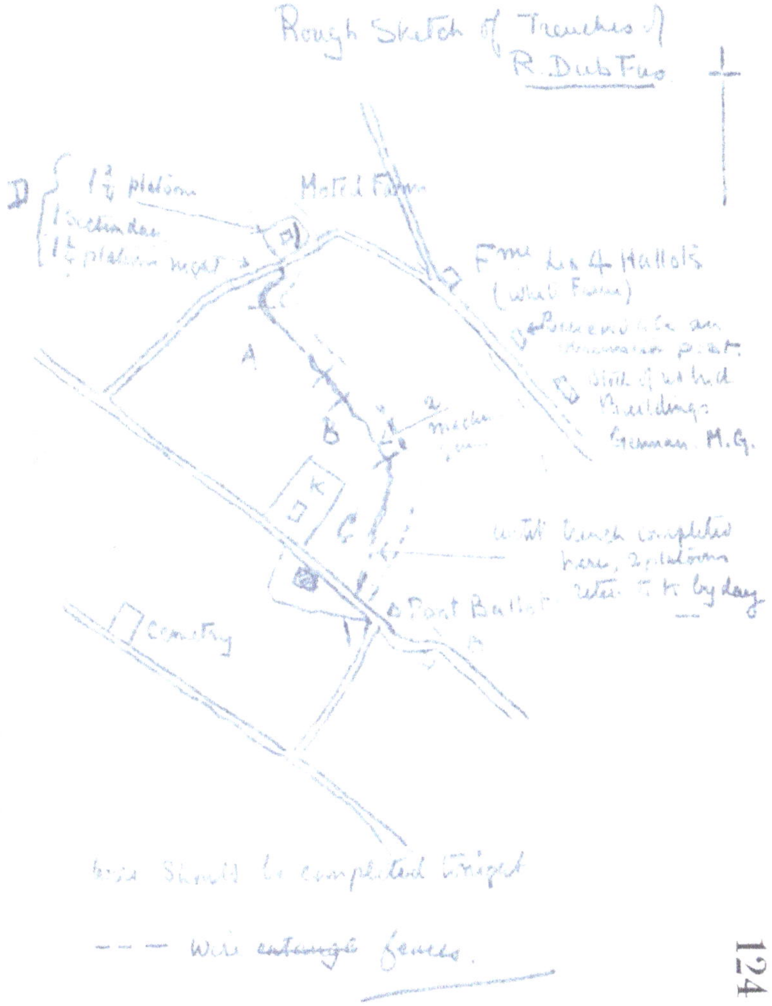

Rough Sketch of Trenches of
R. Dub Fus

D
1 3/4 platoon
1 section
1 1/4 platoon

Moated Farm

Fme Les 4 Hallots
(White Farm)

Buildings
German M.G.

A

B

2
machine guns

K

C

Until trench completed here, 2 platoons enter by day

Pont Ballot

Cemetery

--- Wire fences.

124

4th Div.

10th Bde.

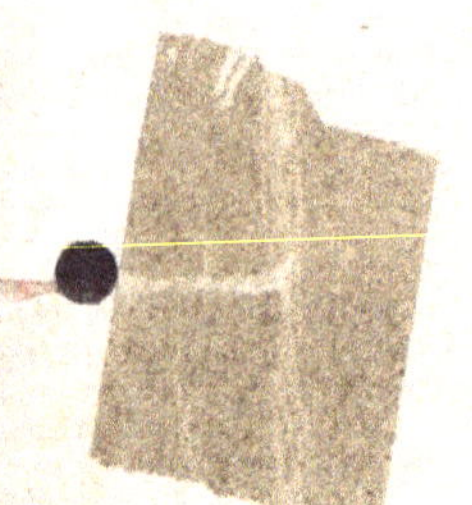

W A R   D I A R Y.

2nd BATT. ROYAL DUBLIN FUSILIERS.

NOVEMBER

1914.

Instructions regarding War Diaries and Intelligence Summaries are contained in F. S. Regs., Part II. and the Staff Manual respectively. Title pages will be prepared in manuscript.

WAR DIARY
or
INTELLIGENCE SUMMARY
(*Erase heading not required.*)

Army Form C. 2118.

Hour, Date, Place	Summary of Events and Information	Remarks and References to Appendices
November 1st	[illegible]	
3rd.	During last few days heavy fighting going on in direction of [illegible].	
[illegible]	[illegible] ARMENTIERES doing some damage. In [illegible] the Germans were heard singing in their trenches the Austrian National Anthem and other hymns.	
6th	Heavy fighting [illegible] going on [illegible] this morning [illegible] day. Heavy firing [illegible] LE TOUQUET [illegible] to the North.	
8th. 9th.	[illegible] Brigade has been heavily engaged the last 2 days in PLOEGSTEERT wood by Germans. [illegible] Major [illegible] went out on patrol [illegible] night but has not returned.	
11th.	At 11.30 am a German battery [illegible] headquarters but most of [illegible]. About 8.30 pm. heavy firing [illegible] the line [illegible] "hot air". [illegible] in bringing out the [illegible]	

49 26 6 W 257 976 100,000 4/12 H W V 79/3298

Instructions regarding War Diaries and Intelligence Summaries are contained in F. S. Regs., Part II. and the Staff Manual respectively. Title pages will be prepared in manuscript.

WAR DIARY
or
INTELLIGENCE SUMMARY
(Erase heading not required.)

Army Form C. 2118.

Hour, Date, Place	Summary of Events and Information	Remarks and References to Appendices
November 11th	and dirt getting into breach and on to chargers.	
13th	Enemy shelled headquarters again to-day dropping shells near headquarters just as a few F G C M s had assembled there. The Court adjourned to a safer place. Heavy rain trenches in a very bad ~~condition~~ condition	
14th	Draft of 100 men mostly 5th Battalion under Lieut J. R. F. Hall 3/rd arrived in evening.	
15th	Bitterly cold. started to snow but turned into rain. Intermittent shelling by enemy. Trenches in bad condition mud and water. Dug outs rapidley falling in repairs being carried out with timber, braziers are being provided for trenches so as the men can cook there and make themselves more comfortable.	103
16th	Received warning to-day that we were to be relieved to-morrow by 19th Brigade. In evening 2Lieut. A. C. Haines, late Motor Cyclist, joined for duty.	
17th. 6 p.m.	19th Brigade arrived to take over trenches. Relief of our trenches by R. W. F and A. & S. Hdrs. quickly and quietly carried out. Battalion marched to ROMARIN where we billeted. Roads in dreadful condition.	

Army Form C. 2118.

Instructions regarding War Diaries and Intelligence Summaries are contained in F. S. Regs., Part II. and the Staff Manual respectively. Title pages will be prepared in manuscript.

WAR DIARY or INTELLIGENCE SUMMARY

(Erase heading not required.)

Hour, Date, Place	Summary of Events and Information	Remarks and References to Appendices
November 18th	Sharp frost last night. 6 pm. Battalion [illegible] to PLOEGSTEERT and billeted there.	
19th.	Snow fell all day. At [illegible] pm [illegible] R B in position at ST IVES. A [illegible] C Companies in front line D Company in support. The position is a pronounced salient, trenches somewhat scattered and not very good. Left on [illegible] with Irish [illegible] Right with Somerset L I.	
20th.	Hard frost last night and freezing hard today. Battalion suffered [illegible] from [illegible] [illegible] 10 wounded.	[illegible]
22nd.	Still freezing. In afternoon enemy subjected [illegible] East of ST IVES [illegible] bombardment [illegible] 2 killed 7 wounded. In evening R War R [illegible] over the trenches and [illegible] moved in [illegible] at 63.	
23rd.	Enemy [illegible] in the vicinity of [illegible] today [illegible] 6" Howitzers. In the evening we [illegible] the [illegible] and [illegible]	
24th.	This morning [illegible] arrangements have been made [illegible] hot water [illegible] clothing [illegible] taken away to be cleaned and the [illegible].	

9 26 6 W 257 976 100,000 1/12 H W V 79 [illegible]

4

Army Form C. 2118.

WAR DIARY
or
INTELLIGENCE SUMMARY
(*Erase heading not required.*)

Instructions regarding War Diaries and Intelligence Summaries are contained in F. S. Regs., Part II. and the Staff Manual respectively. Title pages will be prepared in manuscript.

Hour, Date, Place	Summary of Events and Information	Remarks and References to Appendices
24th	of their trousers and coats ironed. On emerging from bath men are issued with clean underclothing and march to new billets on the outskirts of ARMENTIERES. Father Dowling joined. a thaw has set in.	
25th	Still thawing. at 2-30pm Battalion marched to ·63. Slight frost again in evening	
26th	Relieved R. War. R at 5pm. Trenches owing to thaw are in many places in a very bad condition. During the night the Germans opened a fairly heavy fire lasting about 10 minutes.	
28th	Last two days have been quite. Today we had 1 killed and 4 wounded by shell fire. all companies busy at repairing their trenches. It has been necessary in some places to build up from the bottom of the trench with sandbags. parts of the communication trenches are full of water which cannot be removed. This evening a ~~[illegible]~~ Retrenchment was started behind. Battalion HdQrs	103
30th	Relieved by R. War. Regt between 5 and 7pm and went to ·63.	

A. Loveband Lt Col
Comdg 2/R Dub Fus.

(9 26 6) W 257—976 100,000 4/12 H W V 79/3298

4th Div.

10th Bde.

WAR DIARY.

2nd BATT. ROYAL DUBLIN FUSILIERS.

DECEMBER

1914.

Attached:-

Casualties.

Instructions regarding War Diaries and Intelligence Summaries are contained in F. S. Regs., Part II. and the Staff Manual respectively. Title pages will be prepared in manuscript.

WAR DIARY
or
INTELLIGENCE SUMMARY
(*Erase heading not required.*)

Army Form C. 2118.

Hour, Date, Place			Summary of Events and Information	Remarks and references to Appendices
December 1st	ST. YVES.		Battalion moved to Billets at NIEPPE	For Casualties see Appendix. 1.
" 2nd	NIEPPE	2.30pm	" lined streets for visit of His Majesty The King.	
" 3rd	"		" moved to point .63	
" 4th			" Relieved R War Regt in Trenches	
" 5th	ST. YVES.		Very wet Day. Trenches in an appalling state, some parts had to be evacuated owing to the water, others were filled with debris from crumbling parapets.	
" 6th	"		Fine night, worked at bailing and preparing trenches. Germans were also seen bailing and were heavily sniped.	
" 7th	"		Wet Day. Trenches worse than ever!	
" 8th	"		Moved to point .63. Capt. Le Mesurier joined the Battalion	
" 9th	Point .63.		Capt Smithwick & Lt Rush joined Battalion, moved to LA CRÈCHE.	
" 10th	La. CRÈCHE.		Good Billetts.	
" 11th	"		Lt Col. Loveband went to Hospital. Capt Frankland then took over Command. Bn moved to .63	
" 12th	.63.		Relieved R War Reg. Trenches in a very bad state.	
" 13th	ST. YVES.		Trenches shelled and sniped.	
" 14th	"		Nil	
" 15th	"		Germans very nervous and throwing up many lights. think Germans only holding front line very lightly	
" 16.			moved to .63.	
" 17th			" LA CRÈCHE	103
" 18th			Orders issued for an attack by 11th Brigade	
" 19th		12 Noon	Moved to ROMARIN. remained there as Divisional reserve, 6pm moved to .63.	
20th			1½ Coys. sent up to support R War Regt, relieved R War. Reg. Trenches in better condition	
" 21st	ST. YVES		Quiet day	
" 22nd	"		Quiet day, Strengthened wire	
" 23rd	"		Brigadier came up to discuss placing men in houses on account of wet state of Trenches. Capt. Digby-Johnston & 74 NCO's & men joined the Bn	
" 24th			Relieved by R War. Regt. Moved to .63.	
" 25th	Point .63.		Very quiet day, no shelling or sniping heard. (Christmas Day). Slight frost.	
" 26th	"		Quiet day: Snow: turned to rain later.	
" 27th	"		Quiet day.	
" 28th	"		Relieved R War Reg in Trenches. Commenced putting ST. YVES in a state of defence heavy gale,	
" 29th	St YVES.		Quiet day no sniping	
" 30th			do do	
" 31st			do	

A. Loveband Lt Col
Comdg 2nd Bn ...

1247 W 3299 200,000 (E) 8/14 J.B.C. & A. Forms/C. 2118/11.

APPENDIX I.

C A S U A L T I E S.

War Diary December 1914

Appendix 1.

Casualties.

	OR Killed	OR Wounded	Officers
5th.	—	2	
6th	3	5.	
7th	1.	1.	
8th	–	2.	
12th.		1.	1. R O C Bush (accidental).
13th	2	3.	[illegible] French
14th.	4.	6.	
15th	2	5	(1 Missing) [illegible]
16th	–	2	
20th.	–	1	
22nd	–	1.	
23rd	1.	2.	
24th	2.	1	
29th.	–	3	
30th	1	–	
Total OR.	16	35.	1.
Officers		2.	

A. Loveband Lt Col

2/1/15 Comdg 2/R Dub Fus

4th Division

10th Infantry Bde

2nd Battn Royal Dublin Fus.

January, to 30th June

1915

10th Inf.Bde.
4th Div.

2nd BATTN. THE ROYAL DUBLIN FUSILIERS.

J A N U A R Y

1 9 1 5

Attached:

Appendices 1 & 2.

Instructions regarding War Diaries and Intelligence Summaries are contained in F. S. Regs., Part II. and the Staff Manual respectively. Title pages will be prepared in manuscript.

WAR DIARY
or
INTELLIGENCE SUMMARY
(Erase heading not required.)

Army Form C. [illegible]

Hour, Date, Place	Summary of Events and Information	Remarks and References to Appendices
January 1st ST. YVES	Quiet day. Relieved by R.War.R. and moved to LA CRECHE	
" 2nd LA CRECHE	Nothing to report	
" 3rd "	Battalion bathed at NIEPPE.	
" 4th "	Parade at 12 Noon Capt. Frankland left Bn. Capt. Wheeler took over duties of Brigade Major	
" 5th "	Relieved R.War.R. in Trenches.	For Casualties see Appendix I.
" 6th ST. YVES.	Quiet day very little sniping. enemies light gun shelled left trench.	
" 7th "	Rained all day: trenches very bad: left trench was shelled rather more than usual, sniping more active	For reports see Appx II
" 8th "	Fine morning: rained again in evening: rather more sniping.	
" 9th "	Wet morning: moved to [illegible] in evening.	
" 10th 11th 12th LA COURTE DREVE		
" 12th	Relieved R.War.R. in Trenches.	
" 13th ST. YVES.	H.d.Qrs. shelled for about 1½ hrs from 10 a.m., very little damage; [illegible] morning fine afternoon	
" 14th "	" " " with heavy shrapnel at 8.45 am more sniping during night than usual weather still fine ground dried up a lot. heavy firing on our left at 6 pm nothing apparently became of it.	
" 15th "	A few of Bouquets of shells round Hd Qrs during day. usual sniping; wet evening	
" 16th "	Bouquet of shells at 7.20 am on Hd Qrs. and more during the day; Relieved by R.War.R in evening.	
	Centre company reported that mining had been heard opposite them this was reported to R.War.R. who investigated it. apparently no foundation in report	
17th 18th 19th LA CRECHE	Bn bathed at NIEPPE on the 18th	
20th "	Relieved R.War.R. in trenches [illegible] night	
21st ST. YVES	very wet day. Hd Qrs shelled intermittently. trenches in very bad condition	
22nd "	Fine morning. Centre Company reported that the wire in front of them had been cut this was the same place that reported mining. wire was repaired at night. Trenches & Hd Qrs shelled during day. 3 miners from R.E. [illegible] came up to again investigate reported mining. same opinion without foundation. [illegible] without any sniping. as they strike water [illegible] feet down.	
23rd "	Quiet day.	
24th "	3 [illegible] shells fired near Hd Qrs at 12.15 am. exploded into very small fragments. gave out large number of small balls of [illegible] did no damage. Trenches shelled during afternoon. Relieved by R.War.R.	
25th 26th 27th LA COURTE DREVE	Trial [illegible] by Brigade on 27th men turned out very well	
28th "	Relieved R.W.R	
29th ST. YVES	Very little sniping: usual shelling	
30th "	[illegible] sniping rather less than usual; usual shelling, trenches in excellent condition for [illegible] in trenches	
31st "	Quiet day. Trenches & Hd Qrs shelled for a short time	

[signature illegible]

(9 26 6) W 257—976 100,000 4/12 H W V 79/3298

A P P E N D I C E S 1 & 2.

APPENDIX . I.

Casualties for month of January

Day of Month	Killed in Action	Wounded in Action
6th	11520 Pte [illegible] 9431 - Fitzgerald	NIL
7th	9308 L/C [illegible]	5305 Pte Joseph 7533 - Higgins
12th	5334 Pte Byrne	7126 Pte McGuire. 9072 - Webb
14th	5615 Sgt McDonnell	10464 Sgt Dunn 7000 Pte Healy 11426 - McEvoy 6782 - Morrissey 6695 - Nesbitt. 7320 - Nolan
15th	5079 Pte Clarke	9831 Sgt O'Higgins 8817 Pte Harrington 5458 - O'Connor 8887 Dmr Westwood 11462 Pte Owens (Died of wounds 16/1/15 at 10th F.A)
16th	NIL	9717 L/C O'Donnell 8779 Pte Gorman 5265 - Doyle
21st	NIL	7802 Pte Young
23rd	NIL	Capt. E. G. Smithwick 8002 Cpl Meehan 8686 Pte Davis
26th	NIL	5024 Pte Kavanagh 5880 Sgt Ryan (Died of wounds 25/1/15 at 10th F.A). 5134 Pte Campbell 5353 - Fenley 11790 - Keaney
29th	10600 Pte Knobbs	9216 Pte Fitzharris 9372 - English. 9998 - Tuite 8763 - O'Brien 16743 L/C House 8556 Pte Byrne
30th	11672 Pte Foley 5478 - Shirley	6168 Pte Cardiff. Lieut. D. C. Persse. (Died of wounds 1-2-15 at No 2 Clearing Hospl).
31st	NIL K 1+11	W 2+34 7866 Cpl Bell 0882 Pte Bramble 9505 - Tyrrell 6412 - Elliott.

10th Inf.Bde.
4th Div.

2nd BATTN. THE ROYAL DUBLIN FUSILIERS.

F E B R U A R Y

1 9 1 5

Attached:

Appendix 1.

Army Form C. 2118.

Instructions regarding War Diaries and Intelligence Summaries are contained in F. S. Regs., Part II. and the Staff Manual respectively. Title pages will be prepared in manuscript.

WAR DIARY
or
INTELLIGENCE SUMMARY
(Erase heading not required.)

Hour, Date, Place		Summary of Events and Information	Remarks and References to Appendices
1st Feb	ST YVES	Quiet day. Hd Qrs shelled heavily for ten minutes about 11.45 am. Relieved by R.War.R	No 1. Casualties in action during February 1915
2nd	LA CRECHE	Billets	
3rd	"	do	
4th	"	do	
5th	"	Relieved R.W.R. 5.30 pm	
6th	ST YVES	Quiet day	
7th	"	Very Quiet day. 6 Heavy Shells behind left trench. Wet night.	
8th	"	Very little sniping; eight light shells on left trench at one pm. Trenches drier.	
9th	"	Usual shelling & sniping. Relieved in evening by R.War.R. Moved to ·63	
10th 11th & 12th	·63	Brigade Reserve.	
13th Feb	·63	Relieved R.War.R in evening. Very wet day. Trenches fair	
14th	ST YVES	Very wet. Little sniping; reserve trench shelled intermittently during the day.	
15th	"	Quiet day; usual shelling	
16th	"	Fine day. Hd Qrs & ST YVES shelled during afternoon. Germans singing during night.	
17th	"	Quiet day. Wet afternoon. Relieved by R.War.R in evening & moved to LA CRECHE	
18th 19th & 20th	LA CRECHE	Mentioned in Despatches 17.2.15. Lt Col Loveband; Captains H.P. Clarke, J.H.C. Frankland, R.M. Watson. 2nd Lt G. de C. Wheeler. Lt F.S.P. Campbell (att'd Pathans); Major Burke. SM Hall, CSM Henderson, Sgt O'Hagan & Cpl Cooke. Capt J.H.C. Frankland to be Brevet Major. Lt-Col Loveband awarded C.M.G. Capt R.M. Watson awarded D.S.O. CSM Henderson awarded Military Cross.	
21st Feb	"	Relieved R.War.R in evening. Trenches in very good condition after 4 fine days. Heavy sniping during evening.	
22nd "	ST YVES	Foggy morning. Heavier sniping than usual. Six shells near Hd Qrs at 3 pm	
23rd	"	Usual sniping & shelling.	
24th	"	" " Bn & Hd Qrs ST. YVES shelled during afternoon.	
25th	"	" Right trenches were shelled; enfilade in afternoon. Very little damage. Only 4 men wounded. Relieved by R.War.R & moved to point ·63 in evening.	
26th "	·63	Brigade Reserve.	
27th & 28th	·63		

G. de C. Wheeler

A P P E N D I X 1 .

Appendix I.

10th Inf.Bde.
4th Div.

2nd BATTN. THE ROYAL DUBLIN FUSILIERS.

M A R C H

1 9 1 5

Attached:

Appendices 1 & 2.

Sheet No 1

Instructions regarding War Diaries and Intelligence Summaries are contained in F. S. Regs., Part II. and the Staff Manual respectively. Title pages will be prepared in manuscript.

WAR DIARY
or
INTELLIGENCE SUMMARY
(Erase heading not required.)

Army Form C. 2118

Hour, Date, Place		Summary of Events and Information	Remarks and References to Appendices
1st MARCH 1915	PT. 63.	Relieved R War R. in Trenches at Night.	For Casualties see appendix No. 1.
2nd "	ST. YVES.	Quiet day, Hd Qrs shelled at 3pm.	
3rd "	"	No Shelling, rather more sniping than usual.	Reinforcement see appendix No. 2.
4th "	"	Six shells at Hd Qrs at 12.30 pm. Usual sniping	
5th "	"	Usual Sniping: ST YVES shelled in the afternoon. Relieved by 1/R War R. in evening & Marched to LA CRECHE	
6th 7th 8th "	LA. CRECHE.	Bn bathed on 7th	
9th "	"	Relieved R War R in trenches at Night.	
10th "	ST. YVES.	Our Guns shelled enemies Trenches at 4.30 pm. Bn co-operated with rifle fire about six shells were fired near breast-work & Reserve Trench. about 7pm. Heavy firing on our left enemy put about 6 shells round ST YVES & Hd Qrs in return. No Damage. [reports were called for to-day for every Two hours from 6.30 am to 8.30 pm. as well as the morning & evening ones.]	
11th "	"	Usual sniping. Our Guns fired from 12 Noon: enemy shelled St Yves from 12.30 to 1.30 pm.	
12th "	"	less sniping than usual. Reserve Trenches heavily shelled	
13th "	"	Usual sniping: ST YVES shelling: Our Guns shelled "factory" (Sheet 28 U 16 C. 0.3.) with good effect. [At 7pm we were informed that the Bde would be relieved on the 14th by 84th Bde & that we would march to an unknown destination on the 15th] Relieved by 1/R War R & moved to 63.	103
14th "	PT. 63.	At 7 am ~~Bn~~ was ordered to march to PONT. NIEPPE. at 12 Noon, we are to take over the lines held by 18th Bde at HOUPLINES. 10.30 pm relief cancelled, the Bn might have to move back to 63 during night	
15th "	PONT. NIEPPE.	No orders were received during the night to move] 12 Noon relief ordered to proceed.	
16th "	"	Relief was permanently Cancelled. Bn is to go back to old Section	
17th "	"	ST. Patrick's day] Bn moved back to ST. YVES. & took trenches over from 84th Bde.	
18th "	ST. YVES.	St. Outlon's Trench was heavily shelled at 1pm. fortunately with little damage, only 1 Man killed & wounded.	
19th "	"	Very quiet day. little sniping no shelling.	
20th "	"	Quiet day, left trenches were lightly shelled during afternoon, received orders at night, that we were to be relieved on the 21st by Rifle Bde, & are to take up a line North of River DOUAVE in conjunction with R War Regt.	
21st "	"	Very quiet day, relieved in evening by Rifle Bde moved to LA CRECHE.	
22nd 23rd 24th "	LA. CRECHE	In evening of 24th CO & Coy Commanders visited the new Trenches, the line runs from the River DOUAVE to the WULVERGHEM. Messines Rd. inclusive it is day at present	

A. Loveband Lt Col
Comdg 2nd Bn Royal Dublin Fusiliers

9 26 6) W 257—976 100,000 4/12 H W V 79
3298

Sheet, No. 2.

Army Form C. 2118.

Instructions regarding War Diaries and Intelligence Summaries are contained in F. S. Regs., Part II. and the Staff Manual respectively. Title pages will be prepared in manuscript.

WAR DIARY
or
~~INTELLIGENCE SUMMARY~~

(*Erase heading not required.*)

Hour, Date, Place		Summary of Events and Information	Remarks and References to Appendices
24th March	LA CRECHE	but all the line is constructed on the breastwork principal & the parapets are rather low. The enemies line is above ours. Any movement by day is immediately detected.	
25th "	STEENBEQUE	Relieved R.War.R. in evening.	
26th "	"	Very quiet day: little sniping	
27th "	"	Very quiet: practically no sniping except at dusk & before dawn.	
28th "	"	Four shells near Reserve Company at 6.15 pm	
29th "	"	Little sniping: 57 shells were fired at Centre Company at 4pm. Parapets was blown down in several places: Relieved by R.W.R in evening & moved to .63.	
30th & 31st "	PT. 63.		

103

1/4/15

A. Loveband Lt. Col.

Comdg. 2 Bn. Royal Dublin Fus.

(9 26 6). W 257—976 100,000 4/12 H W V 79/3298

A P P E N D I C E S 1 & 2 .

APPE[illegible]DIX No 1.

2nd Bn Royal Dublin Fusiliers

List of Casualties for the Month of March 1915.

Date	Officers Wounded	Other ranks Killed in Action			Other ranks Wounded in Action		
1st					12055	Pte	Corbury
2nd		11587	Pte	Moore			
3rd					7692	-	Byrne
					7727	-	Reagan
4th		5224	-	Dugan	7415	-	Allen
					5393	-	Warwick
					[illegible]		MCabey
					1621	-	Furlong
					4311	-	Scott
					2625	-	Murphy
9th					11675	-	Byrne
10th					7160	-	McDonnell
11th		5576	-	O'Hanlon	9617	-	Conway
					6100	-	Flynn
12th		12037	-	Smith	10969	L/S	Morris
13th		11211	Cpl	Page	5505	Pte	Bates
					9342	-	Connolly
					7027	-	Doyle
					7768	-	Connell
					5760	Cpl	McCabe
					5643	Pte	Keogh
					7030	-	McCarthy
15th					9087	Sgt	Goufrey
					9436	L/C	Stallman
					7354	Pte	Healey
					8570	-	Tomney
19th					12029	-	Mason
20th					7755	Cpl	Murphy (died of wounds 21/3/15)
					7425	Sgt	Hampson
21st	Lieut. H.S. J.C. Hazledine	3615	Pte	Crosby	7177	Cpl	Bell
					4852	Pte	Moore
26th		9715	Pte	Breen	11479	Pte	Bolger
		9227	-	Maher			

P.T.O

[illegible]

[illegible]

APPENDIX No 2

2nd Bn Royal Dublin Fusiliers

Reinforcements of Officers & other ranks during March, 1915

Date on which joined	Officers	Numbers of Other ranks.
10th March 20th Reinforcement	——	50 Other Ranks.
16th March 21st Reinforcement	Capt [illegible] Mansel	25 Other Ranks.
25th March 22nd Reinforcement	Capt [illegible] [illegible]	17 Other Ranks.
28th March 23rd Reinforcement	Capt [illegible]	31 Other Ranks.
31st March	[illegible]	——
Total	Officers - 5	Other ranks - 123.

A. Loveband Lt Colonel
Commanding 2nd Bn Royal Dublin Fusiliers.

10th Inf.Bde.
4th Div.

2nd BATTN. THE ROYAL DUBLIN FUSILIERS.

A P R I L

1 9 1 5

Instructions regarding War Diaries and Intelligence Summaries are contained in F. S. Regs., Part II. and the Staff Manual respectively. Title pages will be prepared in manuscript.

WAR DIARY

~~OF~~

~~INTELLIGENCE SUMMARY~~

(Erase heading not required.)

Army Form C. 2118.

10

2nd R Dublin Fus

April 1915

Hour, Date, Place		Summary of Events and Information	Remarks and references to Appendices
1st April 1915.	Billets at LA HUTTE (Pt. 63)	Battn. was in reserve here. Last day in these billets.	
2nd —"—	Trenches	Relieved 2 War. Rgt that evening ~~[illegible]~~ (DOUVE Trenches)	
3rd —"—	Trenches	Very quiet day. Nothing to report	
4th —"—	Trenches	Very little sniping. Six shells over centre coy.	
5th —"—	Trenches	Usual sniping. Enemy put about 20 heavies 200 yds N. of H. Qrs.	
6th —"—	Trenches	Very quiet day. No shelling. Relieved in evening by R. War. Rgt and marched to LA CRECHE	
7th 8th 9th —"—	Billets at LA CRECHE.	Nothing of any interest took place.	
10th —"—	Billets at —"—	Informed that Bde is to be relieved night 12–13th. Relieved R. War Rgt. in trenches that evening.	
11th —"—	Trenches (DOUVE)	Very quiet day. Centre coy. had 12 shells on it during the morning. British aeroplane came over H. Qrs. at 6.15 pm flying very low, about 200 ft. up. Enemy fired with rifles and M. Gs. but he rose and got safely away.	
12th —"—	Trenches.	Usual sniping. Centre coy. was heavily shelled in afternoon. Relieved in evening by 4th R. War. Rgt and Battn. marched to billets at BAILLEUL. A Zeppelin passed over BAILLEUL at 11.30 pm: dropping about 12 bombs (3 women 1 child & 7 horses killed) (1 soldier wounded). Battn. H.Q. fired at the Zeppelin. The bombs made very large holes when they pitched but effect was most local.	[signature]

1247 W 3299 200,000 (E) 8/14 J.B.C. & A. Forms/C. 2118/11.

Army Form C. 2118.

Instructions regarding War Diaries and Intelligence Summaries are contained in F. S. Regs., Part II. and the Staff Manual respectively. Title pages will be prepared in manuscript.

WAR DIARY
or
INTELLIGENCE SUMMARY

(Erase heading not required.)

Hour, Date, Place	Summary of Events and Information	Remarks and references to Appendices
[illegible]	[illegible]	
[illegible]	[illegible]	
[illegible]	[illegible]	
[illegible]	[illegible]	
[illegible]	[illegible]	
[illegible]	[illegible]	
[illegible]	[illegible]	

Army Form C. 2118.

Instructions regarding War Diaries and Intelligence Summaries are contained in F. S. Regs., Part II. and the Staff Manual respectively. Title pages will be prepared in manuscript.

WAR DIARY ~~or~~ INTELLIGENCE SUMMARY

(Erase heading not required.)

Hour, Date, Place	Summary of Events and Information	Remarks and references to Appendices
26th April 1915 St JULIEN (Trenches facing)	Quiet morning up to 11 am. Northumbrian INF. BDE attacked through our trenches. Capt BANKS was killed. Capt BASIL MACLEAR assumed command. Heavy shelling throughout the day, and intermittent musketry. Occasional shelling throughout the night.	
27th April 1915 — " —	Quiet day, no sniping, shelling commenced at 8 pm. and continued intermittently throughout the night.	
28th April 1915 — " —	Enemy shelled with gas-shells. Battn suffered little. Quiet night.	
29th April 1915 — " —	Quiet day. Enemy shows signs of attack at 5 pm. Intermittent musketry followed by shelling. Enemy's attack did not develop.	
30th April 1915	Quiet day. LT. COL. LOVEBAND C.M.G. returned.	

[illegible]

10th Inf.Bde.
4th Div.

2nd BATTN. THE ROYAL DUBLIN FUSILIERS.

M A Y

1 9 1 5

Attached:

Report on Action of
24th May.
Casualty List.

Army Form C. 2118

Instructions regarding War Diaries and Intelligence Summaries are contained in F. S. Regs., Part II. and the Staff Manual respectively. Title pages will be prepared in manuscript.

WAR DIARY
~~or~~
~~INTELLIGENCE SUMMARY~~

(Erase heading not required.)

Hour, Date, Place	Summary of Events and Information	Remarks and references to Appendices
1st MAY 1915. Trenches (facing St JULIEN)	Enemys sniping ~~more~~ accurate than usual. Quiet night.	
2nd MAY 1915 — " —	Enemy attacked under cover of gas. Men of left coy were most affected. Enemy did not reach our trenches. Shelling ceased at 4 pm. Quiet night.	
3rd MAY 1915 — " —	Intermittent Shelling throughout the day and night.	
4th MAY 1915 — " —	Quiet day. Battn. withdrew from line & passing through new line 1/2 mile in rear bivouacked on East bank of canal 1/2 mile N-W of LA BRIQUE. arriving there 2 am. 5th May. Two bombs dropped by hostile aeroplane near canal bridge – two men slightly wounded.	
5th MAY 1915. BIVOUAC (E. Bank of Canal).	Moved at dusk to bivouac round CHATEAU DES TROIS TOURS.	
6th MAY 1915 BIVOUAC (CHATEAU DES TROIS TOURS)	Quiet day	
7th MAY 1915 — " —	Quiet day	
8th MAY 1915 — " —	At noon warned to be prepared to support 84th Inf. Bde. At 1.30 pm. left bivouac (in fighting order) joined with 1st Q. Vic. Rgt outside Ypres and marched in artillery formation through LA BRIQUE and ST JEAN to wood by POTIJZE CHATEAU. Battn. was under heavy shell fire throughout afternoon and evening. Battn. deployed for attack N of POTIJZE WOODS and advanced to attack with left on WIELTJE. Three times the Battn. was extended beyond our barbed wire ready to assault the German trenches and each time the attack was cancelled. Enemys M. Guns did considerable damage. NO rations came up.	
9th MAY 1915 TRENCHES (WIELTJE)	At 2.15 a.m. Battn. finally occupied [illegible] left of G.H.Q. LINE with left 150 yards S-E of SHELL TRAP [illegible] – one coy. being in reserve in trenches N. of POTIJE WOOD. Shelling started at 11 am. One of the worst days shelling Battn. experienced. During afternoon sniping was accurate and machine gunfire made the reconstruction of trenches that night accurate.	[illegible signature]

Instructions regarding War Diaries and Intelligence Summaries are contained in F. S. Regs., Part II. and the Staff Manual respectively. Title pages will be prepared in manuscript.

WAR DIARY

or

~~INTELLIGENCE SUMMARY~~

(Erase heading not required.)

Army Form C. 21[illegible]

Hour, Date, Place	Summary of Events and Information	Remarks and References to Appendices
10th May 1915 TRENCHES (WIELTJE)	Intermittent Shelling throughout Day and [illegible] sniping [illegible] evening. Quiet night.	
11th May 1915 TRENCHES (WIELTJE)	Heavy Shelling from [illegible] [illegible] [illegible] of Day [illegible] sniping [illegible] during the evening. [illegible] [illegible] throughout the night. No damage done by Shelling	
12th May 1915 TRENCHES (WIELTJE)	Intermittent shelling throughout [illegible] [illegible] sniping [illegible] [illegible] evening. [illegible] [illegible] [illegible] [illegible] BDE. Battn marched [illegible] [illegible] bivouac in VLAMERTINGHE CHATEAU GROUNDS.	
13th MAY 1915 BIVOUAC VLAMERTINGHE CHATEAU 14th MAY [illegible] 15th MAY 1915	[illegible]	
16th MAY 1915 BIVOUAC VLAMERTINGHE CHATEAU	Battn left bivouac at [illegible] [illegible] [illegible] [illegible] [illegible] [illegible] [illegible] as Divisional support [illegible] [illegible] Battn [illegible] [illegible] [illegible] [illegible] Quiet night. Battn relieved [illegible]	
17th MAY 1915 TRENCHES (DIV. SUPPORT LINE) 18th MAY 1915	} Quiet Day [illegible] [illegible] [illegible] [illegible]	
19th MAY 1915	[illegible] Battn [illegible] [illegible] [illegible] [illegible] from [illegible] [illegible] [illegible] [illegible] (left) [illegible] [illegible] [illegible] [illegible] [illegible] [illegible] ([illegible]) [illegible] [illegible] [illegible] [illegible]	
[illegible] MAY 1915 TRENCHES (FRONT LINE)	[illegible] [illegible] [illegible] [illegible] [illegible] [illegible] [illegible] [illegible] [illegible] [illegible] day & night	[illegible]

9 26 6 W 257—976 100,000 4/12 H W V 70 3298

Instructions regarding War Diaries and Intelligence Summaries are contained in F. S. Regs., Part II. and the Staff Manual respectively. Title pages will be prepared in manuscript.

WAR DIARY
or
INTELLIGENCE SUMMARY
(Erase heading not required.)

Army Form C. 2118.

Hour, Date, Place	Summary of Events and Information	Remarks and References to Appendices
22nd MAY 1915 TRENCHES (FRONT LINE)	Enemy shelled right and centre of Battn line. No damage done during day. Trench mortar put two shells into SHELL TRAP Fm at 11.30pm. Intermittent shelling throughout night. Enemys aeroplane passed very low down over SHELL TRAP Fm 4 pm	
23rd MAY 1915 TRENCHES (FRONT LINE)	Enemys aeroplane flew low over SHELL TRAP Fm 5.30pm Quiet Day and night	
24th MAY 1915 TRENCHES (FRONT LINE)	At 2.45 am. enemy attacked with gas. Area round SHELL TRAP Fm and to N-W of Fm was most affected. Enemy advanced in small numbers 4.30 am. occupied & held British line North, and to left of Battn trenches. Battn. subjected to heavy shelling and enfilade fire. Battn supported by part of 2 coys 9th A+S. Highrs. Battn held to their trenches to the end. Germans advancing, under cover of enfilade fire, in small parties finally occupied Battn line by 2.30 pm. Shelling ceased but rifle and M.G. fire remained accurate and constant whenever a target presented itself, until dusk. What remained of Battn. was withdrawn from the line at 9.30 pm. and bivouaced on west bank of canal 1½ mls W. of LA BRIQUE. Battn strength in trenches in the morning was Officers 17, Other Ranks 651. When Battn. was withdrawn that evening one officer and 20 other ranks crossed the canal	
25th MAY 1915 BIVOUAC (CANAL BANK)	What remained of Battn (reinforced by draft) moved into bivouac in VLAMERTINGHE CHATEAU Grounds 12 noon. Strength including draft officers 2, Other ranks 190. (also Chaplain and medical officer)	
26th MAY 1915 BIVOUAC (VLAMERTINGHE CHATEAU Grounds)	Battn moved to bivouac with 1st L. of T. 1 mile N. of VLAMERINGHE CHATEAU.	
27th MAY 1915 BIVOUAC (with 1st L. of Transport)	Quiet Day.	[signature] 2nd [illegible]

(9 26 6) W 257—976 100,000 4/12 H W V 79/3298

Army Form C. 2118.

WAR DIARY
or
INTELLIGENCE SUMMARY

(Erase heading not required.)

Instructions regarding War Diaries and Intelligence Summaries are contained in F. S. Regs., Part II, and the Staff Manual respectively. Title pages will be prepared in manuscript.

Hour, Date, Place	Summary of Events and Information	Remarks and References to Appendices
28th May [illegible]	[illegible]	
29th		
30th		
31st	[illegible]	

[illegible signature]

C A S U A L T Y   L I S T .

[illegible]

Date	Officers		[illegible]	[illegible]	[illegible]
25-4-15	Killed	[illegible]	45	70	[illegible]
	Wounded	[illegible]			
26-4-15	Killed	Capt E.R. [illegible]	–	5	–
28-4-15			–	6	–
30-4-15			–	6	–
1-5-15			–	18	–
2-5-15			–	7	–
3-5-15			5	20	–
4-5-15	Wounded	[illegible]	–	10	2
9-5-15	Killed	Capt [illegible]	21	50	155
10-5-15	Killed	[illegible]	[illegible]	[illegible]	–
	Wounded	[illegible]			
11-5-15			–	4	–
13-5-15			–	5	–
15-5-15			–	1	–
16-5-15	[illegible]	[illegible]			
17-5-15			–	24	–
19-5-15			4	5	1
20-5-15	Killed	[illegible]	3	6	–
21-5-15			–	12	–
22-5-15			4	11	–
24-5-15	Killed	Lieut-Col A. Loveband, [illegible]	9 + 5	2 + 88	546
	Wounded	[illegible]			
	Gassed	[illegible]			
	Missing	[illegible]			
	[illegible]	[illegible]			
25-5-15	[illegible]	2/Lt M. Young			
	K. 24 W. 14 M. 2		103	291	1094

REPORT ON ACTION OF 24TH MAY.

War Diary from Col. Loveband Carter

2nd Royal Dublin Fusiliers.

Report on action of 24th May 1915.

Col. Lovesand, Major Magan (2nd in C), Russell (R.A.M.C and I (A/Adj) had just finished dinner in our H.Qr. dug outs (C.22. central) at 2:30 a.m. Previous to this the Col. and Magan had been round all the front line trenches and spent considerable time in SHELL TRAP FARM. Something suggested "gas" to the Col. during his round of the trenches as he personally warned all coy. officers to be prepared and Russell had inspected all the Vermoral sprayers and warned each company about damping their respirators. There were ten (10) sprayers in working order that night - one with each M.G. and remainder distributed along the trenches.

At about 2:45 a.m. the Col. and I were standing outside our dug out, some 400 yds behind the first line of trenches, looking in the direction of Shell Trap Farm, when we saw a red light thrown up in the German lines to the N.W. of the Farm, and immediately three lights (Red) were seen directly over Shell Trap Farm, and a few more lights (Red) in the German lines from the direction of C.30 - (S.E. from where we were standing). A few seconds later a dull roar was heard - more of an explosion (certainly not a shell) and we saw the gas coming on either side of Shell Trap Farm. The Col. shouted "Get your respirators boys, here comes the gas". We had only just time to get our respirators on before the gas was over us - the Doctor (Russell) who was seeing to other people got some gas before his own respirator was adjusted.

In the trenches the "Stand To" was just over and Rum was being issued, so there could not have been any element of surprise other than the sudden appearance of the gas - everyone was awake. There was a very gentle breeze, the gas was very dense and took considerable time to pass over, about $\frac{3}{4}$ Hr. From the nature of the ground - a gradual slope towards Bn. H.Qrs. from the first line of trenches. I do not think that the gas lasted as long over the trenches as it did over us at H.Qrs. or the troops (2 coys 9th Argyls) in the Retrench ment. Also our right coy.(A) under Capt. Basil Maclear did not get such a heavy gassing as the remainder. While the gas was at its height with us some of the 9th Argyls retired from the Retrenchment. Col. Lovehand and I ran out to stop them, there were five Dublins with them, who came to us and three of them were employed later as orderlies, the other two were gas effected, but I regret to say we could'nt stop those of the Argyls. By this time the gas was clearing a little but was still fairly thick and Russell drew our attention to the trench on the left of Shell Trap Farm out of which men were(pmx) pouring and almost immediately saw 3 Germans in the right corner of Shell Trap Farm, close against the buildings.

The Col. sent the following messages :-

1. To 9th Argyls Retrenchment.

"Enemy are in Shell Trap Farm, counter attack at once" (4:45 a.m.)

2. A verbal message to Kings Own on left of 18th R.Irish :-

"Enemy are occupying some of 18th R.I. trenches, and there are a few in Shell Trap Farm" - (or orders to that effect - it was a verbal message.)

3. To O.C. 9th Argyls.

"Enemy are in Shell Trap Farm. Send forward 2 coys to reinforce Retrenchment line and counter attack at once" (4:45 a.m.)

Almost immediately we received a verbal reply from Kings Own saying that they could deal with enemy in 18th R.I. trench if we could deal with those in Farm - (or words to that effect). We had also asked King's Own to inform 10th Inf. Bde. as our(kimmm) wires by that time were all out. Just before they were cut Kings Own sent another message saying that they were all right.

By this time gas had quite cleared and enemy were shelling heavily, a good many of 9th Argyls in Retrenchment had moved up but had gone rather in support of A and -- coys. i.e. to our right and centre trenches instead of to Shell Trap Farm and I think an Argyl officer with M.G. and team had moved up to one of our support trenches, but to which trench I cannot say.

Verbal messages then started coming in from the front trenches, all full of confidence; and Basil Maclear told us about enemy in Shell Trap Farm. This was the first time he could see them there, as they had previously kept under cover of the buildings out of his sight. Colonel then sent 2nd message to

O.C. 9th Argyls.

"Enemy are in Shell Trap Farm, please send up two coys at once and counter attack and reoccupy Farm A A A Germans are in right side of Farm A A A Inform 10th Inf. Bde. (5:55 a.m.)

Meanwhile "heavies" were being dumped into our trenches and there was a severe enfilade M.G. fire opened on us from 18th R.I. trenches left of Farm. Getting messages down to Battn. H.Q. was a difficulty and it was impossible to get an orderly back to Div. Support line without him being badly hit - every orderly who came to and went from us was hit, yet every time there was a message to go there was a volunteer to take it. My orderlies were used up by then so I had to use gassed men and signallers.

Colonel then sent following message to 10th Inf. Bde:-

"Germans are in Shell Trap Farm and I can see a few in small building in right of Farm A A A Get artillery to shell it A A A I believe my 2 platoons are still holding trench to left of Farm A A A Germans have occupied the right trench of 18th R.I. A A A Have been unable to get up the 2 coys of Argyls in support line so far A A A Argyls in Retrenchment have moved up but I fear to my centre and right but I am not sure if any went up to the Farm A A A Reinforcements are required A A A Situation not satisfactory ".

This message was untimed but I think it was sent about ½ hr. before Burt - Marshall arrived with us.

The enemy were now using gas shells, which disturbed our eyes, but did not appear to have any other effect.

Meanwhile the Col. Russell, and I were standing at back of our dug out (C.22.centre) - Major Magan was inside gassed and out of action since about 4 a.m. Russell was hit with piece of shell, but remained at duty. He did most gallant work throughout.

Col. Poole then came up and Col. Loveband explained the situation. As far as I can remember Col. Poole had not gone very long before Burt - Marshall arrived. The Col. Burt - Marshall and I were standing at back of dug out - the Doctor was inside - when the bullets came from behind and presently Col Loveband was hit through the heart. He died without a word though he tried to say something. Burt Marshall was hit in the shoulder from a bullett coming from the same direction. He was most pluckly - would'nt wait, but raced off to stop the firing. Our guns were shelling Shell Trap Farm heavily by this and our shrapnell appeared to be bursting well clear of our trenches. The enemy recommenced their shelling and "heavies" were being dumped into our right trenches and the rifle and M.G. fire was very accurate from the 18th R.I. trench which the Germans held in force. It was marvellous how quickly they converted the parapet and everything was done without confusion and with proper method.

Basil Maclear then sent following message :-

"Must have more men on left between B Coy and Shell Trap

Farm ".

This particular spot was occupied by D coy and they were in a bad state. It was obvious now that the 9th A & S Highlanders who had supported us had gone too much to their right, very few had supported D coy. or Major Digby Johnson with C coy in front of Farm.

Some Argyls started coming back on right i.e. from trenches in C.22.b., and C.23.b. Russell and I ran out to stop them. Russell was perfectly splendid and could'nt have given more help had he been a combatant officer, but it was useless. A few of our men were with them, and some of these stopped when they saw their own officers and obeyed orders. The remainder were dropping like flies and very few reached the Div support line. I should think there were about six Dublins I could'nt turn at once, and they came with me when the others started. On arriving back at the dug out I found Lieut Gerald Tarleton had just managed to crawl down with a message from D coy (Capt.J.Harold-Barry) Barry had sent Tarleton down with the message as he was badly wounded in the trenches. D coy was in a bad state one man per 5 yards capable of using a rifle and this with all supports in front line. Tarleton was mad with gas and badly hit, but he had the heart of a lion and delivered his message - it was the only thing on him which was not covered with blood and mud. He had about 10 wounds but was quite happy when his messahge was safe. Later in the day when he recovered somewhat there was something on his mind but we could not discover what - he was too done to talk but when we produced his Very pistol from his haversack he was quite happy - he knew that Very pistols were very important.

A message arrived then from 2/Lt. Wright (9th A & S. Highlanders) -

"I have a M.G. and a few men of 9th A & S Highlanders and R.I.F. in the support trench which guide will show you - almost due west of the Farm. Are you going to relieve us or shall we retire".

I sent him a message telling him to hold on and that I expected supports up. The R. War. R$\frac{1}{8}$ had a few men coming up on the left of where I was, though Farm in C.22.b. Wright evidently mistook the few 18th R.I. men he had with him for R.I.Fus.

Shanks - (our M.G. officer) sent following message :-
"Enemy are strongly entrenching themselves between Shell Trap Farm and D coy trenches. We are extremely weak. Reinforcements are urgently needed. Reference attached message Two coys did reinforce us but they have been considerably weakened".

Basil Maclear sent following :-
"Very many of men are surrounded. We must have reinforcements".

Basil was on left of A coy. and right of B coy. and when the Germans got into D coy. trench, as they did about this time he gallantly led a party to grenade them out. He was killed doing this.

Next message came from 2/Lt. Kempston who was with B coy?.(2/Lt. Ramsey Fitzgibbon Hall had been killed):-
"For God's sake send us some help. We are nearly done".

Meanwhile I had scribbled other messages of which I have no copies and at 12:45 p.m. sent following to 10th Inf. Bde :-
"Reinforce or all is lost".

Shanks (M.G. officer) sent one as follows :-
"Our artillery are firing into our trenches. Please hasten Reinforcements. All along the line they are needed. The Germans hold our trenches from Shell Trap Farm for about 200 yards towards us. Maclear, Thomas, Hall are killed ".

Just after that Kenyiston was killed, but Shanks was still fighting with B coy. and that is the last I heard of him.

A coy. were also holding out, presumably under 2/Lt. Y oung. This officer was got away by someone in the evening as he died of wounds in Hospital on 25th. Of C coy. in front of Shell Trap Farm I heard little, but they were still fighting at 12 noon though they were having a bad time from M.Guns in 18th R.I. trenches. Major Digby Johnson died of gas early in the morning and 2/Lt. Considine was killed about 8 a.m. 2/Lt. Moran was off his head with gas with me about 2 p.m.

When the wounded were sent away after dark there were no Dublins in front of Battn. H.Qrs. From about 2:30 p.m. there was no fighting in our trenches. Everyone held on to them to the last. There was no surrender, no retirement and no quarter given or accepted. They all died fighting at their posts.

At 9:30 p.m. I received the following message:- "Please withdraw your H.Qrs. and all men in the Retrenchment if any are still there, and report at Bde. H.Qrs. west of Canal".

I have not put in all the messages I sent to 10th Inf. Bde and R.War. Regt. as they are already known.

(signed) Thomas V Linky. Capt.

2 R. Dublin Fusiliers.

10th Inf.Bde.
4th Div.

2nd BATTN. THE ROYAL DUBLIN FUSILIERS.

J U N E

1 9 1 5

Attached:

Casualty & Reinforcement List.

Instructions regarding War Diaries and Intelligence Summaries are contained in F. S. Regs., Part II. and the Staff Manual respectively. Title pages will be prepared in manuscript.

WAR DIARY
or
INTELLIGENCE SUMMARY
(Erase heading not required.)

Army Form C. 2118.

Hour, Date, Place	Summary of Events and Information	Remarks and references to Appendices
1st June 1915 Canal Bank, West of La Brique	Peaceful Day. Men bathing in the afternoon. Digging parties in evening 200 men.	
2nd June 1915 ″	ditto ditto ditto 300 men.	
3rd ″ ″	″ ″ ″ 100 ″	
4th ″ ″	Left for Vlamertinghe Chateau 12.30 noon. Bivouac in Woods.	
5th ″ Bivouac in Woods Vlamertinghe Chateau.	Nothing to report.	
6th ″ ″	Left to take over position from French, Canal West Bank Zwaanhof Bridge, 10 pm.	
7th ″ Canal West Bank Zwaanhof Bridge.	Annoyed with small shells & slight casualties digging that night.	
8th ″ ″	Major Higginson arrived and ~~[illegible]~~ took over Command from Capt T. S. Healy.	
9th ″ ″	Night shelling.	
10th ″ ″	Quiet day. Wet.	
11th ″	Battalion relieved at night by East Lancashire Regiment, marched to Billets at A.18.D. Sheet 28, arriving there 4AM 12 instant.	
12th 13th 14th & 15th		
16th ″ Reserve Trenches Canal Bank.	Battalion took over Reserve Trenches from East Lancs.	
17th June 1915 ″	Fine Quiet day.	
18th ″	Nothing to report.	
19th ″		

Instructions regarding War Diaries and Intelligence Summaries are contained in F. S. Regs., Part II. and the Staff Manual respectively. Title pages will be prepared in manuscript.

WAR DIARY
or
INTELLIGENCE SUMMARY
(Erase heading not required.)

Army Form C. 2118.

Hour, Date, Place		Summary of Events and Information	Remarks and references to Appendices
20th June 1915.	Canal Bank Reserve Trenches	Heavily shelled. 3 AM. Little damage	
21st "	"	Quiet Day. Shelled Little Willies 2.30 AM. 5.9., 5.30. pm.	
22nd "	"	Quiet Day. Relieved Warwicks in evening.	
23rd "	C.19.B. (Sheet 27)	Quiet Day. Few shells. Trenches in bad state, require cleaning and rebuilding.	
24th "	"	" "	
25th "	"	Slight shelling in afternoon.	
26th "	"	Nothing to report.	
27th "	"	Fine Day Intermittent shelling all day	
28th "	"	Relieved in evening by 1st R. War. R. marched to Billets A.16.A. arriving there 2 AM. 29th ins[illegible].	
29th + 30th	Billets A.16.A.	Nothing to report.	

[illegible] 1st D. 2.[illegible]

1247 W 3299 200,000 (E) 8/14 J.B.C.&A. Forms/C. 2118/11.

CASUALTY & REINFORCEMENT LIST.

War Diary 1915.

Remarks and References to Appendices.

Date.	Drafts and Casualties etc.
1st June 1915.	4 Officers and 75 Other Ranks taken on strength of Battalion
4th " "	1 Officer and 103 Other Ranks taken on strength of Battalion.
7th " "	2 Officers and 125 Other Ranks taken on strength of Battalion
8th " "	8. Casualties in action
9th " "	3 Officers taken on strength of Battalion.
11th " "	1 Officer ditto 2 Casualties in action.
12th " "	126 Other Ranks ditto.
13th " "	Capt R. M. Watson D.S.O., Adjutant, rejoined.
14th " "	2 Officers taken on strength of Battalion.
15th " "	50 Other Ranks ditto
18th " "	2 Officers ditto
19th " "	29 Other Ranks ditto
20th " "	2. Casualties in action
21st " "	1. Officer taken on strength of Battalion.
23rd " "	11 Casualties in action.
24 " "	2. Casualties in action
25th " "	Lieut J. V. Holland accidently wounded. + 1. Casualty in action.
26th " "	2 Officers and 21. Other Ranks taken on strength of Battalion
27th " "	3. Casualties in action.
30th " "	3 Killed and 5 wounded in action.

4th D[illegible]

[illegible]

2nd Batt [illegible]

July [illegible]

17

10th Inf.Bde.
4th Div.

2nd BATTN. THE ROYAL DUBLIN FUSILIERS.

J U L Y

1 9 1 5

Attached:

Casualty & Reinforcement List.

Instructions regarding War Diaries and Intelligence Summaries are contained in F. S. Regs., Part II. and the Staff Manual respectively. Title pages will be prepared in manuscript.

WAR DIARY
or
INTELLIGENCE SUMMARY

(Erase heading not required.)

Army Form C. 2118.

Hour, Date, Place	Summary of Events and Information	Remarks and references to Appendices
JULY 1st 2nd + 3rd A.16.A	BILLETS.	
" 4th	Relieved 1/R War. Regt	
" 5th	Quiet day	
5am " 6th	Guns opened fire on German Trenches, which the 11th Bde were assaulting at 6 am kept it up without ceasing till 6 am and then lengthened range, and kept firing till 7 am. We had removed lengths of wire in front of our trenches during the night and showed Bayonets at intervals in the morning, so as to appear as if attack was coming from our trenches, we were shelled steadily between 5.30 am and 6.30 am & afterwards intermittently till 7 am. Enemy massed for counter attack on their lost trenches in afternoon but were dispersed by the FRENCH and our Guns.	
July 7th	Good deal of damage was done to our Parapets by shelling on 7th. Quiet morning; Officers of the West Riding Regt (T.F.) who were going to relieve us visited trenches. Counter attacks by the enemy were all dispersed by the French and our Guns. Our trenches shelled during afternoon between 6.45 & 7.30 pm. Battn Head Quarters and Reserve trenches shelled with "STINK SHELLS".	
" 8th	FUSILIER ~~[illegible]~~ and Lancashire Lanes bombarded with trench mortars between 9.30 and 10.30 am. Otherwise quiet day. Relieved at night by 6th Bn West Riding Regt T.F. and marched to A.16.A.	
" 9th A.16.A	Battalion marched by companies to HOUTKERQUE.	
" 10th 11th 12th 13th HOUTKERQUE.	BILLETS.	
" 14th "	Lt General Sir Herbert PLUMER Commanding 2nd Army inspected the 10th Inf Brigade. Battalion looking well [illegible] Sir Herbert addressed the Brigade after the Parade [illegible] complimented it on its doings in April 25th [illegible]	

5

1247 W 3299 200,000 (E) 8 14 J.B.C. & A. Forms/C. 2118/11.

Instructions regarding War Diaries and Intelligence Summaries are contained in F. S. Regs., Part II. and the Staff Manual respectively. Title pages will be prepared in manuscript.

WAR DIARY
or
INTELLIGENCE SUMMARY
(Erase heading not required.)

Army Form C. 2118.

Hour, Date, Place	Summary of Events and Information	Remarks and references to Appendices
July 15th 16th 17th HOUTKERQUE	Billets	
" 18th HOUTKERQUE	Billets. Maj: H.W. Higginson returned from leave & assumed Command	
" 19th "	"	
" 20th "	" Field Marshal Sir John French C-in-C inspected Bde 11.30 am	
" 21st "	"	
" 22nd "	Battn. left HOUTKERQUE 3.15 pm. & marched to GODEWAERSVELDE (8½ mls) arriving 7 pm., bivouacked until 11 pm. & then entrained. Heavy rain from 4 p.m. onwards. Entrainment carried on without any difficulty.	
" 23rd Line of March	Battn. left GODERSVELDE 2.23 am. arriving DOULLENS 9.15 am. detrained & marched to bivouac near FRESCHEVILLERS. Heavy rain until 11 am. At 4 pm Battn marched to billets at VAUCHELLES-LES-AUTHIE, accomodation was limited & billets indifferent	
" 24th VAUCHELLES-LES-AUTHIE	Billets. Lieut-Gen Sir C.C. Monro Comdg. IIIrd Army inspected Bde. Battn. drawn up in line outside billets. He expressed himself very pleased with the appearance of the Battn.	
" 25th "	Battn. moved to billets at BERTRANCOURT.	
" 26th BERTRANCOURT	Billets. C.O. Adj. M.O. & Coy. Commanders left BERTRANCOURT at 3 am. to visit French trenches, moving via BEAUSSART & MAILLY-MAILLET to SUCRERIE (H.Q. 64th Rgt Infantrie) they proceeded to trenches of 3rd Battn 64th Rgt (C.O. Capt. TESSIER.) Battn. took over trenches that night without any difficulty.	
" 27th TRENCHES.	Quiet day. Battn. spent day adjusting themselves in new trenches. Reserve [illegible] was in old German line which had been captured by the French on 7th June & contained numerous very deep 'dug outs' – some 20 feet deep. Front line was well planned but the parapets poor and inadequate.	

1247 W 3299 200,000 (E) 8/14 J.B.C. & A. Forms/C. 2118/11.

Instructions regarding War Diaries and Intelligence Summaries are contained in F. S. Regs., Part II. and the Staff Manual respectively. Title pages will be prepared in manuscript.

WAR DIARY
or
INTELLIGENCE SUMMARY
(Erase heading not required.)

Army Form C. 2118.

Hour, Date, Place	Summary of Events and Information	Remarks and references to Appendices
July 28th TRENCHES	Quiet Day	
" 29th "	Quiet Day. C.O. at [illegible]	
30th	Quiet Day. Battn relieved by [illegible]	
	[illegible]	
31st [illegible]	Billets	

H. W. Higginson Lt Col.
Comdg 2nd R Dub Fus

1247 W 3299 200,000 (E) 8/14 J.B.C. & A. Forms C. 2118/11.

CASUALTY & REINFORCEMENT LIST.

[illegible]

[illegible] (9am to 7.15)

[illegible] 2 Other ranks wounded

[illegible]

10th Inf.Bde.
4th Div.

2nd BATTN. THE ROYAL DUBLIN FUSILIERS.

A U G U S T

1 9 1 5

Attached:

Casualty & Reinforcement List.

2nd Bn Royal Dublin Fusiliers

Instructions regarding War Diaries and Intelligence Summaries are contained in F. S. Regs., Part II. and the Staff Manual respectively. Title pages will be prepared in manuscript.

WAR DIARY

or

~~INTELLIGENCE SUMMARY~~

(Erase heading not required.)

Army Form C. 2118.

1915 Hour, Date, Place	Summary of Events and Information	Remarks and References to Appendices
August 1st BERTRANCOURT.	BILLETS.	
" 2nd "		
" 3rd LEALVILLERS	Battalion moved to LEALVILLERS	
" 4th 5th 6th 7th "	On 6th inst at 2.30 pm Capt Massy-Westropp was giving a bomb demonstration and a Mills Hand Grenade exploded prematurely. Capt Massy-Westropp & 12 other Ranks being wounded.	
" 8th "	Relieved 1/8 War. R. in trenches on the right of line previously occupied.	
" 9th TRENCHES	nothing to report	
" 10th "	Not [illegible].	
" 11th 12th "	Nothing to report.	
" 13th "	Trenches shelled by field guns between 3.20 & 4.00 pm.	
" 14th 15th "	Nothing to report.	
" 16th "	Enemy fired about 20 large Trench Mortar Bombs into Bay Trench. 3 men Buried One Killed.	
" 17th 18th 19th 20th & 21st "	Nothing to report.	
" 22nd "	Relieved in evening by 1/8 War. R. went into billets in [illegible]	
" 23rd to 31st MAILLY, MAILLET.	BILLETS.	

H. [illegible] Higginson [illegible]
[illegible]

CASUALTY & REINFORCEMENT LIST.

Remarks and References to Appendices

6-8-15	Capt Harvey Wethold and 12 Other Ranks injured through the [illegible] of a No 5 Hand Grenade while Instructing Bomb Throwing
8-8-15	1 Other Rank Killed in action
11-8-15	1 Other Rank wounded in action
12-8-15	1 Other Rank wounded in action
15-8-15	4 Other Ranks wounded in action
16-8-15	2 Other Rank killed and 8 Wounded in action
17-8-15	1 Other Rank Wounded in Action
20-8-15	3 Other Ranks Wounded in action
21-8-15	1 Other Rank Wounded accidentally.
13-8-15	17 O.R. Joined Battalion.
17-8-15	15 O.R. Joined Battalion
23-8-15	2/Lieut A.W. Sainsbury joined Battalion.
24-8-15	Lieut W.R. Morgan Joined Battalion
25-8-15	24 O.R. Joined Battalion

Strength of Battalion on 1-8-15 Officers 25 Other Ranks 817
31-8-15 " 25 " " [illegible]20

10th Inf.Bde.
4th Div.

2nd BATTN. THE ROYAL DUBLIN FUSILIERS.

S E P T E M B E R

1 9 1 5

Attached:

Casualty & Rein-
forcement List.

Confidential

Instructions regarding War Diaries and Intelligence Summaries are contained in F. S. Regs., Part II. and the Staff Manual respectively. Title pages will be prepared in manuscript.

WAR DIARY 2nd Bn Royal Dublin Fusiliers
or
~~INTELLIGENCE SUMMARY~~
(*Erase heading not required.*)

Army Form C. 2118.

Hour, Date, Place	Summary of Events and Information	Remarks and References to Appendices
September 1st MAILLY-MAILLET	"BILLETS."	
" 2nd "AUCHONVILLERS"	Relieved [illegible] in Trench in front of AUCHONVILLERS [illegible]	
" 3, 4, 5, 6th	Nothing of importance occurred.	
" 7th	Lt Ingoldby, L.C. Brennan & Pte Beatty went out at 7.30 pm on patrol and laid out about 150 yards beyond "REDAN" [illegible] they saw a party of about 20 Germans coming towards them, when the Germans had approached within 20 yards the patrol opened fire and 2 Germans fell: the remainder immediately [illegible] [illegible] [illegible] surround our patrol which had to retire. Pte Beatty was wounded. At [illegible] a patrol went out to see if they could find any dead or wounded Germans, but reported the Enemy had removed the 2 men who fell: traces of blood were found.	
" 8th	Nothing to report.	
" 9th	Battn relieved by 2/Monmouthshire Regt, and marched to Billets at FORCEVILLE.	
" 10th, 11th, 12th, 13th, 14th, 15th FORCEVILLE	BILLETS.	
" 16th to 22nd Trenches	Relieved 2/Monmouthshire R. at [illegible]. Quiet Tour, usual [illegible] patrolling: nothing of [illegible] to report. Relieved on 22nd by 8 South Lancs. Battn marched to billets in "VARENNES."	
" 24th VARENNES	[illegible] to COURCELLES-AUX-BOIS.	
" 25th COURCELLES	Nothing to report.	
" 26th, 27th & 28th — do —	BILLETS. Relieved [illegible] in Trenches on [illegible]	
30th TRENCHES	Nothing to report.	

[illegible signature]

CASUALTY & REINFORCEMENT LIST.

Appendix to War Diary Sept [illegible]

[illegible]

10th Inf.Bde.
4th Div.

2nd BATTN. THE ROYAL DUBLIN FUSILIERS.

O C T O B E R

1 9 1 5

Attached:

Casualty & Reinforcement List.

Instructions regarding War Diaries and Intelligence Summaries are contained in F. S. Regs., Part II. and the Staff Manual respectively. Title pages will be prepared in manuscript.

WAR DIARY
~~or~~
~~INTELLIGENCE SUMMARY~~
(Erase heading not required.)

Army Form C. 2118.

2nd Bn Royal Dublin Fusiliers

Hour, Date, Place	Summary of Events and Information	Remarks and references to Appendices
Trenches Oct 1st 1915	Applied under Lt [illegible] R I R succeeded in cutting the [illegible] of enemy wire N. of RAVIN-EN-Y. [illegible] about 10 yards before they were discovered & [illegible] we had no casualties.	
2nd 3rd 4th 5th 6th	Nothing of interest to report. Bn relieved on 6th by [illegible], and marched to billets in ACHEUX.	
ACHEUX 7th - 13	On Oct 13th General Sir C. C. Monro K.C.B. Comdg 3rd Army inspected the Bn in chateau grounds in [illegible] noon. The Bn was drawn up in Quarter Column, & after inspection was formed in three sides of a square & addressed. The General said it was always a pleasure to be able to say nice things to people, he then went on to say that he had very good accounts of the Bn from everywhere, both on account of its bravery in action, its conduct in trenches, and its [illegible]. He [illegible] the Bn would live up to its [illegible]. The Bn [illegible] [illegible] in the trenches on the same day.	
14th 20th In the trenches	Nothing of interest to report. Bn was relieved on 20th by [illegible] and went to billets in MAILLY.	
21st - 30th MAILLEY-MAILLET	On Oct 25th several units of the VII Corps were inspected by His Majesty the King in ACHEUX. His Majesty was accompanied by M. Poincaré the President of the French Republic. On Oct 29th received orders that we [illegible] take over [illegible] Lancashire Fusiliers [illegible]. This line is immediately on the left of our old line & includes THE REDAN	
30th 31st Trenches	Relieved Lancashire Fusiliers in trenches. Nothing to report.	

1247 W 3299 200,000 (E) 8/14 J.B.C. & A. Forms/C. 2118/11.

CASUALTY & REINFORCEMENT LIST.

Appendix to War Diary

2-10-15	Draft Other Ranks 9 joined the Battalion
7-10-15	2Lieut G M D D Wolf, Royal Irish Regt. joined the Battalion.
14-10-15	Draft Other Ranks 9 joined the Battalion
15-10-15	Other Ranks 2 Wounded in action
16-10-15	Capt R W Smith [illegible]
20-10-15	2Lieut L G Kettlewell and Other Ranks 4 wounded in action
28-10-15	Draft Other Rank 1 joined the Battalion

10th Inf.Bde.
4th Div.

2nd BATTN. THE ROYAL DUBLIN FUSILIERS.

N O V E M B E R

1 9 1 5

Attached:

Casualty & Reinforcement List.

Instructions regarding War Diaries and Intelligence Summaries are contained in F. S. Regs., Part II. and the Staff Manual respectively. Title pages will be prepared in manuscript.

WAR DIARY

or

~~INTELLIGENCE SUMMARY~~

(Erase heading not required.)

Army Form C. 2118.

2nd Bn Royal Dublin Fusiliers

Hour, Date, Place	Summary of Events and Information	Remarks and references to Appendices
Nov 1st – 7th In the Trenches	On Nov 5th we blew in a German mine at 5 p.m. Otherwise nothing of interest to report. On Nov 7th relieved by 1st Royal Irish Fusiliers & marched to FORCEVILLE	
8th – 14th FORCEVILLE.	Relieved Irish Fusiliers in the trenches Nov 14th	
14th – 20th In the Trenches.	Wet tour. On Nov 19 a patrol of 8th R Irish Rifles, one off of whom was attached to the Bn were fired on by a strong hostile patrol and lost the officer wounded and missing.	
Nov 20th	The Bn relieved by 1st R Irish Fusiliers & marched to VARENNES	
VARENNES 21st to 26th	Relieved 1st Royal Irish Fusiliers in the trenches Nov 26th	
Nov 27 – 30	Very wet tour. At 4.30 p.m. Nov 28th we fired no 2 mine in REDAN. Result not at present known. Enemy put about 10 trench mortars into the REDAN; our 4.5 Howitzers retaliated, otherwise nothing of interest to report during tour.	

1217 W 3299 200,000 (E) 8/14 J.B.C. & A. Forms/C. 2118/11.

CASUALTY & REINFORCEMENT LIST.

Appendices to War Diary

1-11-15	Lieut G.A. Stoney joined the Battalion
"	Other Rank 1 Killed in action
4-11-15	Draft Other Ranks 4 joined the Battalion
8-11-15	Draft " " 1 " " "
10-11-15	Draft " " 6 " " "
12-11-15	2Lieut W T Colyer rejoined the Battalion
17-11-15	Draft Other Ranks 3 joined the Battalion
21-11-15	Other Rank 1 Killed in action.

10th Inf.Bde.
4th Div.

2nd BATTN. THE ROYAL DUBLIN FUSILIERS.

D E C E M B E R

1 9 1 5

Attached:

Casualty & Reinforcement List.

2nd Bn Royal Dublin Fusiliers

Instructions regarding War Diaries and Intelligence Summaries are contained in F. S. Regs., Part II. and the Staff Manual respectively. Title pages will be prepared in manuscript.

WAR DIARY
~~or~~
~~INTELLIGENCE SUMMARY~~

(Erase heading not required.)

Army Form C. 2118.

Hour, Date, Place	Summary of Events and Information	Remarks and references to Appendices
December 1st 1915	Heavy rain last night. Trenches very wet especially in the REDAN.	
" 2nd	Wet most of the day. Heavy rain at night Bn relieved by 1st R Ir Fus. Relief completed at 8-50 pm. Bn proceeded to billets in ACHEUX	
" 3rd	Rained nearly all day	
" 4th to 7th	In billets at ACHEUX. Wet every day.	
" 8th	Fine day. Bn relieved 1st R Ir Fus. in the trenches. One man killed by M. Gun fire during relief	
" 9th	Wet all day. Trenches very bad.	
" 10th	Wet morning but cleared about 7 am.	
" 11th	Very wet last night. The trenches held by the left Co are very bad and all the shelters have fallen in so that it has become necessary to relieve this Co every 24 hours.	
" 12th	Heavy rain last night which turned to snow later. Complete redistribution of Bn. 2 Cos in front line and 2 in Bn Reserve	
" 13th	Fine day. Bn relieved by 1st R Ir Fus and proceeded to billets in MAILLY – MAILLET. Enemy were very quiet during the tour.	

1247 W 3299 200,000 (E) 8/14 J.B.C. & A. Forms/C. 2118/11.

Page 2

Instructions regarding War Diaries and Intelligence Summaries are contained in F. S. Regs., Part II. and the Staff Manual respectively. Title pages will be prepared in manuscript.

WAR DIARY
or
INTELLIGENCE SUMMARY
(Erase heading not required.)

Army Form C. 2118

Hour, Date, Place	Summary of Events and Information	Remarks and References to Appendices
December 1915		
" 14th to 16th	In billets	
" 17th	Bn relieved 8th R. Ir. Fus. in the trenches. Relief completed by 7.15pm	
" 18th, 19th, 20th	Enemy quiet. Weather fine	
" 21st	Enemy exploded a mine in the REDAN at 7 am. Very little damage done to our mines. About 50 yards of parapet in the REDAN front line fell in owing to the shock. Rain on and off all day. Bn relieved in the trenches by the 9th R. Ir. Rifles, and proceeded to billets in FORCEVILLE.	
" 22nd	Bde Machine Gun Section formed. 2nd Lt MATSON, 2nd Lt THOMPSON R. Ir. Rif (attd) 2 Sergts 32 Ptes struck off strength of Bn for service with Machine Gun Corps. Bn Lewis Gun Section formed. Establishment 1 Off. 2 Sergts 1 Cpl 27 Pte. 2 Limbered G.S. Wagons 4 Horses	
" 23rd	Very wet	

(9.26.6) W 257—976 100,000 3/12 H.W.V. 78

Page 3

Instructions regarding War Diaries and Intelligence Summaries are contained in F. S. Regs., Part II, and the Staff Manual respectively. Title pages will be prepared in manuscript.

WAR DIARY
or
INTELLIGENCE SUMMARY
(Erase heading not required.)

Army Form C. 2118.

Hour, Date, Place	Summary of Events and Information	Remarks and References to Appendices
December 1915		
24th	[illegible] most of the day.	
25th	Heavy showers throughout the day. [illegible] left in the trenches.	
27th	Enemy artillery rather more active on our trenches [illegible] noticeable.	
28th	Fine day. Enemy [illegible]	
29th	Enemy shelled [illegible] [illegible] [illegible] ARDENNES	
30th	[illegible]	

CASUALTY & REINFORCEMENT LIST.

Appendices to War Diary for December 1915

Date	Casualties and Drafts.
1-12-15	1 Other Rank wounded in action.
2-12-15	2 Other Ranks wounded in action
3-12-15	2 Lieut C J Morris joined the Battalion
6-12-15	2 Lieuts C B Donovan, A J Franklin joined the Battalion
9-12-15	1 Other Rank Killed and 1 Other Rank Wounded in action
11-12-15	2 Other Ranks Wounded in action
18-12-15	1 Other Rank Killed in action.
25-12-15	2 Other Ranks Wounded in action.
31-12-15.	30 Other Ranks joined the Battalion.

4th Division

10th Bde.

2nd Battn Royal Dublin Fus.

February to June

1916

2nd R Dublins

January 1916

Missing

8th Brigade.

3rd Division.

86--------------

68th BATTALION

10th Brigade.

4th Division.

2nd BATTALION

ROYAL DUBLIN FUSILIERS.

FEBRUARY 1 9 1 6

Appendices attached:-

[illegible]

[illegible] [illegible]

[illegible] [illegible]

Army Form C. 2118.

Instructions regarding War Diaries and Intelligence Summaries are contained in F. S. Regs., Part II. and the Staff Manual respectively. Title pages will be prepared in manuscript.

WAR DIARY
~~or~~
~~INTELLIGENCE SUMMARY~~
(*Erase heading not required.*)

2 Bn Royal Dublin Fusiliers

Hour, Date, Place	Summary of Events and Information	Remarks and References to Appendices
FORCEVILLE Feb 1st 1916	Fine Day. "B" Co carried out Bombing Attack on trenches at BEAUSSART	
" " WEDNESDAY. Feb 2nd	Bn relieved 2nd SEAFORTH HIGHLANDERS in trenches E of TOUVENT FME.	
TRENCHES THURS. Feb 3rd	Quiet night. ENEMY inactive during the day.	
" " FRI. " 4th	Officers of 2nd ESSEX Regt came up and looked over trenches. Fine Day.	
" SAT. " 5th	2/ESSEX Regt relieved Bn in trenches. BRIG-GEN C.P.A. HULL ~~[illegible]~~ vacated command of 10th Inf. Bde on appointment to command of 56th Div.	
Brig Gen	C.A. WILDING CMG assumed command ~~[illegible]~~ of 10th Inf. Bde	
COLINCAMPS SUN 6th	Bn rested in billets. Inspections	
" MON 7th	Bn left COLINCAMPS at 9.30 AM and marched to billets at ORVILLE. Fine day	
ORVILLE TUE 8th	Billets. Very fine weather.	
" WED. 9th		

(9 26 6) W 257—976 100,000 4/12 H W V 79/3298

Instructions regarding War Diaries and Intelligence Summaries are contained in F. S. Regs., Part II, and the Staff Manual respectively. Title pages will be prepared in manuscript.

WAR DIARY
or
~~INTELLIGENCE~~ SUMMARY
(Erase heading not required.)

Army Form C. 2118.

Page 2

Hour, Date, Place	Summary of Events and Information	Remarks and References to Appendices
GRVILLE. THURS. 10th	Fine Day.	
" FRI. 11th	Coy Training in vicinity of GRVILLE. Very wet day – Training in Billets.	
" SAT. 12th	No 17988 Pte E. CALLAGHAN awarded DCM	Appendix No. 2.
" SUN. 13th	Church Parades. Inspections.	
" MON 14th	Coy Training.	
" TUES. 15th	Route March about 9 miles [illegible]	
" WED 16th THURS 17th	Very wet. Parades in Billets. Lectures to NCOs and men	
" FRI 18th " SAT 19th	[illegible] Parades [illegible] Billets	
" SUN 20th	Church Parades. Inspections.	
" MON 21st	Very cold indeed. Slight fall of Snow. Coy Parades. Area round GRVILLE	
" TUES. 22nd	Route March about [illegible] miles. Lectures to NCOs and men in the [illegible] snow [illegible]	

9-26-6 W 257 976 100,000 4/12 H W V 79/3298

Instructions regarding War Diaries and Intelligence Summaries are contained in F. S. Regs., Part II. and the Staff Manual respectively. Title pages will be prepared in manuscript.

WAR DIARY
or
INTELLIGENCE SUMMARY
(*Erase heading not required.*)

Army Form C. 2118.

Page 3

Hour, Date, Place February	Summary of Events and Information	Remarks and References to Appendices
ORVILLE WED. 23rd	Coy Parades in the morning. Snowed heavily all the day. Smoke Bomb Demonstration. Owing to lack of Bombs and Smoke Candles and the inclemency of the weather it was not a great success	
" THURS 24th	Snowing all the day. Very cold indeed. Coy Parades in billets.	
" FRI. 25th	Shortage of Fuel. All leave to U.K. stopped until further notice.	
" SAT. 26th	Thaw set in. Roads very muddy indeed. Weather not quite so cold. Coy Training in vicinity of ORVILLE	
" SUN 27th	Church Parades. Inspections. Thawed all the day. All lorries taken off the roads and waggons are sent with the Column in order to prevent the roads from being torn up.	
" MON 28th	Coy Training in vicinity of Billets. Raining all the day.	
" TUES 29th	Brigade Route March — about 10 miles. Very fine warm day. Lectures to Officers - NCO's & men in the evening.	

H. W. Higginson

[illegible] Comd 2 R. Dub. Fus.

(9 26 6) W 257—976 100,000 4/12 H W V 79/3298

2nd Bn Royal Dublin Fusiliers

Appendix 1. to War Diary. February 1916.

5 - 2 - 16.	Capt W. F. Jeffries joined
7 - 2 - 16	2/Lieut R. H. Ingoldby rejoined from Hospital (Sick)
17 - 2 - 16	Draft of 40 Other Ranks joined.

Casualties - Nil.

2nd Bn Royal Dublin Fusiliers.

Appendix No 2. to War Diary. February 1916.

No: 17988 Pte E. CALLAGHAN.

On the night of Jan 20th 1916.

This Stretcher Bearer had to cross open country [illegible] swept by machine [illegible] to [illegible] wounded men.
[illegible] of Pte RUE he got a badly wounded man to safety, and [illegible] to bring in a man who had been killed when he came across [illegible] badly wounded [illegible]
[illegible] got badly hit himself in the [illegible]
RUE, his companion, bandaged him, but CALLAGHAN refused to be carried in on a Stretcher as he was afraid one of the [illegible] would be hit, so dragged himself [illegible] the [illegible]
[illegible] very bright and [illegible] fire heavy.

~~In the Field. The night of [illegible]~~

In the Field
27. 1. 16.

Sd. [illegible] P. Walsh Capt.
Comg 2/R. Dub. Fus.

No. of Report D 21

Army Form B. 213.

FIELD RETURN.

(To be furnished by all arms, services, and departments (except A.S.C. units) to the A. G.'s Office at the Base in accordance with Field Service Regulations, Part II.)

RETURN showing numbers RATIONED by, and Transport on charge of, 2nd/8th Royal Dublin Fusiliers at in the Field 5th February 16 Date.

Detail	Personnel			Animals								Guns, carriages, and limbers and transport vehicles														Remarks
				Horses				Mules								Horsed		Mechanical								
	Officers	Other ranks	Natives	Riding	Draught	Heavy Draught	Pack	Large	Small	Camels	Oxen	Guns, carriages and limbers, showing description	Ammunition wagons and limbers	Machine guns	Aircraft, showing description	4 Wheeled	2 Wheeled	Motor Cars	Tractors	Lorries, showing description	Trucks, showing description	Trailers	Motor Bicycles	Bicycles		
Effective Strength of Unit	31	976		11	26	9	9						Lewis	4		10	9							9		
Details, *by Arms* attached to unit as in War Establishment:— RAMC	1	5		1																						
AOC		1																								
Total	32	981		12	26	9	9							4		10	9							9		
War Establishment	30	995		13	26	9	9							4		10	9							9		
Wanting to complete (Detail of Personnel and Horses below)	5	14		-	-	-	-							-		-	-							-	Majors or Captains to complete	
Surplus	7																								Subalterns surplus to Establishment	
*Attached (not to include the details shown above)	1	2		1		4 2										2 1									Chaplain R.C. ASC Train Reserve Park	
Civilians:— Employed with the Unit																										
Accompanying the Unit																										
Total Rationed ...	25	823		13	26	15	9																			

Remarks (Details Rationed Away):

Leave	9
Sick on leave	1
Details	1
	4

Leave	45
Rhonkes	27
ADC	1
Survey	1
Flying Corps	1
Sheecoyote	1
Pigeon flyer	1
AG Office	1
Tho Coy	46
M.G.	8
10th Bde	15
Trench Mortar	10
	157

* In the case of field ambulances, hospitals or depots, the number of patients are to be included here, the names being shown in A. F. A. 36.

L P Ward Capt Signature of Commander.

5th February 1916 Date of Despatch.

Perforated Sheet giving detail of personnel and horses wanting to complete, shown on Army Form B. 213.

Number of Report D21

Detail of Wanting to Complete	Drivers						Gunners	Smith Gunners	Range Takers	Farriers		Shoeing, or Shoeing and Carriage Smiths	Cold Shoers	Wheelers			Saddlers or Harness Makers	Blacksmiths	Bricklayers and Masons	Carpenters and Joiners
	R. A.	R. E.	A. S. C.	Car	Lorry	Steam				Serjeants	Corporals			R. A.	H. T.	M. T.				
CAVALRY																				
R. A.																				
R. E.																				
INFANTRY																				
R. A. M. C.																				
A. O. C.																				
A. V. C.																				

Detail of Wanting to Complete	Fitters & Turners (R. E.)		Fitters		Plumbers	Electricians		Signalmen	Engine Drivers		Air Line Men	Permanent Line Men	Operators, Telegraph	Cablemen	Brigade Section Pioneers	General-duty Pioneers	Signallers	Instrument Repairers	Motor Cyclists	Motor Cyclist Artificers
	Wood	Iron	R. A.	Wireless		Ordinary	W. T.		Loco.	Field										
CAVALRY																				
R. A.																				
R. E.																				
INFANTRY																				
R. A. M. C.																				
A. O. C.																				
A. V. C.																				

Detail of Wanting to Complete	Telephonists	Clerks	Machine Gunners	Armament Artificers		Armourers	Storemen	Privates	W.O.'s and N.C.O.'s (by ranks) not included in trade columns	TOTAL to agree with wanting to complete		Horses			
				Fitters	Range Finders					Officers	Other Ranks	Riding	Draught	Heavy Draught	Pack
CAVALRY															
R. A.															
R. E.															
INFANTRY								4		5	4	-	-	-	-
R. A. M. C.															
A. O. C.															
A. V. C.															

Remarks :—

L P Walsh Capt Signature of Commander.

Comdg 2nd Bn Royal Dublin Fusiliers Unit.

10th Inf Bde 4th Division Formation to which attached.

5th February 1916 Date of Despatch.

(82434.) Wt. 4394/2217. 500,000. 6/15. B.M.&S. Forms/B. 213/6.

[P.T.O.

No. of Report D.62 Army Form B. 213.

FIELD RETURN.

(To be furnished by all arms, services, and departments (except A.S.C. units) to the A. G.'s Office at the Base in accordance with Field Service Regulations, Part II.)

RETURN showing numbers RATIONED by, and Transport on charge of, 2nd Bn Royal Dublin Fusiliers in the Field 12th February 1916 Date.

Detail	Personnel: Officers	Personnel: Other ranks	Personnel: Natives	Animals: Horses: Riding	Horses: Draught	Horses: Heavy Draught	Horses: Pack	Mules: Large	Mules: Small	Camels	Oxen	Guns, carriages, and limbers and transport vehicles: Guns, carriages and limbers, showing description	Ammunition wagons and limbers	Machine guns	Aircraft, showing description	Horsed: 4 Wheeled	Horsed: 2 Wheeled	Mechanical: Motor Cars	Tractors	Lorries, showing description	Trucks, showing description	Trailers	Motor Bicycles	Bicycles	Remarks
Effective Strength of Unit	32	968		11	26	9	9						Lewis	4		10	9							9	Details Rationed Away — Officers: Leave 3, Sick on leave 1, Grenade 1; Men: Leave 39, Absentees 23, Grenade 1, A.O.C. 1, Survey 1, Flying Corps 1, [illegible] 1, Pigeon Flyer 1, A.G.'s Office 1, Rec Coy 46, M.G. Course 8, Trench Mortar 10, 10th Inf Bde 15
Details, *by Arms* attached to unit as in War Establishment:— R.A.M.C.	1	5		1																					
A.O.C.		1																							
Total	33	974		12	26	9	9							4		10	9							9	Officers 5; Men 148
War Establishment	30	995		13	26	9	9							4		10	9							9	
Wanting to complete (Detail of Personnel and Horses below)	4	21																							Majors or Captains to complete
Surplus	7																								Subalterns surplus to Establishment
*Attached (not to include the details shown above)	1	2		1		4/2										2/1									Chaplain R.C.; A.S.C. Train; Reserve Park
Civilians:— Employed with the Unit																									
Accompanying the Unit																									
Total Rationed ...	29	828		13	26	15	9																		

* In the case of field ambulances, hospitals or depots, the number of patients are to be included here, the names being shown in A. F. A. 36.

H. W. Higginson Lieut Colonel Signature of Commander.

12th February 1916 Date of Despatch.

For information of the A.G.'s Office at the Base.

Officers and men who have become casuals, been transferred or joined since last report.

Place In the Field   Date 18th February 1916

Regtl. Number	Rank	Name	Corps	Nature of casualty, or name of unit from or to which transferred	Date of being struck off or coming on the ration return	Remarks*
	Capt	William Farmer-Jeffares	2nd Bn Royal Dublin Fusiliers	[illegible]	5-2-16	
	Lieut	R.A. [illegible]	2nd Bn Roy Dublin Fusiliers	Wounded [illegible] Hospital	7-2-16	
8591	Private	Byrne	2nd Bn R.D.F.	Absent from leave reported [illegible]	9-2-16	
18462	Private	Dillon	" "	Absent from trenches	3-2-16	
8[illegible]	Private	Fox	" "	To Prison	10-2-16	
5042	Private	Doyle	" "	To Base [illegible]	6-2-16	for Discharge

* State whether absence is of a permanent or temporary nature, adding, in the case of casuals from wounds or disease, any available information for communication to the relatives.

Perforated Sheet giving detail of personnel and horses wanting to complete, shown on Army Form B. 213.

Number of Report D22

Detail of Wanting to Complete	Drivers R. A.	Drivers R. E.	Drivers A. S. C.	Drivers Car	Drivers Lorry	Drivers Steam	Gunners	Smith Gunners	Range Takers	Farriers Serjeants	Farriers Corporals	Shoeing, or Shoeing and Carriage Smiths	Cold Shoers	Wheelers R. A.	Wheelers H. T.	Wheelers M. T.	Saddlers or Harness Makers	Blacksmiths	Bricklayers and Masons	Carpenters and Joiners
CAVALRY																				
R. A.																				
R. E.																				
INFANTRY																				
R. A. M. C.																				
A. O. C.																				
A. V. C.																				

Detail of Wanting to Complete	Fitters & Turners (R. E.) Wood	Fitters & Turners (R. E.) Iron	Fitters R. A.	Fitters Wireless	Plumbers	Electricians Ordinary	Electricians W. T.	Signalmen	Engine Drivers Loco.	Engine Drivers Field	Air Line Men	Permanent Line Men	Operators, Telegraph	Cablemen	Brigade Section Pioneers	General-duty Pioneers	Signallers	Instrument Repairers	Motor Cyclists	Motor Cyclist Artificers
CAVALRY																				
R. A.																				
R. E.																				
INFANTRY																				
R. A. M. C.																				
A. O. C.																				
A. V. C.																				

Detail of Wanting to Complete	Telephonists	Clerks	Machine Gunners	Armament Artificers Fitters	Armament Artificers Range Finders	Armourers	Storemen	Privates	W.O.'s and N.C.O.'s (by ranks) not included in trade columns									TOTAL to agree with wanting to complete Officers	TOTAL Other Ranks	Horses Riding	Horses Draught	Horses Heavy Draught	Horses Pack
CAVALRY																							
R. A.																							
R. E.																							
INFANTRY								21										4	21	-	-	-	-
R. A. M. C.																							
A. O. C.																							
A. V. C.																							

Remarks :—

A W Higginson Lieut Colonel Signature of Commander.

2nd Bn Royal Dublin Fusiliers Unit.

10th Inf Bde, 4th Division Formation to which attached.

12th February 1916 Date of Despatch.

(82434.) Wt. 4394/2217. 500,000. 6/15. B.M.&S. Forms/B. 213/6.

[P.T.O.

No. of Report D23

Army Form B. 213.

FIELD RETURN.

(To be furnished by all arms, services and departments (except A.S.C. units) to the A. G.'s Office at the Base in accordance with Field Service Regulations, Part II.)

RETURN showing numbers RATIONED by, and Transport on charge of, 2nd Battalion Royal Dublin Fusiliers at in the Field [illegible] Date.

Detail	Personnel			Animals								Guns, carriages, and limbers, and transport vehicles.												Motor Bicycles	Bicycles	Remarks
				Horses				Mules								Horsed		Mechanical								
	Officers	Other ranks	Natives	Riding	Draught	Heavy Draught	Pack	Large	Small	Camels	Oxen	Guns, carriages and limbers, showing description	Ammunition wagons and limbers	Machine guns	Aircraft, showing description	4 Wheeled	2 Wheeled	Motor Cars	Tractors	Lorries, showing description	Trucks, showing description	Trailers			[illegible]
Effective Strength of Unit	32	[illegible]		10	26	9	9						[illegible]	4		10	0							9	[illegible]
Details, *by Arms* attached to unit as in War Establishment:— [illegible]	1	5		1																					
Total	33	[illegible]		11	26	9	9							4		10	9							9	
War Establishment	30	[illegible]		13	26	9	9							4		10	9							[illegible]	
Wanting to complete (Detail of Personnel and Horses below)	4	12																							[illegible]
Surplus	[illegible]																								[illegible]
*Attached (not to include the details shown above)	1	4		1	4																				[illegible]
Civilians:— Employed with the Unit																									
Accompanying the Unit																									
TOTAL RATIONED ...	[illegible]	850		[illegible]	[illegible]	[illegible]	9							—											

* In the case of field ambulances, hospitals or depots, the number of patients are to be included here, the names being shown in A. F. A. 36.

[illegible] Signature of Commander.

[illegible] Date of Despatch.

For information of the A.G.'s Office at the Base.

Officers and men who have become casuals, been transferred or joined since last report.

Place In the Field Date 10th February 1916

Regtl. Number	Rank	Name	Corps	Nature of casualty, or name of unit from or to which transferred	Date of being struck off or coming on the ration return	Remarks*
[illegible]	Private	Brown	[illegible]	[illegible]	28-1-16	[illegible]
5880	"	[illegible]	C Coy	[illegible]	[illegible]	[illegible]
[illegible]	L/Cpl	Ward	D "	[illegible]	8-1-16	[illegible]
6760	Private	[illegible]	"	[illegible]	[illegible]	[illegible]
[illegible]		[illegible]	A	[illegible]	[illegible]	[illegible]
[illegible]	Private	[illegible]	A Coy	[illegible]		
7030	"	[illegible]		[illegible]		
[illegible]	"	Hayes	C	[illegible]		
[illegible]	"	Hall		[illegible]		
[illegible]	"	May	D	[illegible]		
[illegible]	"	Burrell		[illegible]		
[illegible]	"	[illegible]		[illegible]		
[illegible]	"	[illegible]		[illegible]		
[illegible]	"	[illegible]		[illegible]		
[illegible]	"	[illegible]		[illegible]		
[illegible]		[illegible]	B	[illegible]		
[illegible]	"	[illegible]	"	[illegible]	8-2-16	
[illegible]	[illegible]	[illegible]	[illegible]	[illegible]	[illegible]	
[illegible]	[illegible]	[illegible]	"		[illegible]	
[illegible]	[illegible]	[illegible]	"		[illegible]	
[illegible]	[illegible]	[illegible]	[illegible]	[illegible]	[illegible]	[illegible]

* State whether absence is of a permanent or temporary nature, adding, in the case of casuals from wounds or disease, any available information for communication to the relatives.

Perforated Sheet giving detail of personnel and horses wanting to complete, shown on Army Form B. 213.

Number of Report D93

Detail of Wanting to Complete.	Drivers.									Farriers				Wheelers							Fitters & Turners (R. E.)		Fitters			Electricians			Engine Drivers	
	R. A.	R. E.	A. S. C.	Car	Lorry	Steam	Gunners	Smith Gunners	Range Takers	Serjeants	Corporals	Shoeing, or Shoeing and Carriage Smiths	Cold Shoers	R. A.	H. T.	M. T.	Saddlers or Harness Makers	Blacksmiths	Bricklayers and Masons	Carpenters and Joiners	Wood	Iron	R. A.	Wireless	Plumbers	Ordinary	W. T.	Signalmen	Loco.	Field
CAVALRY																														
R. A.																														
R. E.																														
INFANTRY																														
R. A. M. C.																														
A. O. C.																														
A. V. C.																														

Detail of Wanting to Complete.														Armament Artificers					W.O.'s and N.C.O.'s (by ranks) not included in trade columns.											TOTAL to agree with wanting to complete		Horses			
	Air Line Men	Permanent Line Men	Operators, Telegraph	Cablemen	Brigade Section Pioneers	General-duty Pioneers	Signallers	Instrument Repairers	Motor Cyclists	Motor Cyclist Artificers	Telephonists	Clerks	Machine Gunners	Fitters	Range Finders	Armourers	Storemen	Privates												Officers	Other Ranks	Riding	Draught	Heavy Draught	Pack
CAVALRY																																			
R. A.																																			
R. E.																																			
INFANTRY																		12												4	12	-	-	-	-
R. A. M. C.																																			
A. O. C.																																			
A. V. C.																																			

Remarks :—

A. W. [illegible] Lieut Colonel Signature of Commander.

2nd Battalion Royal Dublin Fusiliers Unit.

10th Inf. Bde 4th Division Formation to which attached.

19th February 1916 Date of Despatch.

(26149.) Wt. W. 10698/4046. 500,000. 10/15. M.R.Co., Ltd. Forms/B. 213/6.

[P.T.O.

No. of Report D724

FIELD RETURN.

Army Form B. 213.

(To be furnished by all arms, services and departments (except A.S.C. units) to the A. G.'s Office at the Base in accordance with Field Service Regulations, Part II.)

RETURN showing numbers RATIONED by, and Transport on charge of, 2nd Bn. Royal Dublin Fusiliers at in the Field 26-2-16 Date.

DETAIL	Personnel			Animals								Guns, carriages, and limbers, and transport vehicles.											Motor Bicycles	Bicycles	REMARKS
				Horses				Mules								Horsed		Mechanical							
	Officers	Other ranks	Natives	Riding	Draught	Heavy Draught	Pack	Large	Small	Camels	Oxen	Guns, carriages and limbers, showing description	Ammunition wagons and limbers	Machine guns	Aircraft, showing description	4 Wheeled	2 Wheeled	Motor Cars	Tractors	Lorries, showing description	Trucks, showing description	Trailers			
Effective Strength of Unit	30	974		10	26	9	9						[illegible]	4		10	9							9	[illegible]
Details, *by Arms* attached to unit as in War Establishment:—																									
R A M C	1	5		1																					
A V C		1																							
Total	31	980		11	26	9	9							4		10	9							9	
War Establishment	30	[illegible]		13	26	9	9							4		10	9							9	
Wanting to complete (Detail of Personnel and Horses below)	4	76		1																					[illegible]
Surplus	[illegible]																								[illegible]
*Attached (not to include the details shown above)	1			1																					[illegible]
Civilians:— Employed with the Unit	1	4			4																				
Accompanying the Unit		1																							
TOTAL RATIONED ...	32	[illegible]		12	30	9	9																		

* In the case of field ambulances, hospitals or depots, the number of patients are to be included here, the names being shown in A. F. A. 36.

[illegible] Signature of Commander.

26th February 1916 Date of Despatch.

For information of the A.G.'s Office at the Base.

Officers and men who have become casuals, been transferred or joined since last report.

Place .... Date ....

Regtl. Number	Rank	Name	Corps	Nature of casualty, or name of unit from or to which transferred	Date of being struck off or coming on the ration return	Remarks*

* State whether absence is of a permanent or temporary nature, adding, in the case of casuals from wounds or disease, any available information for communication to the relatives.

Perforated Sheet giving detail of personnel and horses wanting to complete, shown on Army Form B. 213.

Number of Report D. 24

Detail of Wanting to Complete.	Drivers.						Gunners	Smith Gunners	Range Takers	Farriers		Shoeing, or Shoeing and Carriage Smiths	Cold Shoers	Wheelers			Saddlers or Harness Makers	Blacksmiths	Bricklayers and Masons	Carpenters and Joiners	Fitters & Turners (R. E.)		Fitters		Plumbers	Electricians		Signalmen	Engine Drivers		Air Line Men	Permanent Line Men	Operators, Telegraph	Cablemen	Brigade Section Pioneers	General-duty Pioneers	Signallers	Instrument Repairers	Motor Cyclists	Motor Cyclist Artificers	Telephonists	Clerks	Machine Gunners	Armament Artificers		Armourers	Storemen	Privates	W.O.'s and N.C.O.'s (by ranks) not included in trade columns.										TOTAL to agree with wanting to complete		Horses			
	R. A.	R. E.	A. S. C.	Car	Lorry	Steam				Serjeants	Corporals			R. A.	H. T.	M. T.					Wood	Iron	R. A.	Wireless		Ordinary	W. T.		Loco.	Field														Fitters	Range Finders														Officers	Other Ranks	Riding	Draught	Heavy Draught	Pack
CAVALRY																																																																	
R. A.																																																																	
R. E.																																																																	
INFANTRY																																																	15											4	15	1			
R. A. M. C.																																																																	
A. O. C.																																																																	
A. V. C.																																																																	

Remarks :—

M. Byrne [illegible] Lieut. Colonel Signature of Commander.

2nd/3rd Royal Dublin Fusiliers Unit.

10th Inf. Bde, 4th Divn. Formation to which attached.

26/2/16 Date of Despatch.

(26149.) Wt. W. 10698/4046. 500,000. 10/15. M.R.Co.,Ltd. Forms/B. 213/6.

[P.T.O.

Special Order of the Day by His Majesty the King.

Officers, Non-Commissioned Officers and Men—

I am happy to have found myself once more with my Armies.

It is especially gratifying to me to have been able to see some of those that have been newly created. For I have watched with interest the growth of these Troops from the first days of Recruit Drill and through the different stages of training until their final inspection on the eve of departure for the Front as organised Divisions. Already they have justified the general conviction then formed of their splendid fighting worth.

Since I was last among you, you have fought many strenuous battles. In all you have reaped renown and proved yourselves at least equal to the highest traditions of the British Army.

In company with our noble Allies you have baffled the infamous conspiracy against the law and liberty of Europe, so long and insidiously prepared.

These achievements have involved vast sacrifices. But your countrymen who watch your campaign with sympathetic admiration will, I am well assured, spare no effort to fill your ranks and afford you all supplies.

I have decorated many of you. But had I decorated all who deserve recognition for conspicuous valour, there would have been no limit, for the whole Army is illustrious.

It is a matter of sincere regret to me that my accident should have prevented my seeing all the Troops I had intended, but during my stay amongst you I have seen enough to fill my heart with admiration of your patient cheerful endurance of life in the trenches: a life either of weary monotony or of terrible tumult. It is the dogged determination evinced by all ranks which will at last bring you to victory. Keep the goal in sight and remember it is the final lap that wins.

George, R.I.

November 1st, 1915.

[illegible]

10th Brigade.

4th Division.

2nd BATTALION

ROYAL DUBLIN FUSILIERS

MARCH 1 9 1 6

4

J R Dublin Ins

Vol XIX

Instructions regarding War Diaries and Intelligence Summaries are contained in F. S. Regs., Part II. and the Staff Manual respectively. Title pages will be prepared in manuscript.

WAR DIARY
or
INTELLIGENCE SUMMARY
(*Erase heading not required.*)

Army Form C. 2118.

Hour, Date, Place		Summary of Events and Information	Remarks and References to Appendices
ORVILLE.	MARCH 1st '16	Received orders to move from ORVILLE to St AMAND on 2.3.16. Coy training in vicinity of Billets.	
"	2nd	Battn marched from ORVILLE at 2pm and arrived in St AMAND at 5.30 PM. Good billets for officers and men.	
St AMAND	March 3rd '16.	Snowed very heavily. Roads in a very bad condition.	
"	4th	Very cold day. Snowed during the night. Roads nearly impassable. Coys turned out to clear the roads with snow ploughs.	
"	5th	Voluntary Church Service. Snowed hard. Very cold. Inoculations.	
	6th	Coy training in Billets. Snowed little during the day. Inoculations.	
	7th	Very cold day. Snowed a little. Battn found working parties on the CORPS LINE.	

(9 26 6) W 257—976 100,000 4/12 H W V 79/3298

Instructions regarding War Diaries and Intelligence Summaries are contained in F. S. Regs., Part II. and the Staff Manual respectively. Title pages will be prepared in manuscript.

WAR DIARY
or
INTELLIGENCE SUMMARY
(Erase heading not required.)

Army Form C. 2118.

Hour, Date, Place	Summary of Events and Information	Remarks and References to Appendices

9 26 6 W 257 976 100,000 4/12 H W V 70 3298

Instructions regarding War Diaries and Intelligence Summaries are contained in F. S. Regs., Part II. and the Staff Manual respectively. Title pages will be prepared in manuscript.

WAR DIARY
or
~~INTELLIGENCE SUMMARY~~
(Erase heading not required.)

Army Form C. 2118.

Page 3.

Hour, Date, Place	Summary of Events and Information	Remarks and References to Appendices
TRENCHES Saturday MARCH 18th 1916	Quiet night. Trenches very good [illegible] Bn has [illegible] 11th Inf Bde on RIGHT. 2nd Lea Regt on left. 4 [illegible] slightly wounded in the morning. BRIG-GEN. C.A. WILSON C.M.G. came up to see the ~~trenches~~ in the afternoon. Leave reopened.	
" " Sunday " " 19 "	Quiet night. Enemy artillery fired some 4.2 shells into left Co (D) killing one man and wounding [illegible].	
" " Monday " " 20 "	Quiet night. Coy Comdrs 1st R. Warwickshire Regt came up to see the line. Hostile artillery shelled RIGHT Coy (A) in the forenoon with 5.9 shells. Very active with Rifle Grenades. One man killed and one wounded.	
" TUESDAY " " 21 "	Very quiet night. Misty day. Bn relieved in Trenches by 1st R. War. Regt. Relief complete 7.5 pm. Bn proceeded to billets in BIENVILLERS.	
BIENVILLERS. WEDNESDAY " 22 "	Inspections. Working parties for front line trenches at night.	
" " THURSDAY " 23 "	Very cold day. Snowing slightly. Our artillery bombarded enemy trenches during the night. Working parties. Bathing. Leave closed.	
" " FRIDAY " 24 "	Snowed hard during the night. Hostile artillery shelled BIENVILLERS put 6 4.2 in shells in. No damage done. Working Parties.	

(9 26 6) W 257—976 100,000 4/12 H W V 79/3298

Army Form C. 2118.

Instructions regarding War Diaries and Intelligence Summaries are contained in F. S. Regs., Part II. and the Staff Manual respectively. Title pages will be prepared in manuscript.

WAR DIARY
or
INTELLIGENCE SUMMARY

(Erase heading not required.)

Hour, Date, Place	Summary of Events and Information	Remarks and references to Appendices

1247 W 3299 200,000 (E) 8/14 J.B.C. & A. Forms/C. 2118/11.

Appendices to War Diary
March 1916.

Date.			Remarks.	
7	3	16	Draft 1 other Rank joined Battalion	
9	3	16	" 1 " " " "	
10	3	16	" 50. " Ranks " "	
12.	3.	16	" 1. other Rank " "	
18.	3	16.	Wounded-in-Action 4. other Ranks 1 still at Duty.	
19	3	16.	Killed-in-Action 1 other Rank	
			Wounded-in-Action 5 other Ranks 1 still at Duty.	
20	3	16.	" " " 1 other Rank.	
21	3	16.	Killed-in-Action 1. other Rank.	
			Wounded-in-Action 2 other Ranks.	
22	3	16.	Draft 3 other Ranks joined Battalion.	
24.	3.	16.	Killed-in-action 1 other Rank.	
			Wounded-in-Action 1 other Rank still at Duty.	
26	3	16.	" " " 1 " "	
28	3	16.	Draft 1 other Rank joined Battalion.	
29	3	16.	Wounded-in-Action 1 other Rank.	
31	3	16.	Killed-in-Action 1 other Rank.	
			Wounded-in-Action 1 " "	
~~2~~	~~4~~	~~16~~	~~Draft 1 other Rank.~~	
~~5~~	~~4~~	~~16~~	~~Killed in action 1 other Rank~~	

L P Walsh Major
Comdg 2nd Bn Royal Dublin Fusiliers

10th Brigade.

4th Division.

2nd BATTALION

ROYAL DUBLIN FUSILIERS

APRIL 1 9 1 6

7 R. Dublin Fus

Vol XX

Army Form C. 2118.

WAR DIARY
or
INTELLIGENCE SUMMARY

(Erase heading not required.)

Instructions regarding War Diaries and Intelligence Summaries are contained in F. S. Regs., Part II. and the Staff Manual respectively. Title pages will be prepared in manuscript.

Hour, Date, Place	Summary of Events and Information	Remarks and references to Appendices

1247 W 3299 200,000 (E) 8/14 J.B.C. & A. Forms C. 2118/11.

2nd Bn. Royal Dublin Fusiliers

Original

WAR DIARY
or
~~INTELLIGENCE~~ SUMMARY
(Erase heading not required.)

Page II

Army Form C. 2118.

Instructions regarding War Diaries and Intelligence Summaries are contained in F. S. Regs., Part II. and the Staff Manual respectively. Title pages will be prepared in manuscript.

Hour, Date, Place	Summary of Events and Information	Remarks and references to Appendices
16th April 1916. BIENVILLERS	BILLETS. Quiet day.	
17th " "	" Our Artillery Bombarded Trenches N of MONCHY during bombardment parties from 1/R War Regt & 1/R Irish Fus entered enemy trenches, Bombed Dug-Outs: R.E. blew up a Mine and Machine Gun emplacement: Casualties one man slightly wounded. Enemy retaliation very weak.	Casualties R. Appendix I
18th " " "	Quiet day. Relieved 1/R War Regt in Trenches at 5.45 pm. Enemy Artillery Bombarded left Company doing little damage.	
19th " " Trenches	Raining the whole day: Enemy shelled our Trenches with Field Guns. no damage done.	
20th " " "	Enemy Bombarded B Coy with 4.2 & 5.9 shells: doing much damage to dug-outs and Trenches: Trenches becoming very bad owing to very heavy rain	
21st " "	Rained heavily in the evening: Heavy Trench Mortar Bombs fell in Trenches occupied by A & B Coys damaging Dug-outs. Our Artillery carried out pre-arranged Bombardment of Trenches N of Monchy. Very good results. Enemy Trenches very badly damaged: Hostile retaliation very feeble. Reinforcement 49 O.Ranks.	
22nd	Quiet day.	
23rd	Enemy shelled A Coy with Field Guns. And 3 Aerial Torpedoes fell in B Coy doing little damage. 2/Lt Lyne Wounded in action.	
24th "	Enemy shelled B Coy with 5.9 & 4.2 shells nearly all day little damage done).	
25th " " BIENVILLERS	Quiet day Enemy shelled Bettam N.W. of Bienvillers (Relieved by 1/R War Regt by 7.30 pm 24.4.16)	
26th " " "	Maj Gen. Hon. W. Lambton C.B. visited C.O. in morning.	
27th " "	Very Quiet day	
28th " " "	" " Corps Commander visited the C.O. in afternoon	
29th " " "	" " Orders received that the Battalion will move next day	
30th " " "	" " Battalion relieved by 13th KRR at 11am and marched to Billets at ST. AMAND.	

1247 W 3299 200,000 (E) 8/14 J.B.C. & A. Forms/C. 2118/11.

L P Walsh Maj
Comdg 2 Bn Roy Dublin Fus.

2nd Bn Royal Dublin Fusiliers

Appendix To War Diary Month of April 1916

Date	Remarks
2. 4. 16	Reinforcement 1 other Rank.
5 4 16	1 other Rank Killed in Action
9 4 16	2 other Ranks Wounded-in-Action
"	2Lt F P le Peer Trench Died of Wounds (3rd Leinster Regt att 2nd R.D.F.).
10 4. 16	1 other Rank Killed in Action
"	2 other Ranks Wounded "
14. 4. 16	Reinforcements 2 other Ranks
16. 4 16	Major + 2Lt [illegible] Wounded-in-Action [illegible]
19 4 16	1 other Rank Wounded-in-Action
20 4 16	2 other Ranks Killed-in-Action
"	2Lt R S Wall Wounded-in-Action
"	1 other Rank " "
"	4 other Ranks Shell Shock.
21- 4- 16	1 other Rank Killed-in-Action
"	Draft 49 other Ranks
23 4 16	Reinforcement 1 other Rank.
"	Lieut J C Byrne Wounded-in-Action
24- 4- 16	Reinforcement 2Lt G S T Fleming
23 4 16	1 other Rank Died of Wounds
25 4 16	1 " Wounded in Action

[illegible] Major.

Commdg 2nd Bn Royal Dublin Fusiliers.

10th Brigade.

4th Division.

2nd BATTALION

ROYAL DUBLIN FUSILIERS

M A Y 1 9 1 6

Instructions regarding War Diaries and Intelligence Summaries are contained in F. S. Regs., Part II. and the Staff Manual respectively. Title pages will be prepared in manuscript.

WAR DIARY
or
INTELLIGENCE SUMMARY
(Erase heading not required.)

Army Form C. 2118.

Hour, Date, Place	Summary of Events and Information	Remarks and references to Appendices

1247 W 3200 200,000 (E) 8/14 J.B.C. & A. Forms/C. 2118/11.

WAR DIARY
or
INTELLIGENCE SUMMARY
(Erase heading not required.)

Army Form C. 2118.

Instructions regarding War Diaries and Intelligence Summaries are contained in F. S. Regs., Part II. and the Staff Manual respectively. Title pages will be prepared in manuscript.

Hour, Date, Place	Summary of Events and Information	Remarks and references to Appendices
Sunday May 21st LONGVILLERS	Fine day. Marched to ARGENVILLERS for Divisional training. Good billets.	
Mon " 22 ARGENVILLERS	Fine day. Div. training, from 8 – 1	
Tues " 23 "	Very hot day. Div. training, 1 – 6.30 P.M.	
Wed. " 24 "	Very hot day. Brigade attack scheme. 8 – 2.30 P.M.	
Thurs. " 25 "	Very hot day. Brigade attack scheme. 1 – 7 P.M.	
Frid. " 26 "	Fine day. Bn attack practice 8 – 1.30 P.M.	
Sat " 27 "	Fine day. Bn attack practice 1 – 6.30 P.M.	
Sun " 28 "	Fine day. Bn attack practice. 8 – 1.30. Afternoon Staff ride for all Coy Comdrs.	
Mon " 29 "	Fine day. Div. attack practice with 12th Bde, 2 4th Div. Art. 1 – 6 P.M.	
Tues. " 30 "	Fine day. Demonstration of trench mortar Btty. (Stokes) all officers & 100 men. Afternoon Bn attack practice with new formation of attack, i.e. lines of section, 3 coys in front line.	
Wed. " 31 "	Fine day. Bn attack practice. 8 – 1.30 P.M.	

[illegible] Major & a. adj. for O.C. 2nd [illegible] 31.5.16

1247 W 3299 200,000 (E) 8/14 J.B.C. & A. Forms/C. 2118/11.

Appendix to War Diary

2nd Bn Royal Dublin Fusiliers [illegible]

Date Remarks.

18 5 16 Draft [illegible] joined

19 5 16 2Lt [illegible] Mason 3/RDF joined Bn on this date

20 5 16 [illegible] 3/[illegible] RDF joined on this day

22 5 16 [illegible] joined the Bn.

[illegible] RDF left Bn [illegible]

2[illegible] 5 16 Draft [illegible] Ranks.

2[illegible] 5 16 [illegible] RDF joined [illegible]

27 5 16 Draft [illegible] Ranks.

30 5 16 Lieut [illegible] King 3/RDF joined Bn on this date

[illegible] Major
for O C 2nd Bn Royal Dublin Fusiliers

10th Brigade.

4th Division.

2nd BATTALION

ROYAL DUBLIN FUSILIERS

J U N E 1 9 1 6

Instructions regarding War Diaries and Intelligence Summaries are contained in F. S. Regs., Part II. and the Staff Manual respectively. Title pages will be prepared in manuscript.

WAR DIARY
or
INTELLIGENCE SUMMARY
(Erase heading not required.)

Army Form C. 2118.

2 R Dublin Fus

2 R Dublin Fus 22

4

Hour, Date, Place		Summary of Events and Information	Remarks and references to Appendices
A?SNVILLERS THURS JUNE 1st 1916		Battn at Attack Practices in fine weather [illegible] of scheme.	
BERNAVILLE	4th	Reveille at 4.0 a.m. Parade at 6.15 a.m. when the Bn moved to BERNAVILLE arriving at about 11 a.m. after a march of [illegible] miles. MAJOR-GENERAL LAMBTON, Divisional Commander, met the Bn en route & was pleased with the march discipline.	
AUTHIE	5th	Parade 8 a.m. for march to AUTHIE, 20 miles distant, sultry day with heavy showers. The Corps Commander General HUNTER-WESTON met the Bn en route and was greatly pleased with the men and Transport.	
	6th	Working parties went out. 500 men under Capt. [illegible] moved to BERTRANCOURT with 15 officers for working parties, and remained in tents there.	
	7th	COL. [illegible] and MAJOR WALSH went to TENDERLOIN ST. to [illegible] assembly grounds for the assault. Very showery weather.	
	8th–10th	Very heavy rains.	
BERTRANCOURT	11th	Still very wet. Orders received to move to BERTRANCOURT which was reached at about 3.30 [illegible] Bn being together in huts.	
	12th–13th	Weather still bad but improving [illegible]	
In the trenches TENDERLOIN STREET	14th	In the afternoon Bn moved to trenches via MAILLY and AUCHONVILLERS. Relief complete at 7.30 p.m. Trenches very bad after the rain and dug-out accomodation poor.	
	15th	Generally quiet.	
	16th	Heavy firing on our left. During the night [illegible] CRADDOCK and 2 Lieut INGOLDBY went out and [illegible] which was inscribed in large letters "LORD KITCHENER AND HIS STAFF DROWNED IN THE SEA".	
	17th	Quiet on the whole. The weather [illegible].	
MAILLY-MAILLET.	18th	Relieved in the trenches by 1st Royal Warwick Regt. Daylight relief completed by 6 p.m., the Bn returning to tents at [illegible] end of MAILLY-MAILLET.	
	19th–23rd	Nothing to report. Our working parties [illegible] preparing [illegible] trenches. Artillery on both sides [illegible].	
	Sat 24th	[illegible] active on both sides, especially at night when it was [illegible]. One shell fell just above our lines into [illegible] causing 44 casualties, 5 being killed. This was "U" day of operations, the first day of bombardment [illegible]. Extra bread is provided daily for the men from the [illegible].	
	25th	"V" day of operations. Our Artillery bombarded enemy trenches and [illegible].	
	"	The Bn moved out into the fields, west of MAILLY, as enemy shells were falling in the village in reply to the intense bombardment by our Artillery.	
	26th	"W" day of operations. The bombardment increased in severity. Some enemy shells fell in MAILLY, one setting fire to R.E. Park opposite Bn Headquarters. Weather showery and unsettled.	

Army Form C. 2118.

WAR DIARY
or
INTELLIGENCE SUMMARY
(Erase heading not required.)

Instructions regarding War Diaries and Intelligence Summaries are contained in F. S. Regs., Part II. and the Staff Manual respectively. Title pages will be prepared in manuscript.

Hour, Date, Place		Summary of Events and Information	Remarks and references to Appendices
BEAUSSART	26th (continued)	In the evening the Bn moved by circuitous route to BEAUSSART, the move being completed at 11.20, and bivouaced in orchards.	
"	27th	'X' day of operations. The day was spent quietly in completing arrangements for the assault. A working party went to the trenches in the evening. Weather bad and the camp very muddy. Bombardment continued.	
"	28th	Wet morning. Bn paraded for inspection by Brigadier-General C.A. WILDING who also addressed the men. The Bn was to have proceeded to the trenches in the evening but in the afternoon a wire arrived saying "ZERO postponed 48 hours" ZERO being the hour of attack. The postponement was due to the wet weather. Working parties did not go to the trenches in the evening.	
"	29th	Commanding Officer held conference of officers in the afternoon, and the day was spent in completing arrangements. The weather improved, and the bombardment continued.	
In the Trenches.	30th	Germans sent shells into BEAUSSART near the camp, but only one civilian was killed. At 10.15 p.m. the Bn moved off to the trenches and occupied the Assembly Trenches already prepared.	

1247 W 3299 200,000 (E) 8/14 J.B.C. & A. Forms/C. 2118/11.

2nd Bn Royal Dublin Fusiliers.

Appendix To War Diary.

Month of June, 1916.

6/6/16. Capt.J.O.W.Spine, Joined the Bn.

7/6/16 2Lieut.J.A.H.Melby, " " "

7/6/16. 2Lieut. A.H.West, " " "

12/6/16. Lieut.H.D.K.George, " " "

15/6/16. Draft.50 other ranks" " "

15/6/16. Major.R.G.B.Jeffreys," " "

17/6/16. 2Lieut. G.H.Chandler," " "

17/6/16. Draft.20.other ranks " " "

20/6/16. " 1. " rank " " "

24/6/16. Lieut H.D.K.George, Posted to Flying Corps.

19/6/16. 2Lieut. W.G.Scott, Joined the Bn.

17/6/16. 2Lieut. T.F.Handyside, " " "

17/6/16. 2Lieut.R.C.B.Dillon, " " "

18/6/16. 2Lieut. W.Pedlow, " " "

20/6/16. Lieut. H.E.Andrews, " " "

27/6/16. Capt. J.G.F.Napier-Martin, Joined the Bn.

22/6/16. 2Lieut. G.F.Mulholland, Granted Commission from the Ranks

30/6/16. Casualties, 3 other ranks wounded,(1,(still at duty).

21/6/16. 2Lieut.E.J.Diamond, proceeded to join the Machine Gun Corps, Grantham

Capt.

7/7/16. Adjt. 2nd Bn Royal Dublin Fusiliers.

Unit 2nd Bn Royal Dublin Fusiliers.
Place In the Field
Date 8-6-16

FIELD [illegible]

To be rendered in accordance with Field Service Regulations, Part II.

FIGHTING STRENGTH

This should *not* include details attached to unit, or personnel detailed to march with the **Train,** or any men unfit to go into action with unit

UNIT (1)	Personnel: Officers (2)	Personnel: Other Ranks (3)	Horses and Mules: Riding (4)	Horses and Mules: Draught and Pack (5)	Other Animals (6)	Other Animals (7)	Guns and Ammunition Wagons (stating nature) (8)	Machine Guns (9)	Ambulances (10)	Tool Carts, Technical Carts (stating nature) (11)	Remarks (12)
Strength in Trenches	27.	779.	13	48.			Lewis.	8.			
Bde Machine Gun.		8.									
Stokes Gun Course	-	22.									
School of Instruction [illegible] Army	1	4									
[illegible] Div.	-	1.									
Signalling Course	-	1.									
Bombing School	2	21.									
Instructors Base Depot.	1	2.									
Leave.	1	24.									
Absentees off leave	-	6									
Sick on leave.	-	4.									
16th Inf Bde	1.	14									
Anti Gas School.	-	2									
A.O.C.	-	2									
Survey	-	2									
Pigeon Flyer	-	1.									
R.T.O. G.H.Q.	1	.									
TOTALS ...	34.	892.	13	48.				8.			

RATION STRENGTH

To include **Fighting Strength, Personnel** detailed to march with the **Train,** and all Personnel and animals attached for Rations and Forage

UNIT (1)	Personnel: Total, all Ranks entitled to Rations. (13)	Horses and Mules: Heavy Horses (14)	Horses and Mules: Other Horses and Mules (15)	Other Animals (16)	Other Animals (17)	Mechanically Propelled Vehicles: Motor Cars (18)	Motor Bicycles. (19)	Lorries: 3 Ton (20)	Lorries: 30 Cwt. (21)	Tractors (22)	Remarks (23)
Strength in Trenches	873.	13.	48.								
TOTALS ...	873	13	48.								

Ammunition with Unit:—

·303 inch; approximate number of rounds per Man 200

·303 inch; " " " per Lewis Gun 8300

Gun or Howitzer; approximate number of rounds per Gun or Howitzer —

No. of Men serving with 4th Divn Cav. Coy. 64
Returned during week Nil.

Supplies with Unit:—

Approximate number of days' rations for men of ration strength Two.

" " " forage for Animals " " Two

" " " fuel and lubricants for Mechanically Propelled Vehicles

Signature of Commander [illegible] Lieut. Colonel

(79269.) Wt.W. 5870—621. 900,000 10/14. J. P. & Co. Ltd. Forms B 231/3

Unit 2nd Bn Royal Dublin Fusiliers

Place In the Field

Date 10th June 1916

FIELD STATE.

Army Form B 231

To be rendered in accordance with Field Service Regulations, Part II

UNIT	FIGHTING STRENGTH — This should *not* include details attached to unit, or personnel detailed to march with the Train, or any men unfit to go into action with unit											RATION STRENGTH — To include Fighting Strength, Personnel detailed to march with the Train, and all Personnel and animals attached for Rations and Forage										
	Personnel		Horses and Mules		Other Animals		Guns and Ammunition Wagons (stating nature)	Machine Guns	Ambulances	Tool Carts, Technical Carts (stating nature)	Remarks	Personnel	Horses and Mules		Other Animals		Mechanically Propelled Vehicles					Remarks
	Officers	Other Ranks	Riding	Draught and Pack								Total, all Ranks entitled to Rations.	Heavy Horses	Other Horses and Mules			Motor Cars	Motor Bicycles.	Lorries. 3 Ton	Lorries. 30 Cwt.	Tractors	
(1)	(2)	(3)	(4)	(5)	(6)	(7)	(8)	(9)	(10)	(11)	(12)	(13)	(14)	(15)	(16)	(17)	(18)	(19)	(20)	(21)	(22)	(23)
Strength in Trenches	28	780	13	44			Lewis	8				905.	9	48								
10th Inf Bde	1	14																				
School of Snipers III Army	1	3																				
IV Divn	2	6																				
Base	1	3																				
Sundry	-	1																				
Miners	-	10																				
Trench Mortar Course	-	24																				
Machine Gun Course	-	[illegible]																				
Leave	1	34																				
Absentees	-	2																				
Sick on Leave	-	3																				
Bombers	1	2																				
RE (1) AOC (2)	-	3																				
Visual Signalling	-	2																				
Anti Gas School	-	2																				
Pigeon Flyer	-	1																				
RTO GHQ	1																					
TOTALS ...	36	808	13	44				8				905	9	48								

Ammunition with Unit:—

·303 inch; approximate number of rounds per Man 208

·303 inch; " " " per Machine Gun 8300

Gun or Howitzer; approximate number of rounds per Gun or Howitzer ✓

Supplies with Unit:—

Approximate number of days' rations for men of ration strength Two

" " " forage for Animals " " Two

" " " fuel and lubricants for Mechanically Propelled Vehicles ✓

No of Men serving with 4th Divn Rev Co. 58

returned to unit 3

Signature of Commander [illegible] Lieut Colonel

(79269.) Wt. W. 5870—621. 900,000 10/14. J. P. & Co. Ltd. Forms B 231/3

Army Form B 231.

FIELD STATE.

Unit 2nd Bn Royal Dublin Fus[illegible]

Place In the Field.

Date 17th June 1916.

To be rendered in accordance with Field Service Regulations, Part II.

UNIT	FIGHTING STRENGTH — This should not include details attached to unit, or personnel detailed to march with the Train, or any men unfit to go into action with unit: Personnel		Horses and Mules		Other Animals		Guns and Ammunition Wagons (stating nature)	Machine Guns	Ambulances	Tool Carts, Technical Carts (stating nature)	Remarks	RATION STRENGTH — To include Fighting Strength, Personnel detailed to march with the Train, and all Personnel and animals attached for Rations and Forage: Personnel	Horses and Mules		Other Animals		Mechanically Propelled Vehicles					Remarks
	Officers	Other Ranks	Riding	Draught and Pack								Total, all Ranks entitled to Rations	Heavy Horses	Other Horses and Mules			Motor Cars	Motor Bicycles	Lorries 3 Ton	Lorries 30 Cwt.	Tractors	
(1)	(2)	(3)	(4)	(5)	(6)	(7)	(8)	(9)	(10)	(11)	(12)	(13)	(14)	(15)	(16)	(17)	(18)	(19)	(20)	(21)	(22)	(23)
Strength in Trenches	30	841	13	44			Lewis	8				944	9	48								
10th Inf: Bde	1	13																				
Sch: of Instr II Army	1	3																				
" " IV Div	2	5																				
Base	1																					
Survey / Miners 10.		11																				
Trench mortar class		26																				
M. G. Course		9																				
Leave	1	17																				
Absentees 3 Sick 3		6																				
Bombers	1	2																				
RE 1 ADC 2		3																				
Vis: Sig:		1																				
Anti Gas 2. L.G.S.[illegible]		2																				
Pigeon flyer.		1																				
R.T.O. GHQ	1	.																				
TOTALS ...	~~[illegible]~~ 40	941	13	44				8				944	9	48								

Ammunition with Unit:—

·303 inch; approximate number of rounds per Man ______

·303 inch; " " " per Machine Gun ______

Gun or Howitzer; approximate number of rounds per Gun or Howitzer —

No. of men serving with 4th Div. Res. Co. 52

" " returned to unit —

Supplies with Unit:—

Approximate number of days' rations for men of ration strength Two.

" " " forage for Animals " " Two.

" " " fuel and lubricants for Mechanically Propelled Vehicles —

Signature of Commander [illegible] Capt for Lieut. Col.

(79269.) Wt. W. 5870—621. 900,000 10/14. J. P. & Co. Ltd. Forms B 231 / 3

Unit 2nd Bn Royal Dublin Fus[rs]
Place In the Field
Date 24th June 1916.

FIELD STATE.

Army Form B 231.

To be rendered in accordance with Field Service Regulations, Part II.

UNIT	FIGHTING STRENGTH — This should *not* include details attached to unit, or personnel detailed to march with the Train, or any men unfit to go into action with unit											RATION STRENGTH — To include Fighting Strength, Personnel detailed to march with the Train, and all Personnel and animals attached for Rations and Forage										
	Personnel		Horses and Mules		Other Animals		Guns and Ammunition Wagons (stating nature)	Machine Guns	Ambulances	Tool Carts, Technical Carts (stating nature)	Remarks	Personnel	Horses and Mules		Other Animals		Mechanically Propelled Vehicles					Remarks
	Officers	Other Ranks	Riding	Draught and Pack								Total, all Ranks entitled to Rations	Heavy Horses	Other Horses and Mules			Motor Cars	Motor Bicycles	Lorries 3 Ton	Lorries 30 Cwt.	Tractors	
(1)	(2)	(3)	(4)	(5)	(6)	(7)	(8)	(9)	(10)	(11)	(12)	(13)	(14)	(15)	(16)	(17)	(18)	(19)	(20)	(21)	(22)	(23)
Strength in Trenches	32	873	18	46			Lewis	8				971	11	48								
10th Inf: Bde	2	20																				
4th Army School	1	3																				
4th Div: School	2	5																				
Base	2	4																				
Survey & Vis Sig		2																				
M.G. Course		9																				
T.M. "		27																				
Leave		10																				
Absent 3 Sick 2	1	5																				
French school		1																				
Pigeon flyer		1																				
VIII Corps O.M.		2																				
TOTALS ...	40	964	18	46				8				971	11	48								

Ammunition with Unit:—

·303 inch; approximate number of rounds per Man 208

·303 inch; " " " per Machine Gun 8300.

Gun or Howitzer; approximate number of rounds per Gun or Howitzer —

Supplies with Unit:—

Approximate number of days' rations for men of ration strength Two.

" " " forage for Animals " " Two.

" " " fuel and lubricants for Mechanically Propelled Vehicles

No: of men serving with 4th Div: Res Co: 52

Signature of Commander [illegible] Capt for Lt. Col

Wt. W. 5870—621. 600,000. 10/14. D. P. Wks. (150-3) Forms B 231 / 3

Army Form B 231.

FIELD STATE.

Unit 2nd Bn Roy: Dublin Fus^rs
Place In the Field.
Date 30/6/16.

To be rendered in accordance with Field Service Regulations, Part II.

FIGHTING STRENGTH — This should not include details attached to unit, or personnel detailed to march with the Train, or any men unfit to go into action with unit

RATION STRENGTH — To include Fighting Strength, Personnel detailed to march with the Train, and all Personnel and animals attached for Rations and Forage

UNIT	Fighting: Personnel: Officers	Fighting: Personnel: Other Ranks	Fighting: Horses and Mules: Riding	Fighting: Horses and Mules: Draught and Pack	Fighting: Other Animals	Fighting: Other Animals	Guns and Ammunition Wagons (stating nature)	Machine Guns	Ambulances	Tool Carts, Technical Carts (stating nature)	Remarks	Ration: Personnel: Total, all Ranks entitled to Rations	Ration: Horses and Mules: Heavy Horses	Ration: Horses and Mules: Other Horses and Mules	Ration: Other Animals	Ration: Other Animals	Motor Cars	Motor Bicycles	Lorries: 3 Ton	Lorries: 30 Cwt.	Tractors	Remarks
(1)	(2)	(3)	(4)	(5)	(6)	(7)	(8)	(9)	(10)	(11)	(12)	(13)	(14)	(15)	(16)	(17)	(18)	(19)	(20)	(21)	(22)	(23)
Strength in Trenches	31	870	13	46			Lewis	8				975	9	450								
10th Inf: Bde	3	21																				
4th Army School	1	3																				
4th Div^l School	2	5																				
Base	2	4																				
Survey / Vis: Sig:		2																				
M.G. Course		12																				
T.M.		29																				
Leave		6																				
Absent & Sick	1	10																				
Grenade School		1																				
Pigeon flyer		1																				
VIII Corps O.M.		3																				
IV Div: police		5																				
IV Div R.T. dump	2	-																				
TOTALS ...	42	972	13	46				8				975	9	50								

Ammunition with Unit:—
·303 inch; approximate number of rounds per Man 208
·303 inch; ,, ,, ,, per Machine Gun 8330
Gun or Howitzer; approximate number of rounds per Gun or Howitzer —

Supplies with Unit:—
Approximate number of days' rations for men of ration strength 3.
,, ,, ,, forage for Animals ,, ,, 2.
,, ,, ,, fuel and lubricants for Mechanically Propelled Vehicles

No. of men serving with 4th Div: Res Coy 56
added to during past week 3
Left Nil.

Signature of Commander [illegible] for Lieut-Col.

(79269.) Wt.W. 5870—621. 900,000 10/14. J. P. & Co. Ltd. Forms B 231 / 3

To be made up to and for Sunday in each week.

No. of Report DF.38. **FIELD RETURN.** Army Form B. 213.

(To be furnished by all arms, services, and departments (except A.S.C. units) to the A. G.'s Office at the Base in accordance with Field Service Regulations, Part II.)

RETURN showing numbers (a) Effective strength of Unit. (b) Rationed by Unit. 2nd Bn. Royal Dublin Fusiliers at in the Field 4/6/16 Date.

Detail	Personnel: Officers	Personnel: Other ranks	Personnel: Natives	Horses: Riding	Horses: Draught	Horses: Heavy Draught	Horses: Pack	Mules: Large	Mules: Small	Camels	Oxen	Guns, carriages and limbers, showing description	Ammunition wagons and limbers	Machine guns	Aircraft, showing description	Horsed: 4 wheeled	Horsed: 2 wheeled	Mechanical: Motor Cars	Mechanical: Tractors	Mechanical: Lorries, showing description	Mechanical: Trucks, showing description	Mechanical: Trailers	Motor Bicycles	Bicycles
Effective Strength of Unit	34	1021		11	26	9	9						Lewis	8		10	9							9
Details, *by Arms* attached to unit as in War Establishment:— [illegible]	1	9		1																				
Total	35	1027		12	26	9	9							8		10	9							9
War Establishment	31	995		13	26	9	9							8		10	9							9
Wanting to complete (Detail of Personnel and Horses below)	1	–																						
Surplus	6	32																						
*Attached (not to include the details shown above)	1			1																				
Civilians:— Employed with the Unit		2				4																		
Accompanying the Unit		2																						
Total Rationed...	39	[illegible]		13	26	13	9																	

Remarks:

	Offrs	O.R.
[illegible]		
Brigade Machine Gun Coy	–	8
Stokes Gun Course	–	33
[illegible]	1	[illegible]
[illegible]	[illegible]	1
[illegible]	–	1
[illegible]	2	21
Instructor [illegible] Depot	–	[illegible]
Leave	–	[illegible]
[illegible]	–	6
Sick [illegible]		
[illegible]	–	3
A.G. Office	–	1
[illegible]	1	4
[illegible] School	–	2
[illegible]	–	[illegible]
A.O.C.		
R.T.O. [illegible]	1	[illegible]
	7	[illegible]

Major or Captain to complete

Subalterns over [illegible] to Establishment

[illegible] A.O.C.

[illegible]

* In the case of field ambulance, hospitals or depots, the number of patients are to be included here, the names being shown in A. F. A. 36.

[illegible] Lieut.-Colonel Signature of Commander.

4/6/16 Date of Despatch.

For information of the A.G.'s Office at the Base.

Officers and men who have become casuals, been transferred or joined since last report.

Place In the Field. Date 4/6/16.

Regtl. Number	Rank	Name	Corps	Nature of casualty, or name of unit from or to which transferred	Date of being struck off or coming on the ration return	Remarks*
	Lieut.	L.A. King.	3rd Bn Roy Dub Fus.	joined.	30/5/16.	
	Lieut.	R.J. Dade	5th Bn. " " "	to Hospital.	31/5/16.	
19365	Private	Grogan, C Coy	2nd Bn R.D.F.	rejoined off leave	28-5-16	
17882	"	Sparkes, C "	"	"	30-5-16	
13365	Corpl.	Kyle	" "	posted to D Coy	2-6-16.	Draft.
18506	L/Cpl	Hill	" "	" " C	"	"
6873	Private	Carney	" "	" " A	"	Under escort.
11671	"	Woodhouse	" "	" " C	"	Under escort.
9112	"	Byrne	" "	" " D	"	Under escort.
16878	"	Roberts	" "	" " D	"	"
23820	"	Mc Ardle	" "	" " B	"	"
19143	"	Martin	" "	" " A	"	"
10447	"	Murphy	" "	" " D	"	"
5764	"	Kelly	" "	" " D	"	"
18369	"	Clarke J	" "	B Coy to prison.	29-5-16.	
7122	L/Cpl	Curran W.	"	Performed duties of Battalion Chiropodist for month of May.		
5903	C.Q.M.S.	Partridge A Coy	" "	Performed the duties of Company Q.M. Sgt for month of May		
10809	"	Burke B.	" "			
9884	"	Cahill C.	" "			
10464	"	Boon D.	" "			

* State whether absence is of a permanent or temporary nature, adding, in the case of casuals from wounds or disease, any available information for communication to the relatives.

No. of Report 97 39.

FIELD RETURN.

Army Form B. 213.

(To be furnished by all arms, services and departments (except A.S.C. units) to the A. G.'s Office at the Base in accordance with Field Service Regulations, Part II.)

RETURN showing numbers RATIONED by, and Transport on charge of, [illegible] at [illegible] 1st June 1916 Date.

DETAIL	Personnel			Animals								Guns, carriages, and limbers, and transport vehicles.														REMARKS
				Horses				Mules								Horsed		Mechanical								
	Officers	Other ranks	Natives	Riding	Draught	Heavy Draught	Pack	Large	Small	Camels	Oxen	Guns, carriages and limbers, showing description	Ammunition wagons and limbers	Machine guns	Aircraft, showing description	4 Wheeled	2 Wheeled	Motor Cars	Tractors	Lorries, showing description	Trucks, showing description	Trailers	Motor Bicycles	Bicycles		
Effective Strength of Unit	[illegible]	[illegible]		11	26	9	9						Lewis	8		10	9							9		
Details, *by Arms* attached to unit as in War Establishment:— RAMC / ASC	1	5 / 1		1																						
Total	38	[illegible]		12	26	9	9							8		10	9							9		
War Establishment	30	995		13	26	9	9							8		10	9							9		
Wanting to complete (Detail of Personnel and Horses below)	1			-	-	-	-							-		-									Major or Captain to complete	
Surplus	4	84		-	-	-	-							-		-	-							-	[illegible] to Establishment	
*Attached (not to include the details shown above)				1																					Chaplain R.C. [illegible] Royal Irish Rifles attached	
Civilians:— Employed with the Unit / Accompanying the Unit		3																								
TOTAL RATIONED ...	30	851			26	9	9							-		-	-							-		

Remarks (handwritten, partly illegible): Details Detached Away: Offrs / O.R. — [illegible] 1/9; [illegible] Base 1/4; [illegible] 1/5; [illegible] 2/6; Sniping [illegible] -/62; Mines -/10; Trench Mortar Bty -/24; Machine Gun School -/9; Leave 1/34; [illegible]; Sick [illegible] -/3; Bombers; R.E. [illegible]; [illegible]; [illegible] School; Pigeon [illegible]; [illegible] — Total 170

* In the case of field ambulances, hospitals or depots, the number of patients are to be included here, the names being shown in A. F. A. 36.

[illegible] Signature of Commander.

1st June 1916 Date of Despatch.

For information of the A.G.'s Office at the Base.

Officers and men who have become casuals, been transferred or joined since last report.

Place In the Field Date 10th June 1916.

Regtl. Number	Rank	Name	Corps	Nature of casualty, or name of unit from or to which transferred	Date of being struck off or coming on the ration return	Remarks*
	Capt	J. O. W. Shine	1st Bn Roy Dub Fus	joined Bn	5-6-16	
	2/Lieut	J. A. H. Helby	2nd Bn Roy Dub Fus	" "	7-6-16	
	"	A. H. West	4th Bn " " "	" "	7-6-16	
	"	T. W. H. Mason	3rd Bn " " "	rejoined from Hospl	9-6-16	
5641	Corpl	Behan, A. Coy	2nd Bn Roy Dub F	rejoined from Hospl Base Rest Camp	4-6-16	
18597	"	McCann, B.	" "	" "	"	
17408	L/Cpl	Curran, B.	" "	" "	"	

* State whether absence is of a permanent or temporary nature, adding, in the case of casuals from wounds or disease, any available information for communication to the relatives.

To be made up to and for Sunday in each week.

No. of Report D.F. 40

FIELD RETURN.

Army Form B. 213.

(To be furnished by all arms, services, and departments (except A.S.C. units) to the A. G.'s Office at the Base in accordance with Field Service Regulations, Part II.)

RETURN showing numbers (a) Effective strength of Unit. (b) Rationed by Unit. 2nd Bn Royal Dublin Fus. at In the field. 17th June 1916. Date.

DETAIL	Personnel: Officers	Other ranks	Natives	Animals: Horses: Riding	Draught	Heavy Draught	Pack	Mules: Large	Small	Camels	Oxen	Guns, carriages and limbers, showing description	Ammunition wagons and limbers	Machine guns	Aircraft, showing description	Horsed: 4 wheeled	2 wheeled	Mechanical: Motor Cars.	Tractors	Lorries, showing description	Trucks, showing description	Trailers	Motor Bicycles	Bicycles
Effective Strength of Unit	41	1041		11	26	9	9						Lewis	8		10	9							9
Details, *by Arms* attached to unit as in War Establishment:—																								
R.A.M.C		5		1																				
A.O.C		1																						
Total	42	1047		12	26	9	9							8		10	9							9
War Establishment	30	955		13	26	9	9							8		10	9							9
Wanting to complete (Detail of Personnel and Horses below)	-	-												-		-	-							-
Surplus	12	92												-		-	-							-
*Attached (not to include the details shown above)	1			1																				
Civilians:— Employed with the Unit		2																						
Accompanying the Unit		3																						
TOTAL RATIONED...	34	926		13																				

REMARKS

Details away	Offrs	Men
3rd Army School	1	4
4th Div. School	1	13
[illegible]	1	3
[illegible]	2	5
Survey		1
4th Div. [illegible]		52
Miners		10
Trench Mortar course		26
M. Gun course		9
Leave	1	17
Absentees		3
Sick on leave		3
Bombers	1	3
R.E. [illegible]		3
Visual Signalling		1
Anti-Gas School		2
Pigeon [illegible]		1
R.T.O. G.H.Q.	1	
[illegible]		1
	9	156

Subalterns surplus to Est.

Chaplain R.C.

Interpreter & servant Royal Irish Rifles

* In the case of field ambulances, hospitals or depots, the number of patients are to be included here, the names being shown in A. F. A. 36.

[illegible] Lieut-Col. Signature of Commander.

17th June 1916 Date of Despatch.

For information of the A.G.'s Office at the Base.

Officers and men who have become casuals, been transferred or joined since last report.

Place In the Field   Date 17th June 1916

Regtl. Number	Rank	Name	Corps	Nature of casualty, or name of unit from or to which transferred	Date of being struck off or coming on the ration return	Remarks*
	Lieut	H. D. K. George	3rd Bn Roy: Dub: F.	joined Bn	12-6-16	
	Major	R. G. B. Jeffreys	2nd Bn Roy: Dub. F.	" "	16-6-16	
	2/Lieut	T. F. Honeyside	1st Bn Roy Dub Fus	" "	17-6-16	
	2/Lieut	E. C. B. Dillon	3rd Bn " "	" "	17-6-16	
16930	Pte	Keogh, M. B Coy	2nd Bn Royal Dublin Fus.			
			att. 10th I.B. pioneers	Absent Offshore	10-6-16.	
19735	Pte	Burns J. A Coy	2nd Bn R.D.F.	absent Off leave	10-6-16.	
8107	Pte	Nolan J. D Coy	2nd Bn Roy Dub Fus	rejd. from		
				6th Entrenching Bn	12-6-16.	
16825	Sgt	Donegan W. B	2nd Bn Roy: D. F.	transferred to		
				A.G's Office, Base	13-6-16.	
Draft of		50 other ranks	joined Bn		13-6-16	
"	"	20	" "		16-6-16	

* State whether absence is of a permanent or temporary nature, adding, in the case of casuals from wounds or disease, any available information for communication to the relatives.

To be made up to and for Sunday in each week.

No. of Report D.F. 41

FIELD RETURN.

Army Form B. 213.

(To be furnished by all arms, services, and departments (except A.S.C. units) to the A. G.'s Office at the Base in accordance with Field Service Regulations, Part II.)

RETURN showing numbers (*a*) Effective strength of Unit. (*b*) Rationed by Unit. 2nd Bn Royal Dublin Fusiliers in the field at 24th June 16. Date.

Detail	Personnel: Officers	Personnel: Other ranks	Personnel: Natives	Animals: Horses: Riding	Animals: Horses: Draught	Animals: Horses: Heavy Draught	Animals: Horses: Pack	Animals: Mules: Large	Animals: Mules: Small	Animals: Camels	Animals: Oxen	Guns, carriages and limbers, showing description	Ammunition wagons and limbers	Machine guns	Aircraft, showing description	Horsed: 4 wheeled	Horsed: 2 wheeled	Mechanical: Motor Cars	Mechanical: Tractors	Mechanical: Lorries, showing description	Mechanical: Trucks, showing description	Mechanical: Trailers	Motor Bicycles	Bicycles	Remarks
Effective Strength of Unit	43	10[illegible]		12	26	11	9							8		10	10							8	
Details, *by Arms* attached to unit as in War Establishment:—																									
R.A.M.C.	1	5																							
A.O.C.		1																							
Total	44	1014		12	26	11	9							8		10	10							8	
War Establishment	30	995		13	26	4	4							8		10	4							4	
Wanting to complete (Detail of Personnel and Horses below)	Nil																								
Surplus	14 Subalterns					2																			
*Attached (not to include the details shown above)																									Chaplain R.C.
Civilians:— Employed with the Unit		2																							Interpreter Servant.
Accompanying the Unit																									
Total Rationed...	36	[illegible]		13																					

Details rationed away.

Remarks	O.	O.R.
Hospital	1	
Base	2	
3rd Army School	1	
4th Div: School [illegible]	2	
Survey		
4th Div. [illegible]		
[illegible] Motor [illegible]		
M. G. Course		
Leave		
Absentees		
Sick on Leave		
[illegible]		
Pigeon flyer		
10th I.B.	1	
[illegible]		
[illegible]	1	
	9	143

* In the case of field ambulances, hospitals or depots, the number of patients are to be included here, the names being shown in A. F. A. 36.

[illegible] Lieut.-Col. Signature of Commander.

24th June 1916. Date of Despatch.

For information of the A.G.'s Office at the Base.

Officers and men who have become casuals, been transferred or joined since last report.

Place ______________________ Date ______________________

Regtl. Number	Rank	Name	Corps	Nature of casualty, or name of unit from or to which transferred	Date of being struck off or coming on the ration return	Remarks*
	2/Lieut	W. Pedlow.	3rd Bn R.D.F.	Joined Bn	16-6-16.	
	- -	G.H. Chandler	- - - -	- -	18-6-16.	
	- -	W.G. Scott.	4th - - -	- -	19-6-16.	
	Lieut	J.E. Andrews	3rd - - -	- -	20-6-16.	
	Lieut	H.D.K. George	3rd Bn R.D.F.	to Roy. Fly: Corps	18-6-16.	
	2/Lt.	S.J. Diamond	2nd - -	to M.G. Corps Grantham, U.K.	21-6-16	
19735	Pte	Burns, J.	"D" Coy. absent off leave	Rejoined	17-6-16	
16930	Pte	Keogh, M.	"C" - - -	- -	17-6-16	
7425	L.C.	Scanlon	"B" - - -	- -	22-6-16	
8845	Pte	Shields	"D" - -	- -	22-6-16	
16562	L.C.	Carty	"A" Deserter	- -	24-6-16	
20009	Pte	Mc Glynn J.	"D" Coy. absent off leave		23-6-16.	
18620	-	Mc Geeney M.	- - -	- -	- - -	
8916	L.C.	Cummins	- - -	- -	- - -	
5705	Pte	Murray	- - -	- -	17-6-16.	
18009	Cpl	Kelly	"A" Coy. Rejoined		24-6-16	
9358	Pte	Dowling M.	"D" Coy. -		- - -	
8970	-	Brophy	"C" -	from 32 Bde. R.F.A.	- - -	
No. 9458	Pte	Molyneux	"D" Coy.	Wounded	18-6-16.	
- 9435	-	Reilly	"D" -	-	- - -	
- 21558	-	Doyle	"C" -	-	- - -	

* State whether absence is of a permanent or temporary nature, adding, in the case of casuals from wounds or disease, any available information for communication to the relatives.

No. of Report [illegible]

FIELD RETURN.

Army Form B. 213.

(To be furnished by all arms, services and departments (except A.S.C. units) to the A. G.'s Office at the Base in accordance with Field Service Regulations, Part II.)

RETURN showing numbers RATIONED by, and Transport on charge of, [illegible] at [illegible] 30 [illegible] Date.

Detail	Personnel			Animals								Guns, carriages, and limbers, and transport vehicles.												Motor Bicycles	Bicycles.	Remarks
				Horses				Mules								Horsed		Mechanical								
	Officers	Other ranks	Natives	Riding	Draught	Heavy Draught	Pack	Large	Small	Camels	Oxen	Guns, carriages and limbers, showing description	Ammunition wagons and limbers	Machine guns	Aircraft, showing description	4 Wheeled	2 Wheeled	Motor Cars	Tractors	Lorries, showing description	Trucks, showing description	Trailers			
Effective Strength of Unit	44	1080		12	25	11	9						Lewis	8											
Details, *by Arms* attached to unit as in War Establishment:—																									
R.A.M.C.	1	5																							
A.O.C.		1																							
Total	45	1086		12	25	11	9							8											
War Establishment	30	996		13	26	4	9							8											
Wanting to complete (Detail of Personnel and Horses below)	–																								
Surplus	1	captain																							
	14	subalterns																							
*Attached (not to include the details shown above)	1			1																					
Civilians:— Employed with the Unit / Accompanying the Unit		2				3																			
Total Rationed ...	36	430		13	25	12	9																		

Remarks (handwritten): Details returned [illegible]
- Base
- 3rd Army School
- 4th Div: Sch [illegible]
- 4th Div: Res Co.
- Trench Mortar Bty
- M.G. [illegible]
- [illegible]
- Sick on leave
- [illegible]
- 10th [illegible]
- [illegible] Corps [illegible]
- [illegible]
- [illegible] Div: Police
- [illegible]
- 1045

* In the case of field ambulances, hospitals or depots, the number of patients are to be included here, the names being shown in A. F. A. 36.

[illegible] Signature of Commander.

[illegible] Date of Despatch.

For information of the A.G.'s Office at the Base.

Officers and men who have become casuals, been transferred or joined since last report.

Place In the Field   Date 30-6-16.

Regtl. Number	Rank	Name	Corps	Nature of casualty, or name of unit from or to which transferred	Date of being struck off or coming on the ration return	Remarks*
	Capt	J. G. F. Napier-Martin,	3rd Bn R.D.F.	joined from employment as R.T.O.	[illegible]	
	2/Lieut	J. P. Mulholland.	2nd Bn R.D.F.	commissioned from Ranks.	[illegible]	
	Lieut	R.D.K. George [illegible]	[illegible]	[illegible]	24-6-16.	
	2/Lieut	P. T. Dale	5th Bn R.D.F.	to U.K. Sick	[illegible]	
Pte	4349	Delaney	2nd Bn R.D.F.	Rejoined from prison posted to 'A' Coy	29-6-16.	
15290	Pte	Edwards		Wounded	29-6-16	
26129	"	Williams		"		[illegible]
7100	C.S.M.	Maloney		"	30-6-16	" " "
13624	Pte	McGurney	Rejoined from leave		[illegible]	
8971	"	Cummins	" " "			
5740	"	Murray	Absent off leave, now reported			
			admitted King George V Hospital		16-6-16.	
[illegible]	"	Cahill "D"	missing from camp night of		29-6-16	
[illegible]771	"	O'Brien "C"	working party		28-6-16	

Certified that

5903	C.Q.M.S.	Partridge	acted as Accountant	for 'A' Co June 1 - 30
11809	"	Burke	" " "	" 'B' "
9229	"	Cahill	" " "	" 'C' "
10061	"	Boon	" " "	" 'D' "

* State whether absence is of a permanent or temporary nature, adding, in the case of casuals from wounds or disease, any available information for communication to the relatives.

Perforated Sheet giving detail of personnel and horses wanting to complete, shown on Army Form B. 213.

Number of Report 42

Detail of Wanting to Complete.	Drivers.						Gunners	Smith Gunners	Range Takers	Farriers		Shoeing, or Shoeing and Carriage Smiths	Cold Shoers	Wheelers			Saddlers or Harness Makers	Blacksmiths	Bricklayers and Masons	Carpenters and Joiners	Fitters & Turners (R. E.)		Fitters		Plumbers	Electricians		Signalmen	Engine Drivers		Air Line Men	Permanent Line Men	Operators, Telegraph	Cablemen	Brigade Section Pioneers	General-duty Pioneers	Signallers	Instrument Repairers	Motor Cyclists	Motor Cyclist Artificers	Telephonists	Clerks	Machine Gunners	Armament Artificers		Armourers	Storemen	Privates	W.O.'s and N.C.O.'s (by ranks) not included in trade columns.									TOTAL to agree with wanting to complete		Horses			
	R. A.	R. E.	A. S. C.	Car	Lorry	Steam				Serjeants	Corporals			R. A.	H. T.	M. T.					Wood	Iron	R. A.	Wireless		Ordinary	W. T.		Loco.	Field														Fitters	Range Finders													Officers	Other Ranks	Riding	Draught	Heavy Draught	Pack
CAVALRY																																																															
R. A.																																																															
R. E.																																																															
INFANTRY																																																															
R. A. M. C.																																																															
A. O. C.																																																															
A. V. C.																																																															

Remarks :—

[illegible] Signature of Commander.

2nd Bn Royal Dublin Fusiliers Unit.

10th Inf: Bde 4th Div: Formation to which attached.

30 - 6 - 16 Date of Despatch.

(26149.) Wt. W. 10698/4046. 500,000. 10/15. M.R.Co., Ltd. Forms/B. 213/6.

[P.T.O.

Perforated Sheet giving detail of personnel and horses wanting to complete, shown on Army Form B. 213.

Number of Report DF 41.

Detail of Wanting to Complete	Drivers						Gunners	Smith Gunners	Range Takers	Farriers		Shoeing, or Shoeing and Carriage Smiths	Cold Shoers	Wheelers			Saddlers or Harness Makers	Blacksmiths	Bricklayers and Masons	Carpenters and Joiners	Fitters & Turners (R. E.)		Fitters		Plumbers	Electricians		Signalmen	Engine Drivers		Air Line Men	Permanent Line Men	Operators, Telegraph	Cablemen	Brigade Section Pioneers	General duty Pioneers	Signallers	Instrument Repairers	Motor Cyclists	Motor Cyclist Artificers	Telephonists	Clerks	Machine Gunners	Armament Artificers		Armourers	Storemen	Privates	W.O.'s and N.C.O.'s (by ranks) not included in trade columns	TOTAL to agree with wanting to complete		Horses			
	R. A.	R. E.	A. S. C.	Car	Lorry	Steam				Serjeants	Corporals			R. A.	H. T.	M. T.					Wood	Iron	R. A.	Wireless		Ordinary	W. T.		Loco.	Field														Fitters	Range Finders					Officers	Other Ranks	Riding	Draught	Heavy Draught	Pack
CAVALRY																																																							
R. A.																																																							
R. E.																																																							
INFANTRY																																																							
R. A. M. C.																																																							
A. O. C.																																																							
A. V. C.																																																							

Remarks:—

[illegible] Lieut-Col. Signature of Commander.

2nd Bn Royal Dublin Fusiliers. Unit.

10th Inf Bde. 4th Division Formation to which attached.

24 June 1916 Date of Despatch.

(B 99511.) Wt. W15519/M149. 1,000,000 1/16. J. P. & Co., Ltd. Forms/B 213/7.

[P.T.O.

Perforated Sheet giving deail of personnel and horses wanting to complete, shown on Army Form B. 213.

Number of Report D.F. 40.

Detail of Wanting to Complete	Drivers						Gunners	Smith Gunners	Range Takers	Farriers		Shoeing, or Shoeing and Carriage Smiths	Cold Shoers	Wheelers			Saddlers or Harness Makers	Blacksmiths	Bricklayers and Masons	Carpenters and Joiners	Fitters & Turners (R. E.)		Fitters		Plumbers	Electricians		Signalmen	Engine Drivers		Air Line Men	Permanent Line Men	Operators, Telegraph	Cablemen	Brigade Section Pioneers	General-duty Pioneers	Signallers	Instrument Repairers	Motor Cyclists	Motor Cyclist Artificers	Telephonists	Clerks	Machine Gunners	Armament Artificers		Armourers	Storemen	Privates	W.O.'s and N.C.O.'s (by ranks) not included in trade columns											TOTAL to agree with wanting to complete		Horses			
	R. A.	R. E.	A. S. C.	Car	Lorry	Steam				Serjeants	Corporals			R. A.	H. T.	M. T.					Wood	Iron	R. A.	Wireless		Ordinary	W. T.		Loco.	Field														Fitters	Range Finders															Officers	Other Ranks	Riding	Draught	Heavy Draught	Pack
CAVALRY																																																																	
R. A.																																																																	
R. E.																																																																	
INFANTRY																																																																	
R. A. M. C.																																																																	
A. O. C.																																																																	
A. V. C.																																																																	

Remarks:—

[illegible] Lieut. Col Signature of Commander.

2nd Bn Royal Dublin Fusiliers Unit.

10th Inf: Bde: 4th Division Formation to which attached.

17th June 1916. Date of Despatch.

(B 99511.) Wt. W15519/M149. 1,000,000. 1/16. J. P. & Co., Ltd. Forms/B. 213/7.

[P.T.O.

Perforated Sheet giving detail of personnel and horses wanting to complete, shown on Army Form B. 213.

Number of Report 8730.

Detail of Wanting to Complete.	Drivers. R. A.	Drivers. R. E.	Drivers. A. S. C.	Drivers. Car	Drivers. Lorry	Drivers. Steam	Gunners	Smith Gunners	Range Takers	Farriers Serjeants	Farriers Corporals	Shoeing, or Shoeing and Carriage Smiths	Cold Shoers	Wheelers R. A.	Wheelers H. T.	Wheelers M. T.	Saddlers or Harness Makers	Blacksmiths	Bricklayers and Masons	Carpenters and Joiners	Fitters & Turners (R. E.) Wood	Fitters & Turners (R. E.) Iron	Fitters R. A.	Fitters Wireless	Plumbers
CAVALRY																								
R. A.																								
R. E.																								
INFANTRY																								
R. A. M. C.																								
A. O. C.																								
A. V. C.																								

Detail of Wanting to Complete.	Electricians Ordinary	Electricians W. T.	Signalmen	Engine Drivers Loco.	Engine Drivers Field	Air Line Men	Permanent Line Men	Operators, Telegraph	Cablemen	Brigade Section Pioneers	General-duty Pioneers	Signallers	Instrument Repairers	Motor Cyclists	Motor Cyclist Artificers	Telephonists	Clerks	Machine Gunners	Armament Artificers Fitters	Armament Artificers Range Finders	Armourers	Storemen	Privates	W.O's. and N.C.O's (by ranks) not included in trade columns.								TOTAL to agree with wanting to complete Officers	TOTAL to agree with wanting to complete Other Ranks	Horses Riding	Horses Draught	Horses Heavy Draught	Horses Pack
CAVALRY																																				
R. A.																																				
R. E.																																				
INFANTRY																							-									1	-	-	-	-	-
R. A. M. C.																																				
A. O. C.																																				
A. V. C.																																				

Remarks :—

Signature of Commander.

Unit.

Formation to which attached.

10th June 1916 Date of Despatch.

(26149.) Wt. W. 10698/4046. 500,000. 10/15. M.R.Co., Ltd. Forms/B. 213/6.

[P.T.O.

Perforated Sheet giving detail of personnel and horses wanting to complete, shown on Army Form B. 213.

Number of Report DF38.

Detail of Wanting to Complete	Drivers R.A.	Drivers R.E.	Drivers A.S.C.	Drivers Car	Drivers Lorry	Drivers Steam	Gunners	Smith Gunners	Range Takers	Farriers Serjeants	Farriers Corporals	Shoeing, or Shoeing and Carriage Smiths	Cold Shoers	Wheelers R.A.	Wheelers H.T.	Wheelers M.T.	Saddlers or Harness Makers	Blacksmiths	Bricklayers and Masons	Carpenters and Joiners	Fitters & Turners (R.E.) Wood	Fitters & Turners (R.E.) Iron	Fitters R.A.	Fitters Wireless	Plumbers	Electricians Ordinary	Electricians W.T.	Signalmen	Engine Drivers Loco.	Engine Drivers Field	Air Line Men	Permanent Line Men	Operators, Telegraph	Cablemen	Brigade Section Pioneers	General-duty Pioneers	Signallers	Instrument Repairers	Motor Cyclists	Motor Cyclist Artificers	Telephonists	Clerks	Machine Gunners	Armament Artificers Fitters	Armament Artificers Range Finders	Armourers	Storemen	Privates	W.O.'s and N.C.O.'s (by ranks) not included in trade columns	TOTAL to agree with wanting to complete Officers	TOTAL Other Ranks	Horses Riding	Horses Draught	Horses Heavy Draught	Horses Pack
CAVALRY																																																							
R.A.																																																							
R.E.																																																							
INFANTRY																																																							
R.A.M.C.																																																							
A.O.C.																																																							
A.V.C.																																																							

Remarks:—

[signature] Lieut Colonel Signature of Commander.

2nd/5th Royal Berkshire Battalion. Unit.

10th Inf Bde 4th Divn Formation to which attached.

3/6/16. Date of Despatch.

(B 99511.) Wt. W15519/M149. 1,000,000. 1/16. J. P. & Co., Ltd. Forms/B 213/7.

[P.T.O.

4th Division

10th Bde

2nd Battn Royal Dublin Fus

July to October

~~Trans to 48th Bde 16th Divn~~

~~15th November 1916~~

TO 16 DIV 48 BDE

10th Brigade

4th Division

2nd BATTALION

ROYAL DUBLIN FUSILIERS

J U L Y 1 9 1 6

Instructions regarding War Diaries and Intelligence Summaries are contained in F. S. Regs., Part II. and the Staff Manual respectively. Title pages will be prepared in manuscript.

WAR DIARY
or
INTELLIGENCE SUMMARY
(Erase heading not required.)

Army Form C. 2118.

2 R Dublin Fus
July 1916.
Vol 23

Hour, Date, Place	Summary of Events and Information	Remarks and References to Appendices
TRENCHES. H.Q. TENDERLOIN ST. JULY 1st 1916.	At 9.0 a.m. the Battalion left its Assembly trenches and advanced in the following formation: "B" + "C" Coys. 4 lines of platoons each platoon in sections of fire. The lines 100 yards apart. "D" Coy in Reserve 200 yards in rear of 4th line. [illegible] Coy [illegible] formation, each platoon being in column of fours. Immediately after leaving their assembly trenches, each line came under a heavy enfilade fire from machine guns in BEAUMONT-HAMEL [illegible] the Reserve Coy having casualties as they left YOUNG STREET. At [illegible] a.m. the order [illegible] by message "[illegible]" Two runners were immediately sent after each Coy and the C.O. personally went to "A" Coy [illegible] a Sergt who was a little in rear of the 4th line [illegible] with the verbal message. [illegible] first line trenches [illegible] In the meantime the Battalion had lost [illegible] [illegible]	
	It had been impossible to stop all the Platoons and some had got into the ground between the enemy and our own trenches – these without exception became casualties including 5 officers.	
	At 12 noon orders as follows were received: "You will attack the German trenches and consolidate line from point 86 to 88 inclusive. The Seaforth Highdrs are attacking north of THE REDAN. Point 89 is held by our own troops. The 29th Divn are attacking BEAUMONT-HAMEL at 12.30. Take care of your left flank as there are still some Germans in position opposite THE REDAN."	
	It was found impossible to collect more than 60 men during the Advance out of 23 officers and 480 men going into action 14 officers and 311 men had become casualties. The Advance having been in lines of sections on a front of 400 yards the remainder were scattered about in the trenches, and mixed up with those troops which remained of the 11th Brigade. The C.O. was therefore ordered to collect all the men possible and put them into the original assembly trenches. This was done. During the evening the Carriers and the 10% Reinforcements rejoined the Battalion.	
2nd	During the morning the remnants of the Battalion were reorganised. Three Lewis guns had been lost but Sergeant DOWNIE succeeded in finding one belonging to another Corps making our total 6. At 2.0 p.m. the Battalion was posted as follows: One Coy in trench immediately in front of TENDERLOIN STREET, one Coy in YOUNG STREET, 2 Coys in SUNKEN ROAD.	
MAILLY-MAILLET. 3rd	At 5.0 p.m. the Battalion returned to billets in MAILLY-MAILLET. The weather throughout the operations was fine and warm.	

9 26 6 W 257 976 100,000 4/12 H W V 79/3298

Army Form C. 2118.

Instructions regarding War Diaries and Intelligence Summaries are contained in F. S. Regs., Part II. and the Staff Manual respectively. Title pages will be prepared in manuscript.

WAR DIARY
or
~~INTELLIGENCE SUMMARY~~

(Erase heading not required.)

Hour, Date, Place		Summary of Events and Information	Remarks and References to Appendices
MAILLY-MAILLET.	July 4th	Capt REDMOND with his Coy went to AUCHONVILLERS and acted as garrison	
	5th–6	Wet weather, some shells fell in MAILLY but with no damage to the Bn.	
Bn H.Q. TENDERLOIN.	7th	Bn left for the trenches at 3.0 in the afternoon, the relief being concluded at 5.10 pm. Trenches were very wet after the recent rain, and heavy rain fell at night.	
	8th	Improvement at night after a dull day. The Artillery made a demonstration at 8.0 a.m. and again at night.	
	9th	In the afternoon smoke was sent over to the German lines which caused heavy shelling.	
	10th–12th	Frequent short and intense bombardments by our Artillery but the enemy response caused no trouble. The weather much improved.	
	13th	Lieut-Col H.M. Cliff relinquished Command of the Bn having found the strain too great for his age. He left for Headquarters Reserve Army "A" leaving a message of appreciation to be conveyed to the troops. Major R. G. B. Jeffreys took over Command of the Battalion.	
	14th	Short intense bombardments at 9.30 a.m., 1 p.m., 3.30 p.m. and 6.15 p.m.	
FORCEVILLE ROAD	15th	Fine weather. Bn relieved by 1st R. Warwickshire Regt as usual, and the Bn went into tents on the FORCEVILLE ROAD.	
	16th	Nothing to report.	
BERTRANCOURT.	17th	The Bn was addressed by Corps Commander VIII Corps at 3.30, after which the Bn moved to BERTRANCOURT into huts at the bottom of the village.	
	18th	Nothing to report.	
	19th	Major Jeffreys received permission to wear the badges of Lieut-Col pending appearance in London Gazette of official notification of appointment.	
BEAUVAL	20th	Orders to move received at 6.0 a.m. Bn moved off at 2.15 p.m. in hot and summerlike weather. Roads very dusty. 54 fell out on the line of march. BEAUVAL was reached at about 8.0 p.m. Bn in billets, rather cramped but otherwise good.	
	21st	The Bn rested.	
	22nd	Parade at 9.0 a.m and the Coys marched to training area headed by the band.	
PROVEN.	23rd	Bn marched to CANDAS where it entrained. Dinner was served at ST POL during a halt. Bn detrained at PROVEN and marched to N Camp about 3 miles East of POPERINGHE, arriving at 7.45. The men were accomodated in tents and the officers in huts, the Camp was in an excellent state, Capt H.R.H. the PRINCE OF WALES being Camp Commandant.	
	24th	A route march in the morning under CAPT W.A. REDMOND.	
	25th	Companies drilled in the morning.	
	26th	Route march under CAPT W.A. REDMOND. The weather is fine but the roads extremely dusty.	
YSER CANAL BANK.	27th	Bn entrained at 8.30 p.m. and detrained at Railhead 10 p.m. taking over position of Right Reserve Bn on CANAL BANK from 1st R. WARWICKS & formerly held by the Guards Brigade. One Platoon of "A" Coy at FRASCATI: one Platoon "B" Coy X 10 Trench: remainder of Bn on CANAL BANK.	

For information of the A.G.'s Office at the Base.

Officers and men who have become casuals, been transferred or joined since last report.

Place ______________________ Date ______________________

Regtl. Number	Rank	Name	Corps	Nature of casualty, or name of unit from or to which transferred	Date of being struck off or coming on the ration return	Remarks*

* State whether absence is of a permanent or temporary nature, adding, in the case of casuals from wounds or disease, any available information for communication to the relatives.

2nd Bn Royal Dublin Fusiliers

Appendix 5 War Diary.

Month of July 1916.

Date	Remarks
1-7-16	Lt Col J. P. [illegible] [illegible] Killed in Action
	Major L. P. Walsh Wounded in Action, since died of wounds
	Captains — T. [illegible], W. F. Jeffries, J. O. S. [illegible], Wd in Action
	Lt. H. [illegible] Andrews, 2/Lt. W. B. [illegible], G. F. Holland,
	[illegible] A. [illegible], [illegible] Franklin, [illegible] [illegible],
	Lt. W. T. Colyer, 2/Lt [illegible] J. Chadwick, Wounded in Action.
	311 other Ranks, Killed, Wounded & Missing
2-7-	[illegible] [illegible] died of wounds
4-7-16	Major L. P. Walsh.
8-7-16	2 other Ranks Wounded in Action.
9-7-16	92 joined the Battalion
	1 " rank Killed in Action
	2 " ranks Wounded in Action
9-7-16	1 " rank " " "
10-7-16	2 " ranks " " "
11-7-16	9 " " joined the Battalion (6/Connaught Rangers)
13-7-16	1 " rank Wounded in Action
14-7-16	2 " ranks " " "
16-7-16	1 " rank " " "
	2/Lt R. G. Rourke joined the Battalion
	2/Lt R. F. Hudder " " "
	2/Lt H. W. Gibson " " "
	42 other Ranks " " "
18-7-16	56 " " " " "
19-7-16	2/Lt L. G. Doran " " "
	2/Lt W. H. Ayres " " "
	2/Lt W. H. Hinchy " " "
	2/Lt A. R. Henry " " "
	2/Lt J. D. Sheehan " " "
	2/Lt H. J. James " " "
23-7-16	Lt J. A. Noblett " " "
25-7-16	2/Lt P. N. Gordon " " "
	2/Lt D. P. Glancy " " "
26-7-16	Lieut. R. D. Moffat (R.A.M.C.) joined the Bn.

28-7-16 2/Lt G. H. Chandler, Wounded in Action.
5 other ranks joined the Battalion.
29-7-16 1 " " sent

R. [illegible]

31/7/1916 O.C. 2nd Bn Royal Dublin Fusiliers.

No. of Report 43.

FIELD RETURN.

Army Form B. 213.

(To be furnished by all arms, services and departments (except A.S.C. units) to the A. G.'s Office at the Base in accordance with Field Service Regulations, Part II.)

RETURN showing numbers RATIONED by, and Transport on charge of, 2nd Royal Dublin Fus. at In the Field 8th July 1916. Date.

DETAIL	Personnel: Officers	Personnel: Other ranks	Personnel: Natives	Animals: Horses: Riding	Animals: Horses: Draught	Animals: Horses: Heavy Draught	Animals: Horses: Pack	Animals: Mules: Large	Animals: Mules: Small	Animals: Camels	Animals: Oxen	Guns, carriages and limbers, showing description	Ammunition wagons and limbers	Machine guns	Aircraft, showing description	Horsed: 4 Wheeled	Horsed: 2 Wheeled	Mechanical: Motor Cars	Mechanical: Tractors	Mechanical: Lorries, showing description	Mechanical: Trucks, showing description	Mechanical: Trailers	Motor Bicycles	Bicycles	REMARKS
Effective Strength of Unit	30	770		11	25	9	9						Lewis	8										4	
Details, *by Arms* attached to unit as in War Establishment:— R.A.M.C.	1	5		1																					
Total	31	775		12	25	9	9							8										8	
War Establishment	30	995			26	9	9							8										9	
Wanting to complete (Detail of Personnel and Horses below)	3				1																			1	Majors or Capt. to complete Subalterns
Surplus	4																								Subalterns
*Attached (not to include the details shown above)	1			1																					Chaplain R.C.
Civilians:— Employed with the Unit / Accompanying the Unit		1																							Interpreter & Servant
TOTAL RATIONED ...	32	643		13	25	9	9																	8	

Details rat. away	Offrs.	O.R.
R.I.S.		53
Base	3	4
4th Army School	1	3
4th Div. School		2
Brigade Signal		2
T.M. Attached		26
M.G.		10
Leave		5
Absentees		5
Sick on leave	1	3
Pioneers		1
10th I.B.	2	17
8th Corps		3
R. Trans.	1	1
A.O.C.		1
	10	134

* In the case of field ambulances, hospitals or depots, the number of patients are to be included here, the names being shown in A. F. A. 36.

[illegible] for Lieut-Col. Signature of Commander.

8th July 1916. Date of Despatch.

For information of the A. G.'s Office at the Base.

Officers and men who have become casuals, been transferred or joined since last report.

Place In the Field Date 8th July 1916.

Regtl. Number	Rank	Name	Corps	Nature of casualty, or name of unit from or to which transferred	Date of being struck off or coming on the ration return	Remarks*
	Major	L. P. Walsh	Died of	Wounds 4/7/16		
	Capt	J. O. W. Shine	Wounded	in Action 1/7/16.		
	–	W. F. Jeffries	–	– –		
	–	T. Brady	–	– –		
	Lieut	A. E. Andrews	–	– –		
	2/Lt	J. W. R. Morgan	Killed	in Action – –		
	–	W. H. A. Damiano	Died	of Wounds 2/7/16.		
	–	R. H. Ingoldby	Killed	in Action 1/7/16.		
	–	J. C. J. Chadwick	Wounded & bruised.	1/7/16.		
	–	T. W. H. Mason	–	Shell shock – – –		
	–	A. W. Sainsbury	–	– – –		
	–	A. J. Franklin	–	– – –		
	–	G. F. Mulholland	–	– –		
	–	W. T. Colyer	–	2/7/16		
	–	Lieut J. B. Moffat	To Hospital	4-7-16		
		2/Lt W. G. Scott	– –	– – –		
		– C. B. Donovan	– –	5-7-16.		
11771	Pte	O'Brien reported	missing, rejoined	30-6-16.		
11361	–	Cahill –	–	now reported wd. in Action 24/6/16.		
7122	L.C.	Curran performed the duties of Chiropodist				
		to the Bn during month of June.				
		~~Draft of 93 other ranks arrived 7/7/16.~~				

* State whether absence is of a permanent or temporary nature, adding, in the case of casuals from wounds or disease, any available information for communication to the relatives.

Perforated Sheet giving detail of personnel and horses wanting to complete, shown on Army Form B. 213.

Number of Report 43

Detail of Wanting to Complete.	Drivers. R. A.	Drivers. R. E.	Drivers. A. S. C.	Drivers. Car	Drivers. Lorry	Drivers. Steam	Gunners	Smith Gunners	Range Takers	Farriers Serjeants	Farriers Corporals	Shoeing, or Shoeing and Carriage Smiths	Cold Shoers	Wheelers R. A.	Wheelers H. T.	Wheelers M. T.	Saddlers or Harness Makers	Blacksmiths	Bricklayers and Masons	Carpenters and Joiners	Fitters & Turners (R. E.) Wood	Fitters & Turners (R. E.) Iron	Fitters R. A.	Fitters Wireless	Plumbers
CAVALRY																									
R. A.																									
R. E.																									
INFANTRY																									
R. A. M. C.																									
A. O. C.																									
A. V. C.																									

Detail of Wanting to Complete.	Electricians Ordinary	Electricians W. T.	Signalmen	Engine Drivers Loco.	Engine Drivers Field	Air Line Men	Permanent Line Men	Operators, Telegraph	Cablemen	Brigade Section Pioneers	General-duty Pioneers	Signallers	Instrument Repairers	Motor Cyclists	Motor Cyclist Artificers	Telephonists	Clerks	Machine Gunners	Armament Artificers Fitters	Armament Artificers Range Finders	Armourers	Storemen	Privates	W.O.'s and N.C.O.'s (by ranks) not included in trade columns.									TOTAL, to agree with wanting to complete Officers	TOTAL, to agree with wanting to complete Other Ranks	Horses Riding	Horses Draught	Horses Heavy Draught	Horses Pack
CAVALRY																																					
R. A.																																					
R. E.																																					
INFANTRY																							220														
R. A. M. C.																																					
A. O. C.																																					
A. V. C.																																					

Remarks :—

[illegible] Lieut.-Col. Signature of Commander.

2nd Bn Royal Dublin Fus. Unit.

10th Inf. Bde, 4th Div. Formation to which attached.

8th July 1916. Date of Despatch.

(26149.) Wt. W. 10698/4046. 500,000. 10/15. M.R.Co., Ltd. Forms/B. 213/6.

[P.T.O.

FIELD RETURN.

Army Form B. [illegible]3.

No. of Report 144

(To be furnished by all arms, services and departments (except A.S.C. units) to the A. G.'s Office at the Base in accordance with Field Service Regulations, Part II.)

RETURN showing numbers RATIONED by, and Transport on charge of, 2nd Bn Roy. Dublin Fus. at In the Field 16th July 1916 Date.

DETAIL	Personnel			Animals								Guns, carriages, and limbers, and transport vehicles.													REMARKS
				Horses				Mules								Horsed		Mechanical							
	Officers	Other ranks	Natives	Riding	Draught	Heavy Draught	Pack	Large	Small	Camels	Oxen	Guns, carriages and limbers, showing description	Ammunition wagons and limbers	Machine guns	Aircraft, showing description	4 Wheeled	2 Wheeled	Motor Cars	Tractors	Lorries, showing description	Trucks, showing description	Trailers	Motor Bicycles	Bicycles	
Effective Strength of Unit	28	663		11	26	9	9						2 Limbers	8										8	
Details, *by Arms* attached to unit as in War Establishment:—																									
R.A.M.C.	1	5		1																					
Total	29	668		12	26	9	9							8										8	
War Establishment	30	993		13	26	9	9							8										9	
Wanting to complete (Detail of Personnel and Horses below)	4	325																						1	
Surplus	4																								
*Attached (not to include the details shown above)	1			1	1																				
Civilians:— Employed with the Unit / Accompanying the Unit		2																							
TOTAL RATIONED ...	23	723		13	26	9	9							8											

* In the case of field ambulances, hospitals or depots, the number of patients are to be included here, the names being shown in A. F. A. 36.

[illegible] Signature of Commander.

[illegible] Date of Despatch.

Perforated Sheet giving detail of personnel and horses wanting to complete, shown on Army Form B. 213.

Number of Report 44

Detail of Wanting to Complete.	Drivers. R. A.	Drivers. R. E.	Drivers. A. S. C.	Drivers. Car	Drivers. Lorry	Drivers. Steam	Gunners	Smith Gunners	Range Takers	Farriers Serjeants	Farriers Corporals	Shoeing, or Shoeing and Carriage Smiths	Cold Shoers
CAVALRY													
R. A.													
R. E.													
INFANTRY													
R. A. M. C.													
A. O. C.													
A. V. C.													

Detail of Wanting to Complete.	Wheelers R. A.	Wheelers H. T.	Wheelers M. T.	Saddlers or Harness Makers	Blacksmiths	Bricklayers and Masons	Carpenters and Joiners	Fitters & Turners (R. E.) Wood	Fitters & Turners (R. E.) Iron	Fitters R. A.	Fitters Wireless	Plumbers	Electricians Ordinary	Electricians W. T.	Signalmen	Engine Drivers Loco.	Engine Drivers Field
CAVALRY																	
R. A.																	
R. E.																	
INFANTRY																	
R. A. M. C.																	
A. O. C.																	
A. V. C.																	

Detail of Wanting to Complete.	Air Line Men	Permanent Line Men	Operators, Telegraph	Cablemen	Brigade Section Pioneers	General-duty Pioneers	Signallers	Instrument Repairers	Motor Cyclists	Motor Cyclist Artificers	Telephonists	Clerks	Machine Gunners	Armament Artificers Fitters	Armament Artificers Range Finders	Armourers	Storemen	Privates
CAVALRY																		
R. A.																		
R. E.																		
INFANTRY																		
R. A. M. C.																		
A. O. C.																		
A. V. C.																		

Detail of Wanting to Complete.	W.O's. and N.C.O's (by ranks) not included in trade columns.									TOTAL. to agree with wanting to complete Officers	TOTAL. to agree with wanting to complete Other Ranks	Horses Riding	Horses Draught	Horses Heavy Draught	Horses Pack
CAVALRY															
R. A.															
R. E.															
INFANTRY										4	127				
R. A. M. C.															
A. O. C.															
A. V. C.															

Remarks :—

[illegible] Major Signature of Commander.

2nd Bn Royal Dublin Fus. Unit.

10th Inf: Bde. 4th Divn Formation to which attached.

15th July 1916 Date of Despatch.

(26149.) Wt. W. 10698/4046. 500,000. 10/15. M.R.Co., Ltd. Forms/B. 213/6.

[P.T.O.

To be made up to, and for Sunday in each week.

No. of Report 45

FIELD RETURN.

Army Form B. 213.

(To be furnished by all arms, services, and departments (except A.S.C. units) to the A. G.'s Office at the Base in accordance with Field Service Regulations, Part II.)

RETURN showing numbers (a) Effective strength of Unit. (b) Rationed by Unit. 2nd Bn Royal Dub. Fus. at In the Field 23rd July 1916. Date.

Detail	Personnel: Officers	Personnel: Other ranks	Personnel: Natives	Animals: Horses: Riding	Animals: Horses: Draught	Animals: Horses: Heavy Draught	Animals: Horses: Pack	Animals: Mules: Large	Animals: Mules: Small	Animals: Camels	Animals: Oxen	Guns, carriages, and limbers and transport vehicles: Guns, carriages and limbers, showing description	Ammunition wagons and limbers	Machine guns	Aircraft, showing description	Horsed: 4 wheeled	Horsed: 2 wheeled	Mechanical: Motor Cars	Mechanical: Tractors	Mechanical: Lorries, showing description	Mechanical: Trucks, showing description	Mechanical: Trailers	Motor Bicycles	Bicycles
Effective Strength of Unit	38	[illegible]		[illegible]	26	9	9						[illegible]	8										8
Details, *by Arms* attached to unit as in War Establishment:—																								
R.A.M.C.	1	5		1																				
Total	39	[illegible]		[illegible]	26	9	9							8										8
War Establishment	30	[illegible]		[illegible]	26	9	9							8										9
Wanting to complete (Detail of Personnel and Horses below)				1																				1
Surplus	[illegible]																							
*Attached (not to include the details shown above)		2																						
Civilians:— Employed with the Unit				1		[illegible]																		
Accompanying the Unit																								
Total Rationed...		[illegible]		[illegible]	26	[illegible]	9																	

Remarks

Details Ration Away	Offrs	Men
10th Inf. Bde	2	18
Base	2	4
[illegible] Reserve Army	1	1
10th Inf. Bde Res Coy.		55
T. Mortar Attd		29
M. Gun "		8
L. Gun School		1
Surveys Signals		3
4 Divl School	1	5
A O C		2
Army Troops		1
[illegible]		5
[illegible]		3
Total	6	[illegible]

* In the case of field ambulances, hospitals or depots, the number of patients are to be included here, the names being shown in A. F. A. 36.

[illegible] Lieut-Col Signature of Commander.

23rd July 1916. Date of Despatch.

For information of the A.G.'s Office at the Base.

Officers and men who have become casuals, been transferred or joined since last report.

Place In the Field Date 23rd July 016.

Regtl. Number	Rank	Name	Corps	Nature of casualty, or name of unit from or to which transferred	Date of being struck off or coming on the ration return	Remarks*
	2/Lieut	R. G. Bourke	10th Bn R.D.F.	Joined Bn	16-7-16	
	"	R. T. Holder	10th Bn			
	"	H. W. Gibson	10th Bn			
	"	J. G. Doran	3rd Bn		19-7-16	
	"	W. H. Hynes	3rd Bn			
	"	D. N. Hensley	3rd Bn			
	"	A. R. Henry	3rd Bn			
	"	J. B. Sheehan	3rd Bn			
	"	H. J. Lemass	3rd Bn			
12891	Pte	Whelan				
18224	"	Maher		Serving with 4th Div Res [illegible]		
18239	"	Mooney		marked Permanent Base,		
21390	"	Monaghan		under Authority of Reserve Army		
21523	"	Hogan		Struck off strength 16/7/16		
16901	"	Lally		(Authy 10th Inf Bde A/1265 d 19/7/16		
18263	"	Doyle				
21394	"	Casey				
8833	"	Lambe				
11689	"	Ward				
19449	"	Colgan				
9349	Pte	Hayes	A,	Rejoined from VII Corps	15-7-16	
11322	"	Doolan	"	Cycle Bn		
21655	Pte	Greenaway	B,	Wounded	16-7-16	At Duty
26444		O'Hara		Missing from Camp	20-7-16.	

* State whether absence is of a permanent or temporary nature, adding, in the case of casuals from wounds or disease, any available information for communication to the relatives.

Perforated Sheet giving detail of personnel and horses wanting to complete, shown on Army Form B. 213.

Number of Report 45

Detail of Wanting to Complete	Drivers						Gunners	Smith Gunners	Range Takers	Farriers		Shoeing, or Shoeing and Carriage Smiths	Cold Shoers	Wheelers			Saddlers or Harness Makers	Blacksmiths	Bricklayers and Masons	Carpenters and Joiners	Fitters & Turners (R.E.)		Fitters		Plumbers	Electricians		Signalmen	Engine Drivers		Air Line Men	Permanent Line Men	Operators, Telegraph	Cablemen	Brigade Section Pioneers	General-duty Pioneers	Signallers	Instrument Repairers	Motor Cyclists	Motor Cyclist Artificers	Telephonists	Clerks	Machine Gunners	Armament Artificers		Armourers	Storemen	Privates	W.O.'s and N.C.O.'s (by ranks) not included in trade columns					TOTAL to agree with wanting to complete		Horses			
	R.A.	R.E.	A.S.C.	Car	Lorry	Steam				Serjeants	Corporals			R.A.	H.T.	M.T.					Wood	Iron	R.A.	Wireless		Ordinary	W.T.		Loco.	Field														Fitters	Range Finders									Officers	Other Ranks	Riding	Draught	Heavy Draught	Pack
CAVALRY																																																											
R.A.																																																											
R.E.																																																											
INFANTRY																																															0	4						4	4				
R.A.M.C.																																																											
A.O.C.																																																											
A.V.C.																																																											

[illegible]

Remarks:—

[illegible] Lieut.-Col Signature of Commander.

2nd Bn Royal Dublin Fusrs Unit.

4th Div, Reserve Army Formation to which attached.

25-7-16. Date of Despatch.

(B 99511.) Wt. W15519/M149. 1,000,000. 1/16. J. P. & Co., Ltd. Forms/B. 213/7.

[P.T.O.

No. of Report

FIELD RETURN.

Army Form B. 213.

(To be furnished by all arms, services and departments (except A.S.C. units) to the A. G.'s Office at the Base in accordance with Field Service Regulations, Part II.)

RETURN showing numbers RATIONED by, and Transport on charge of ______ at ______ ______ Date.

DETAIL	Personnel			Animals									Guns, carriages, and limbers, and transport vehicles.												Motor Bicycles	Bicycles	REMARKS
				Horses				Mules									Horsed		Mechanical							
	Officers	Other ranks	Natives	Riding	Draught	Heavy Draught	Pack	Large	Small	Camels	Oxen	Guns, carriages and limbers, showing description	Ammunition wagons and limbers	Machine guns	Aircraft, showing description	4 Wheeled	2 Wheeled	Motor Cars	Tractors	Lorries, showing description	Trucks, showing description	Trailers			
Effective Strength of Unit																									
Details, *by Arms* attached to unit as in War Establishment:—																									
Total																									
War Establishment																									
Wanting to complete (Detail of Personnel and Horses below)																									
Surplus																									
*Attached (not to include the details shown above)																									
Civilians:— Employed with the Unit; Accompanying the Unit																									
TOTAL RATIONED ...																									

* In the case of field ambulances, hospitals or depots, the number of patients are to be included here, the names being shown in A. F. A. 36.

Signature of Commander.

Date of Despatch.

For information of the A.G.'s Office at the Base.

Officers and men who have become casuals, been transferred or joined since last report.

Place In the Field   Date July 30th 1916.

Regtl. Number	Rank	Name	Corps	Nature of casualty, or name of unit from or to which transferred	Date of being struck off or coming on the ration return	Remarks*
	Lieut	J. A. Noblett	3rd Bn R.D.F.	Joined Bn	23.7.16.	
	2/Lt.	P. N. Gordon	" "	" "	25.7.16	
	"	B. P. Glancy	" "	" "	" " "	
	"	A. H. West	Admitted to Hospital		24-7-16.	
	"	J. A. Tobin	Struck off strength on appt R.T.O.			
	"	G. H. Chandler	Wounded-in-Action		28.7-16.	
11294	Sgt	Carley	"A" Coy	Rejoined (wounded)	28-7-16	
8895	Cpl	Nugent	" "	"	" " "	
8794	Sgt	Ward	"B" "	"	" " "	
20234	L/Sergt	Anderson	"C" "	"	" " "	
10416	Sgt	Carolan	"D" "	"	" " "	
26444	Pte	O'Hara	Missing from camp 20/7/16 apprehended at Arras, not yet rejoined.			
1	Lieut	H. J. G. Rutherford	R.A.M.C.	To Hospital	25.7-16.	
	"	A. B. Moffat	R.A.M.C.	Joined	25.7-16.	
5814	A/Cpl	Glen	R.A.M.C.	To Hospital	27-7-16.	

* State whether absence is of a permanent or temporary nature, adding, in the case of casuals from wounds or disease, any available information for communication to the relatives.

Perforated Sheet giving detail of personnel and horses wanting to complete, shown on Army Form B. 213.

Number of Report 46.

Detail of Wanting to Complete.	Drivers.									Farriers				Wheelers							Fitters & Turners (R. E.)		Fitters			Electricians			Engine Drivers															Armament Artificers					W.O.'s and N.C.O.'s (by ranks) not included in trade columns.										TOTAL to agree with wanting to complete		Horses			
	R. A.	R. E.	A. S. C.	Car	Lorry	Steam	Gunners	Smith Gunners	Range Takers	Serjeants	Corporals	Shoeing, or Shoeing and Carriage Smiths	Cold Shoers	R. A.	H. T.	M. T.	Saddlers or Harness Makers	Blacksmiths	Bricklayers and Masons	Carpenters and Joiners	Wood	Iron	R. A.	Wireless	Plumbers	Ordinary	W. T.	Signalmen	Loco.	Field	Air Line Men	Permanent Line Men	Operators, Telegraph	Cablemen	Brigade Section Pioneers	General-duty Pioneers	Signallers	Instrument Repairers	Motor Cyclists	Motor Cyclist Artificers	Telephonists	Clerks	Machine Gunners	Fitters	Range Finders	Armourers	Storemen	Privates											Officers	Other Ranks	Riding	Draught	Heavy Draught	Pack
CAVALRY																																																											[illegible]					
R. A.																																																																
R. E.																																																																
INFANTRY																																																											4	19		1		
R. A. M. C.																																																																
A. O. C.																																																																
A. V. C.																																																																

Remarks :—

[signature] Lt. Col. Signature of Commander.

2nd Bn. Royal Dublin Fus.rs Unit.

10th Inf: Bde. 4th Divn. Formation to which attached.

July 29. Date of Despatch.

(26149.) Wt. W. 10698/4046. 500,000. 10/15. M.R.Co., Ltd. Forms/B. 213/6.

[P.T.O.

Only additional information regarding "wanting to complete" is to be entered on this side.

1 Second-in-Command urgently required.

Unit 2nd Bn. Royal Dublin Fus^rs

Place In the Field

Date 8th July 1916.

FIELD STATE.

Army Form B 231

To be rendered in accordance with Field Service Regulations, Part II.

UNIT	FIGHTING STRENGTH — This should *not* include details attached to unit, or personnel detailed to march with the Train, or any men unfit to go into action with unit											RATION STRENGTH — To include Fighting Strength, Personnel detailed to march with the Train, and all Personnel and animals attached for Rations and Forage										
	Personnel		Horses and Mules		Other Animals		Guns and Ammunition Wagons (stating nature)	Machine Guns	Ambulances	Tool Carts, Technical Carts (stating nature)	Remarks	Personnel	Horses and Mules		Other Animals		Mechanically Propelled Vehicles					Remarks
	Officers	Other Ranks	Riding	Draught and Pack								Total, all Ranks entitled to Rations	Heavy Horses	Other Horses and Mules			Motor Cars	Motor Bicycles	Lorries 3 Ton	Lorries 30 Cwt.	Tractors	
(1)	(2)	(3)	(4)	(5)	(6)	(7)	(8)	(9)	(10)	(11)	(12)	(13)	(14)	(15)	(16)	(17)	(18)	(19)	(20)	(21)	(22)	(23)
Strength in Trenches	18	561	13	43			Lewis	8				642	9	47								
10th I.B.	2	17																				
Hospital	3																					
R. Tramways	1	1																				
Base	2	4																				
A.O.C.		1																				
4th Army School	1	3																				
Survey / Vis: Sig:		2																				
Trench Mortar Bty		26																				
M.G. Attached		10																				
Leave & Absents		10																				
Sick on Leave	1	3																				
D. Hqrs. [illegible] 3		4																				
TOTALS ...	28	642	13	43				8				642	9	47								

Ammunition with Unit:—

·303 inch; approximate number of rounds per Man 208

·303 inch; " " " per Machine Gun 8300

Gun or Howitzer; approximate number of rounds per Gun or Howitzer —

Supplies with Unit:—

Approximate number of days' rations for men of ration strength Two

" " " forage for Animals " " Two.

" " " fuel and lubricants for Mechanically Propelled Vehicles

Signature of Commander [illegible] Lieut-Col.

No: of men serving with Res: Co: 53

Returned [illegible] Nil

Wt. W. 5870—621. 600,000. 10/14. D. P. Wks. (150-3) Forms B 231 / 3

Unit 2nd Bn Royal Dublin Fus[illegible]
Place In the Field
Date 16th July 1916.

FIELD STATE.

Army Form B. 231.

To be rendered in accordance with Field Service Regulations, Part II.

FIGHTING STRENGTH — This should *not* include details attached to unit, or personnel detailed to march with the **Train**, or any men unfit to go into action with unit

RATION STRENGTH — To include **Fighting Strength, Personnel** detailed to march with the **Train**, and all **Personnel** and **animals** attached for Rations and Forage

UNIT	Personnel: Officers	Personnel: Other Ranks	Horses ~~and Mules~~: Riding	Horses ~~and Mules~~: Draught and Pack	Other Animals	Other Animals	Guns and Ammunition Wagons (stating nature)	Machine Guns	Ambulances	Tool Carts, Technical Carts (stating nature)	Remarks	Personnel: Total, all Ranks entitled to Rations.	Horses ~~and Mules~~: Heavy Horses	Horses: Other Horses and Mules	Other Animals	Other Animals	Mechanically Propelled Vehicles: Motor Cars	Motor Bicycles	Lorries: 3 Ton	Lorries: 30 Cwt.	Tractors	Remarks
(1)	(2)	(3)	(4)	(5)	(6)	(7)	(8)	(9)	(10)	(11)	(12)	(13)	(14)	(15)	(16)	(17)	(18)	(19)	(20)	(21)	(22)	(23)
Strength in Trenches.	18	647	13	46			Lewis	8				753	9	48								
10th Inf: Bde	3	14																				
Base	2	4																				
4th Army School	1	1																				
4th Divn School		3																				
T.M. Attached		29																				
M.G. Attached.		7																				
L.G.I. Grenade Schl	1	22																				
VIII Corps [illegible]		3																				
Sick on leave & Absent		7																				
[illegible] A.O.C. R.E.		3																				
TOTALS ...	25	740	13	46				8				753	9	48								

Ammunition with Unit:—

·303 inch; approximate number of rounds per Man 208

·303 inch; „ „ „ per Machine Gun 8300

Gun or Howitzer; approximate number of rounds per Gun or Howitzer —

No: of men serving with Reserve Coy 52
Returned during week 2

Supplies with Unit:—

Approximate number of days' rations for men of ration strength Two

„ „ „ forage for Animals „ „ Two.

„ „ „ fuel and lubricants for Mechanically Propelled Vehicles

Signature of Commander [illegible signature] Major.
O.C. 2nd Bn Royal Dublin Fusiliers

(79269.) Wt. W. 5870—621. 900,000 10/14. J. P. & Co. Ltd. Forms B 231 / 3

Army Form B 231.

FIELD STATE.

Unit 2nd Bn Royal Dublin Fus^o
Place In the Field
Date 25th July 1916.

To be rendered in accordance with Field Service Regulations, Part II.

FIGHTING STRENGTH — This should *not* include details attached to unit, or personnel detailed to march with the Train, or any men unfit to go into action with unit

RATION STRENGTH — To include Fighting Strength, Personnel detailed to march with the Train, and all Personnel and animals attached for Rations and Forage

UNIT	Personnel		Horses and Mules		Other Animals		Guns and Ammunition Wagons (stating nature)	Machine Guns	Ambulances	Tool Carts, Technical Carts (stating nature)	Remarks	Personnel	Horses and Mules		Other Animals		Mechanically Propelled Vehicles					Remarks
	Officers	Other Ranks	Riding	Draught and Pack								Total, all Ranks entitled to Rations.	Heavy Horses	Other Horses and Mules			Motor Cars	Motor Bicycles	Lorries. 3 Ton	Lorries. 30 Cwt.	Tractors	
(1)	(2)	(3)	(4)	(5)	(6)	(7)	(8)	(9)	(10)	(11)	(12)	(13)	(14)	(15)	(16)	(17)	(18)	(19)	(20)	(21)	(22)	(23)
Strength in Trenches	29	827	13	44								887	9	48								
10th Inf: Bde	2	18											5									Attached.
Base.	2	4																				
H.Q. Reserve Army "A"	1	1																				
T.M. Att^d		29																				
M. Gun Att^d		8																				
L. Gun Sch 1. Survey 1		2																				
Signals 2. A.O.C. 2		4																				
IV Div: School	1	5																				
Other details		10																				
TOTALS ...	35	908	13	44								887	14	48								

Ammunition with Unit:—

·303 inch; approximate number of rounds per Man 208

·303 inch; " " " per Machine Gun 8300

Gun or Howitzer; approximate number of rounds per Gun or Howitzer —

Supplies with Unit:—

Approximate number of days' rations for men of ration strength Two

" " " forage for Animals " " Two.

" " " fuel and lubricants for Mechanically Propelled Vehicles

No: of men at present with 4th Div: Res Co^y 53
Rejoined from " " nil.

Signature of Commander [illegible]
Lieut-Col,
[illegible] Royal Dublin Fus^o

(90988.) Wt. W. 5216—2140. 900,000 7/15. J. P. & Co. Ltd. Forms B 231 / 3

Unit
Place In the Field
Date 30-7-16

FIELD STATE.

Army Form B231.

To be rendered in accordance with Field Service Regulations, Part II.

UNIT	FIGHTING STRENGTH — This should not include details attached to unit, or personnel detailed to march with the Train, or any men unfit to go into action with unit											RATION STRENGTH — To include Fighting Strength, Personnel detailed to march with the Train, and all Personnel and animals attached for Rations and Forage										
	Personnel		Horses and Mules		Other Animals							Personnel	Horses and Mules		Other Animals		Mechanically Propelled Vehicles					
	Officers	Other Ranks	Riding	Draught and Pack			Guns and Ammunition Wagons (stating nature)	Machine Guns	Ambulances	Tool Carts, Technical Carts (stating nature)	Remarks	Total, all Ranks entitled to Rations.	Heavy Horses	Other Horses and Mules			Motor Cars	Motor Bicycles	Lorries. 3 Ton	Lorries. 30 Cwt.	Tractors	Remarks
(1)	(2)	(3)	(4)	(5)	(6)	(7)	(8)	(9)	(10)	(11)	(12)	(13)	(14)	(15)	(16)	(17)	(18)	(19)	(20)	(21)	(22)	(23)
Strength in Trenches	29	741	13	43			Lewis	8				896	14	48								
10th Inf: Bde.	1	12																				
Base	1	3																				
3rd Army School	1	2																				
T.M. Attached		29																				
M.G. "		8																				
A.P.M.	2	22																				
177 Tunnel Co		15																				
H.Q. Res. Army Hosp	2	1																				
Other Details		27																				
TOTALS ...	36	860	13	43				8				896	14	48								

Ammunition with Unit:—
·303 inch; approximate number of rounds per Man 208
·303 inch; " " " per Machine Gun 8300
Gun or Howitzer; approximate number of rounds per Gun or Howitzer —

Supplies with Unit:—
Approximate number of days' rations for men of ration strength Two.
" " " forage for Animals " Two.
" " " fuel and lubricants for Mechanically Propelled Vehicles —

No: of men serving with 4th Div Res. Co. 44
" " returned to unit Swimpwch[?] Nil.

Signature of Commander Lieut.-Col.

(90968.) Wt.W. 5216—2140. 900,000 7/15. J. P. & Co. Ltd. Forms B231/3

10th Brigade.

4th Division.

2nd BATTALION

ROYAL DUBLIN FUSILIERS

AUGUST 1 9 1 6

Instructions regarding War Diaries and Intelligence Summaries are contained in F. S. Regs., Part II. and the Staff Manual respectively. Title Pages will be prepared in manuscript.

WAR DIARY
or
INTELLIGENCE SUMMARY
(Erase heading not required.)

Army Form C. 2118

2 R Dublin Fus

AUGUST 1916.

Vol 24

Place	Date	Hour	Summary of Events and Information	Remarks and references to Appendices
TRENCHES.	AUGUST 1st–3rd		Situation quiet. In the early morning of 3rd 2/Lieut J.A.H. KERBY and one O.R. were wounded whilst on patrol by bomb splinters. 2/Lieut KERBY died during the day.	
CAMP "P".	4th 5th		The Battalion was relieved late at night by 2nd Bn ESSEX REGT but did not get away till 2.50 a.m. on the morning of Aug 5 and it was 7 a.m. before the last Coy arrived in "P" CAMP A 13 C 4.6 Sheet 27 1/40,000. The Camp is composed of huts, was well made and pleasantly situated. The 1st Bn Royal Dublin Fusiliers was in the vicinity and football matches were arranged.	
	8th		Company training was carried out on the usual lines. The Camp was inspected on the 8th by General LAMBTON the Divisional Commander who afterwards expressed his approval and satisfaction with the upkeep of the same. About midnight there was a GAS alarm and the Battalion "stood to" for about an hour. Company training was carried out and working parties repaired roads and made other improvements to the Camp. The weather throughout the tour was hot and summer like.	
	11th		Orders were received for the Bn to move and motor-buses were to have ~~were to have~~ arrived at 9.30 to take the men away. The buses not having arrived at 10.45 the men were marched off but the relief was not over until 2.40 a.m. morning of 12th.	
H.Q. ELVERDINGHE CHATEAU	12th–13th		Battalion Headquarters were at ELVERDINGHE CHATEAU together with "B" and "D" Coys. 100 men of "C" Coy were at L 2 work: remainder of "C" Coy and "A" Coy were on the Canal Bank. The weather was still fine and warm and the accommodation in the CHATEAU was excellent. Training was carried on as usual and extensive work was carried on by working parties at night.	
H.Q. TROIS TOURS CHATEAU	14th		At 9.0 p.m. Bn Headquarters, "B" and "D" Coys were relieved by 38th Division at the CHATEAU. Battalion Headquarters and "B" Coy proceeded to TROIS TOURS CHATEAU which had been evacuated by 11th Battalion KINGS OWN (LIVERPOOL) REGT. "C" Coy were at L 2, "A" Coy on the CANAL BANK with "D" Coy.	
H.Q. CANAL BANK	15th		The Battalion H.Q. stayed one night only at TROIS TOURS CHATEAU for the Bn took over the trenches from 1st ROYAL WARWICKSHIRE REGT. "A" Coy held the right [illegible] "B" Coy the centre "D" Coy the left with "C" Coy in support 2 platoons on the CANAL BANK and 2 platoons at LANCASHIRE FARM. Relief was quick being complete at 12.30 a.m.	
	16th 17th		Very quiet all day. Late at night the GAS ALERT was received and the Bn "stood to" from midnight till about 3.0 a.m. and again at about [illegible] a.m. but there were no effects of gas. The weather was threatening and cooler.	
	18th 19th		Quiet. GAS ALERT for most of the night as the wind was coming from the direction of the enemy. An enemy patrol came to our lines but were dispersed [illegible] when the patrol was returning the men were [illegible] by their own comrades.	
	20th		Quiet. The Battalion has an extra day in the trenches as the 38th WELSH DIVn is taking over from 4th Divn	
"M" CAMP.	21st		The Bn was relieved by 14th ROYAL WELSH FUSILIERS in the early hours of the morning and entrained at the ASYLUM. The Bn detrained at L 5 C. and marched to "M" CAMP F 27 C 5.9 where the men were accommodated partly in huts and partly in tents.	
	22/3		Training as usual	
"E" CAMP "WINNIPEG" CAMP DICKEBUSH AREA 19 b 3.5.	24th		The VIII Corps Commander decorated CAPT LAURIE of the SEAFORTH HGHLDRS with the D.S.O. and Capt ~~PEAROTT~~ of the R.I.F. with the Military Cross. The Bn arrived at WINNIPEG CAMP at 7.30 p.m. and took over from 52nd CANADIAN Bn; the camp was not in a sanitary condition & swarmed with flies and rats.	

BEAUFORT

1875 Wt. W593/826 1,000,000 4/15 J.B.C. & A. A.D.S.S./Forms/C. 2118.

Army Form C. 2118

Instructions regarding War Diaries and Intelligence Summaries are contained in F. S. Regs., Part II. and the Staff Manual respectively. Title Pages will be prepared in manuscript.

WAR DIARY
or
INTELLIGENCE SUMMARY
(Erase heading not required.)

Place	Date	Hour	Summary of Events and Information	Remarks and references to Appendices
	AUGUST.			
WINNIPEG CAMP	25th		A large number of improvements were made during the day, including opening up of drains, repair of bridges & trench-boards etc.	
	26th		Company training carried on daily with improvements to the Camp.	
	28th		The weather was showery. Capt W. A REDMOND injured himself by falling on the cobbled road and was admitted to Hospital next morning with an injured shoulder.	
TRENCHES, opposite HILL 60	29th		The Bn went into the trenches opposite HILL 60, "D" Coy held the Right position, "C" Coy the Left front, "A" Coy were in Support and "B" Coy in Reserve. 1st Bn Kings Own LIVERPOOL Regt were on the Right of the Bn, and 2nd Bn SEAFORTH HGHLDRS on the Left of the Bn. The C.O. and Company Officers left for the trenches at 2 p.m. The first Coy left at 6.15 p.m. in drenching rain and a heavy thunderstorm so that the trenches were in a terrible state. The relief was effected without any casualties.	
	30th		The morning was showery, the afternoon was worse rain fell incessantly until after dark had set in, a strong wind driving the rain over the country, so that dug-outs were flooded. The enemy was quiet in consequence.	
	31st		The day was fine and warm so that things dried up somewhat. The enemy sent over a lot of minnewerfer and a few shells but no damage was done. There were 3 cases of trench feet. Some officers of the 3rd AUSTRALIAN Bn arrived to look over the trenches as a preparation for taking over the trenches on the morrow.	

R G Biggs Lt Col
Comdt 2 R Dublin Fus

1875 Wt. W593/826 1,000,000 4/15 J.B.C. & A. A.D.S.S./Forms/C. 2118.

2nd Bn. Royal Dublin Fusiliers

Appendix to War Diary Month of August 1916.

Date	Remarks.
1-8-16	2nd Lieut G. H. Chandler To England (wounded)
"	2 Other Ranks wounded in action.
"	18 " " Reinforcements.
5-8-16	2nd Lieut J. A. Hetley Wounded in Action. Died of the same day
"	1 Other Rank Killed in Action, 2 Other Ranks wounded.
"	2nd Lieut T. J. Beaumont joined the Battalion.
"	2nd Lieut A. H. West, to England (sick).
10-8-16	Lieut J. G. Letherwell, To Headquarters [illegible] Bde.
11-8-16	2nd Lieut H. N. Gandy To Hospital (sick).
13-8-16	Capt. T. A. Redmond To Hospital (sick).
"	2nd Lieut T. E. Handy " "
14-8-16	7 Other Rank wounded in action.
15-8-16	" " " " " (Self inflicted).
20-8-16	" " " " "
21-8-16	2nd Lieut T. E. Handy rejoined Battalion from Hospital.
24-8-16	Capt T. A. Redmond " " " "
28-8-16	Capt. T. A. Redmond To Hospital (sick).
"	Lieut J. C. Lyons Rejoined Battalion from Wounded.
29-8-16	Draft 21 Other Ranks.
31-8-16	1 Other Rank wounded in action.

H. Ryhner for

Lieut Colonel.

3-9-16 Cmdg 2nd Bn. Royal Dublin Fusiliers

Unit 2nd Bn Royal Dublin Fus.

Place In the Field

Date 6/8/16

FIELD STATE.

Army Form B 231.

To be rendered in accordance with Field Service Regulations, Part II.

UNIT	FIGHTING STRENGTH — This should **not** include details attached to unit, or personnel detailed to march with the Train, or any men unfit to go into action with unit											RATION STRENGTH — To include Fighting Strength, Personnel detailed to march with the Train, and all Personnel and animals attached for Rations and Forage										
	Personnel		Horses and Mules		Other Animals		Guns and Ammunition Wagons (stating nature)	Machine Guns	Ambulances	Tool Carts, Technical Carts (stating nature)	Remarks	Personnel	Horses and Mules		Other Animals		Mechanically Propelled Vehicles					Remarks
	Officers	Other Ranks	Riding	Draught and Pack								Total, all Ranks entitled to Rations.	Heavy Horses	Other Horses and Mules			Motor Cars	Motor Bicycles.	Lorries. 3 Ton	Lorries. 30 Cwt.	Tractors	
(1)	(2)	(3)	(4)	(5)	(6)	(7)	(8)	(9)	(10)	(11)	(12)	(13)	(14)	(15)	(16)	(17)	(18)	(19)	(20)	(21)	(22)	(23)
Trench Strength	28	728																				
Bombers & Bayonet men	2	26	13	43								837	10	41								
3rd Army & Central School	2	3																				
16th Inf. Bde	0	14																				
2nd Cliff & APM Att	2	2																				
Tunnel Co		16																				
Trench Mortar Bty		29																				
M Gun Att		8																				
Hospital Sick	2																					
Other details		20																				
TOTALS ...	36	846																				

Ammunition with Unit:—

·303 inch; approximate number of rounds per Man 208

·303 inch; „ „ „ per Machine Gun 8300

Gun or Howitzer; approximate number of rounds per Gun or Howitzer —

Supplies with Unit:—

Approximate number of days' rations for men of ration strength Two

„ „ „ forage for Animals „ Two

„ „ „ fuel and lubricants for Mechanically Propelled Vehicles

Signature of Commander [signature] Lieut Col

O.C. 2nd Bn Royal Dub Fus.

(90968.) Wt. W. 5216—2140. 900,000 7/15. J. P. & Co. Ltd. Forms B 231 / 3

Army Form B. 231.

FIELD STATE.

Unit 2nd Bn Royal Dublin Fus
Place In the Field
Date 13th Aug: 1916.

To be rendered in accordance with Field Service Regulations, Part II.

UNIT	FIGHTING STRENGTH — This should *not* include details attached to unit, or personnel detailed to march with the Train, or any men unfit to go into action with unit											RATION STRENGTH — To include Fighting Strength, Personnel detailed to march with the Train, and all Personnel and animals attached for Rations and Forage										
	Personnel		Horses and Mules		Other Animals		Guns and Ammunition Wagons (stating nature)	Machine Guns	Ambulances	Tool Carts, Technical Carts (stating nature)	Remarks	Personnel	Horses and Mules		Other Animals		Mechanically Propelled Vehicles					Remarks
	Officers	Other Ranks	Riding	Draught and Pack								Total, all Ranks entitled to Rations.	Heavy Horses	Other Horses and Mules			Motor Cars	Motor Bicycles	Lorries. 3 Ton	Lorries. 30 Cwt.	Tractors	
(1)	(2)	(3)	(4)	(5)	(6)	(7)	(8)	(9)	(10)	(11)	(12)	(13)	(14)	(15)	(16)	(17)	(18)	(19)	(20)	(21)	(22)	(23)
Trench Strength	23	692	13	43								821	8	48								
1st L.B. T.O.s Transport	3	63																				
4th Div: School.	3	5											1	1								Attached
2nd Army -	1	1																				
3rd Army -	1	2																				
10/11 Brigade	2	15																				
T.M. Batt Att		29																				
M.G. 12 Tunnel Co		27																				
Grenade School	1	22																				
Hospital	3																					
Other details.	2	40																				
TOTALS ...	39	896	13	43									9	49								

Ammunition with Unit:—

·303 inch; approximate number of rounds per Man 208.

·303 inch; ,, ,, ,, per Machine Gun 8300

Gun or Howitzer; approximate number of rounds per Gun or Howitzer —

No: of men serving with 4th Div Res Co 43
" " " returned from during week, Nil.

Supplies with Unit:—

Approximate number of days' rations for men of ration strength Two

,, ,, ,, forage for Animals ,, ,, Two

,, ,, ,, fuel and lubricants for Mechanically Propelled Vehicles

R.G. [illegible]
Signature of Commander Lieut Col
O.C. 2nd Bn Royal Dublin Fus

(90988.) Wt.W. 5216—2140. 900,000 7/15. J. P. & Co. Ltd. Forms B 231 / 3

Army Form B. 231.

FIELD STATE.

Unit 2nd Bn Royal Dublin Fus.
Place In the Field
Date 19/8/16

To be rendered in accordance with Field Service Regulations, Part II.

UNIT	FIGHTING STRENGTH — This should **not** include details attached to unit, or personnel detailed to march with the Train, or any men unfit to go into action with unit											RATION STRENGTH — To include Fighting Strength, Personnel detailed to march with the Train, and all Personnel and animals attached for Rations and Forage										
	Personnel		Horses and Mules		Other Animals		Guns and Ammunition Wagons (stating nature)	Machine Guns	Ambulances	Tool Carts, Technical Carts (stating nature)	Remarks	Personnel	Horses and Mules		Other Animals		Mechanically Propelled Vehicles					Remarks
	Officers	Other Ranks	Riding	Draught and Pack								Total, all Ranks entitled to Rations.	Heavy Horses	Other Horses and Mules			Motor Cars	Motor Bicycles.	Lorries. 3 Ton	Lorries. 30 Cwt.	Tractors	
(1)	(2)	(3)	(4)	(5)	(6)	(7)	(8)	(9)	(10)	(11)	(12)	(13)	(14)	(15)	(16)	(17)	(18)	(19)	(20)	(21)	(22)	(23)
Trench Strength	19	659	12	43								785	8	47								
10th I.B., T.O., & Transport	3	68											1									Attached
4th Div School	4	5																				
2/4 Army Schools	2	3																				
10/11 Brigade	2	15																				
Hospital	4																					
T.M. Batt. Att.		29																				
M.G. 12 Tunnellers R.E.		45																				
Grenade School	1	22																				
Other Details	3	20																				
TOTALS ...	38	866																				

Ammunition with Unit:—

·303 inch; approximate number of rounds per Man 208

·303 inch; " " " per Machine Gun 8300

Gun or Howitzer; approximate number of rounds per Gun or Howitzer —

Supplies with Unit:—

Approximate number of days' rations for men of ration strength Two

" " " forage for Animals " " Two

" " " fuel and lubricants for Mechanically Propelled Vehicles

Signature of Commander R.G. Griffin Lieut. Col.

(90988.) Wt. W. 5216—2140. 900,000 7/15. J. P. & Co. Ltd. Forms B 231 / 3

Unit 2nd Bn Royal Dublin Fusiliers
Place In the Field
Date 27th August 1916

FIELD STATE.

Army Form B 231

To be rendered in accordance with Field Service Regulations, Part II.

UNIT	FIGHTING STRENGTH — This should *not* include details attached to unit, or personnel detailed to march with the Train, or any men unfit to go into action with unit											RATION STRENGTH — To include Fighting Strength, Personnel detailed to march with the Train, and all Personnel and animals attached for Rations and Forage										
	Personnel		Horses and Mules		Other Animals		Guns and Ammunition Wagons (stating nature)	Machine Guns	Ambulances	Tool Carts, Technical Carts (stating nature)	Remarks	Personnel	Horses and Mules		Other Animals		Mechanically Propelled Vehicles					Remarks
	Officers	Other Ranks	Riding	Draught and Pack								Total, all Ranks entitled to Rations	Heavy Horses	Other Horses and Mules			Motor Cars	Motor Bicycles	Lorries 3 Ton	Lorries 30 Cwt.	Tractors	
(1)	(2)	(3)	(4)	(5)	(6)	(7)	(8)	(9)	(10)	(11)	(12)	(13)	(14)	(15)	(16)	(17)	(18)	(19)	(20)	(21)	(22)	(23)
Trench Strength	23	681	12	44								793	9	47								
10th Inf TO & Transport	3	70											5									Attached
4th Div School	4	5																				
3rd Army School	1	4																				
10/11 Brigade	2	15																				
Hospital	2	[illegible]																				
T.M. Batt attd	–	26																				
M.G. & Tunnelling Coy		28																				
Grenade School	1	22																				
Other Details	1	23																				
TOTALS ...	37	984	12	44									14	47								

Ammunition with Unit:—

·303 inch; approximate number of rounds per Man 208

·303 inch; " " " per Machine Gun 8300

Gun or Howitzer; approximate number of rounds per Gun or Howitzer

Supplies with Unit:—

Approximate number of days' rations for men of ration strength Two

" " " forage for Animals " " Two

" " " fuel and lubricants for Mechanically Propelled Vehicles

Signature of Commander R G A Jeffreys Lieut Col
Comdg 2nd Bn Roy Dub Fusrs

Wt. W. 5870—621. 600,000. 10/14. D. P. Wks. (150-3) Forms B 231 / 3

No. of Report 467. **FIELD RETURN.** Army Form B. 213.

(To be furnished by all arms, services and departments (except A.S.C. units) to the A. G.'s Office at the Base in accordance with Field Service Regulations, Part II.)

RETURN showing numbers RATIONED by, and Transport on charge of, 2nd Bn Royal Dub. Fus. at In the Field 6th Aug 1916 Date.

DETAIL	Personnel: Officers	Personnel: Other ranks	Personnel: Natives	Animals: Horses: Riding	Animals: Horses: Draught	Animals: Horses: Heavy Draught	Animals: Horses: Pack	Animals: Mules: Large	Animals: Mules: Small	Animals: Camels	Animals: Oxen	Guns, carriages and limbers, showing description	Ammunition wagons and limbers	Machine guns	Aircraft, showing description	Horsed: 4 Wheeled	Horsed: 2 Wheeled	Mechanical: Motor Cars	Mechanical: Tractors	Mechanical: Lorries, showing description	Mechanical: Trucks, showing description	Mechanical: Trailers	Motor Bicycles	Bicycles.	REMARKS
Effective Strength of Unit	39	961		11	25	9	9						Lewis	8										7	
Details, *by Arms* attached to unit as in War Establishment:—																									
R.A.M.C.	1	4		1																					
Total	40	965		12	25	9	9							8										7	
War Establishment	30	995		13	36	9	9							8										9	
Wanting to complete (Detail of Personnel and Horses below)	[illegible]	[illegible]			1																			2	L.D. Major & Capt.
Surplus	[illegible]																								Subalterns
*Attached (not to include the details shown above)	1			1																					Chaplain R.C.
Civilians:—		3		1																					Interpreter & servants.
Employed with the Unit					1	1																			A.S.C. Attached
Accompanying the Unit		2																							Div: Signal Co.
TOTAL RATIONED ...	[illegible]	[illegible]		14	26	10	9																		

REMARKS:

Details excl Aug	Offrs	O.R.
Bombing School	2	26
3rd Army School	1	2
Central School	1	1
10th Inf: Bde	1	14
Div: Res: Coy		45
T.M.B. Att		29
M.G. Att.		8
A.P.M.	1	
A.O.C. Rly Tpt		4
Survey: Mail...		5
Sick on leave		5
Hosp	2	
Col: Clift & Sew	1	1
Town Majors	1	
77 Tunnel Co		16
Base		2
VIII Corps Ordnance		2
Wireless L.G.I		2
	10	162

* In the case of field ambulances, hospitals or depots, the number of patients are to be included here, the names being shown in A. F. A. 36.

Lieut. Col. Signature of Commander.

6th Aug 1916 Date of Despatch.

For information of the A.G.'s Office at the Base.

Officers and men who have become casuals, been transferred or joined since last report.

Place In the Field   Date Aug 6 16

Regtl. Number	Rank	Name	Corps	Nature of casualty, or name of unit from or to which transferred	Date of being struck off or coming on the ration return	Remarks*
	2/Lieut	J A H Kelly	Died of	Wounds	3-8-16	
	"	W.V. Beaumont	5th Bn R.D.F.	Joined Bn	3-8-16	
	Capt	L G Kettlewell	ex No 2 Inf. Base	Rejoined	4-8-16	
	2/Lieut	R.O Carver	To Hospital Sick	(No date given by A.P.M. 4th Div) to whom party attached		
	Capt	R.M. Patterson	"	"	2-8-16	
7108	Pte	Moran "C"	Joined Bn on	release from Prison	30-7-16	
17759	"	Sullivan "D"	"	"	30-7-16	
18669	"	McNulty "A"	" "	" "	1-8-16	
22691	"	Loughlin "A"	left Bn for	ETAPLES	5-8-16	Under Age
8732	"	Fox "C"	Killed in Action		2-8-16	
16012	"	McGuinness "C"	Wounded "	"	2-8-16	
12151	Cpl	Lillis "A"	" "		1-8-16	
19547	Pte	McEvoy "A"	" "	"	"	
18384	L/Cpl	McGeehan "B"	" "		3-8-16	
21655	Pte	Greenaway "B"	" (Self	inflicted)	2-8-16	
			To Hospital	15 O.R.		
			from "	9 O.R.		
7122	L/C	Curran performed the duties of Bn				
	Chiropodist for the month of July 1916.					
5903	C.Q.M.S	Partridge acted	as Coy Accountant	for "A" Coy	1st - 31st	July
10809	"	Burke "	" "	" "B"	" "	"
9829	"	Cahill "	" "	" "C"	1st July	
7750	a/"	Gilbert "	" "	" "	2nd - 31st "	
10464	C.Q.M.S	Boon "	" "	" D	1st - 29th	
7450	Sgt	Walsh "	" "	" "	30 - 31st	

* State whether absence is of a permanent or temporary nature, adding, in the case of casuals from wounds or disease, any available information for communication to the relatives.

No. of Report

FIELD RETURN.

Army Form B. 213.

(To be furnished by all arms, services and departments (except A.S.C. units) to the A. G.'s Office at the Base in accordance with Field Service Regulations, Part II.)

RETURN showing numbers RATIONED by, and Transport on charge of, ____ at ____ ____ Date.

DETAIL	Personnel			Animals								Guns, carriages, and limbers, and transport vehicles.											Motor Bicycles	Bicycles.	REMARKS
				Horses				Mules								Horsed		Mechanical							
	Officers	Other ranks	Natives	Riding	Draught	Heavy Draught	Pack	Large	Small	Camels	Oxen	Guns, carriages and limbers, showing description	Ammunition wagons and limbers	Machine guns	Aircraft, showing description	4 Wheeled	2 Wheeled	Motor Cars	Tractors	Lorries, showing description	Trucks, showing description	Trailers			
Effective Strength of Unit																									
Details, *by Arms* attached to unit as in War Establishment:—																									
R A M C																									
A O C																									
Total																									
War Establishment	30	495		13	26	9	9																		
Wanting to complete (Detail of Personnel and Horses below)																									
Surplus																									
*Attached (not to include the details shown above)																									
Civilians:— Employed with the Unit																									
Accompanying the Unit																									
TOTAL RATIONED ...	28	765		13	34	9	9																		

* In the case of field ambulances, hospitals or depots, the number of patients are to be included here, the names being shown in A. F. A. 36.

Signature of Commander.

15-8-16. Date of Despatch.

For information of the A.G.'s Office at the Base.

Officers and men who have become casuals, been transferred or joined since last report.

Place In the Field Date 13th Aug. 1916

Regtl. Number	Rank	Name	Corps	Nature of casualty, or name of unit from or to which transferred	Date of being struck off or coming on the ration return	Remarks*
	Lieut	L. G. Kettlewell	15 H.Q.	11th Inf Bde	10-8-16	
	2/Lieut	D. N. Murphy	To Hospital		11-8-16	
5177	Pte	Ryan	Discharged Home ex 16 Bde		10-8-16	
5659	"	Foley "B"	Sent to Base, under age		8-8-16	
	20690	A/Cpl Bosley	R A M C	in lieu A/Cpl Glen[illegible]	11-8-16	
		To Hospital	20 O.R.			
		From "	8 O.R.			

* State whether absence is of a permanent or temporary nature, adding, in the case of casuals from wounds or disease, any available information for communication to the relatives.

To be made up to and for Sunday in each week.

No. of Report 47 — **FIELD RETURN.** — Army Form B. 213.

(To be furnished by all arms, services, and departments (except A.S.C. units) to the A. G.'s Office at the Base in accordance with Field Service Regulations, Part II.)

RETURN showing numbers (*a*) Effective strength of Unit. (*b*) Rationed by Unit. 2nd Bn Royal Dublin Fusiliers at in the Field 17/8/1916 Date.

Detail	Personnel: Officers	Personnel: Other ranks	Personnel: Natives	Animals: Horses: Riding	Animals: Horses: Draught	Animals: Horses: Heavy Draught	Animals: Horses: Pack	Animals: Mules: Large	Animals: Mules: Small	Animals: Camels	Animals: Oxen	Guns, carriages and limbers, showing description	Ammunition wagons and limbers	Machine guns	Aircraft, showing description	Horsed: 4 wheeled	Horsed: 2 wheeled	Mechanical: Motor Cars.	Mechanical: Tractors	Mechanical: Lorries, showing description	Mechanical: Trucks, showing description	Mechanical: Trailers	Motor Bicycles	Bicycles	Remarks
Effective Strength of Unit	38	921		10	26	8	9						4 Limbers	8										7	[illegible]
Details, *by Arms* attached to unit as in War Establishment:—																									
R A M C	1	5		1																					
A. O. C.		1																							
Total	39	927		11	26	8	9																	7	[illegible]
War Establishment	30	995		13	26	9	9																		[illegible]
Wanting to complete (Detail of Personnel and Horses below)	4	68		1		1																		2	[illegible]
Surplus	13																								Subalterns.
*Attached (not to include the details shown above)	1			1																					Chaplain R C
Civilians:— Employed with the Unit / Accompanying the Unit						1																			A S C AH?
Total Rationed...	24	746		12	26	9	9																		

* In the case of field ambulances, hospitals or depots, the number of patients are to be included here, the names being shown in A. F. A. 36.

[illegible signature] Lieut-Col Signature of Commander.

17/8/16 Date of Despatch.

For information of the A.G.'s Office at the Base.

Officers and men who have become casuals, been transferred or joined since last report.

Place In the Field Date 19/8/16

Regtl. Number	Rank	Name	Corps	Nature of casualty, or name of unit from or to which transferred	Date of being struck off or coming on the ration return	Remarks*
	Capt	W.A. REDMOND		To Hospital	13·8·16	Flu
	2/Lt	T F HANDYSIDE		" "	" "	Sprained Ankle
7532	L C	Cassidy		Wd-in-Action	14·8·16	
18190	L C	O'Hara	(Self-Inflicted)	" " "	16·8·16	Discharging Very Pistol

* State whether absence is of a permanent or temporary nature, adding, in the case of casuals from wounds or disease, any available information for communication to the relatives.

To be made up to and for Sunday in each week.

Army Form B. 213.

No. of Report 60

FIELD RETURN.

(To be furnished by all arms, services, and departments (except A.S.C. units) to the A. G.'s Office at the Base in accordance with Field Service Regulations, Part II.)

RETURN showing numbers (*a*) Effective strength of Unit. (*b*) Rationed by Unit. 2nd B. Roy Dub Fus at In the Field 27.8.16 Date.

Detail	Personnel: Officers	Personnel: Other ranks	Personnel: Natives	Animals: Horses: Riding	Horses: Draught	Horses: Heavy Draught	Horses: Pack	Mules: Large	Mules: Small	Camels	Oxen	Guns, carriages, and limbers and transport vehicles: Guns, carriages and limbers, showing description	Ammunition wagons and limbers	Machine guns	Aircraft, showing description	Horsed: 4 wheeled	Horsed: 2 wheeled	Mechanical: Motor Cars.	Tractors	Lorries, showing description	Trucks, showing description	Trailers	Motor Bicycles	Bicycles	Remarks
Effective Strength of Unit Details, *by Arms* attached to unit as in War Establishment:—	37	[illegible]		10	2[illegible]	9	7						[illegible]	[illegible]										7	[illegible]
R A M C	1	5		1																					
A O C		1																							
Total	38	926		11	26	9	9																		
War Establishment	30	992		13	26	9	9																		
Wanting to complete (Detail of Personnel and Horses below)	269																								[illegible]
Surplus	10																								[illegible]
*Attached (not to include the details shown above)	1			1																					Chaplain R C
Civilians:— Employed with the Unit Accompanying the Unit						5																			A.S.C. [illegible]
Total Rationed...	27	761		12	24	14	9																		

* In the case of field ambulances, hospitals or depots, the number of patients are to be included here, the names being shown in A. F. A. 36.

[illegible] Lieut Col. Signature of Commander.

24/8/16 Date of Despatch.

For information of the A.G.'s Office at the Base.

Officers and men who have become casuals, been transferred or joined since last report.

Place In the Field   Date August 27th 1916

Regtl. Number	Rank	Name	Corps	Nature of casualty, or name of unit from or to which transferred	Date of being struck off or coming on the ration return	Remarks*
	Capt	W A REDMOND		from hospital	24-8-16	
	2/Lt	T F HANDYSIDE		" "	24-8-16	

* State whether absence is of a permanent or temporary nature, adding, in the case of casuals from wounds or disease, any available information for communication to the relatives.

Perforated Sheet giving detail of personnel and horses wanting to complete, shown on Army Form B. 213.

Number of Report 50

Detail of Wanting to Complete	Drivers R.A.	Drivers R.E.	Drivers A.S.C.	Drivers Car	Drivers Lorry	Drivers Steam	Gunners	Smith Gunners	Range Takers	Farriers Serjeants	Farriers Corporals	Shoeing, or Shoeing and Carriage Smiths	Cold Shoers	Wheelers R.A.	Wheelers H.T.	Wheelers M.T.	Saddlers or Harness Makers	Blacksmiths	Bricklayers and Masons	Carpenters and Joiners	Fitters & Turners (R.E.) Wood	Fitters & Turners (R.E.) Iron	Fitters R.A.	Fitters Wireless	Plumbers	Electricians Ordinary	Electricians W.T.	Signalmen	Engine Drivers Loco.	Engine Drivers Field	Air Line Men	Permanent Line Men	Operators, Telegraph	Cablemen	Brigade Section Pioneers	General-duty Pioneers	Signallers	Instrument Repairers	Motor Cyclists	Motor Cyclist Artificers	Telephonists	Clerks	Machine Gunners	Armament Artificers Fitters	Armament Artificers Range Finders	Armourers	Storemen	Privates	W.O.'s and N.C.O.'s (by ranks) not included in trade columns	TOTAL to agree with wanting to complete Officers	TOTAL to agree with wanting to complete Other Ranks	Horses Riding	Horses Draught	Horses Heavy Draught	Horses Pack
CAVALRY																																																							
R.A.																																																							
R.E.																																																							
INFANTRY																																																64		2 Captains or Majors		1			
R.A.M.C.																																																							
A.O.C.																																																							
A.V.C.																																																							

Remarks:—

R. B. Gregg [?] Lieut Col Signature of Commander.

2nd Bn Royal Dublin Fusiliers. Unit.

10th Bde. Formation to which attached.

27th August 1916. Date of Despatch.

(B 99511.) Wt. W15519/M149. 1,000,000. 1/16. J. P. & Co., Ltd. Forms/B 213/7.

P.T.O.

Only additional information regarding "wanting to complete" is to be entered on this side.

A second in command urgently required

Only additional information regarding "wanting to complete" is to be entered on this side.

1 Second-in-Command urgently Required.

1 Rider for C.O. To suit officer 5ft 10 in height
12½ stones weight

Reason for deficiency: Evacuation for Veterinary reasons.

Perforated Sheet giving detail of personnel and horses wanting to complete, shown on Army Form B. 213.

Number of Report ____________

Detail of Wanting to Complete	Drivers R. A.	Drivers R. E.	Drivers A. S. C.	Drivers Car	Drivers Lorry	Drivers Steam	Gunners	Smith Gunners	Range Takers	Farriers Serjeants	Farriers Corporals	Shoeing, or Shoeing and Carriage Smiths	Cold Shoers	Wheelers R. A.	Wheelers R. T.	Wheelers M. T.
CAVALRY															
R. A.															
R. E.															
INFANTRY															
R. A. M. C.															
A. O. C.															
A. V. C.															

Detail of Wanting to Complete	Saddlers or Harness Makers	Blacksmiths	Bricklayers and Masons	Carpenters and Joiners	Fitters & Turners (R. E.) Wood	Fitters & Turners (R. E.) Iron	Fitters R. A.	Fitters Wireless	Plumbers	Electricians Ordinary	Electricians W. T.	Signalmen	Engine Drivers Loco.	Engine Drivers Field	Air Line Men	Permanent Line Men	Operators, Telegraph	Cablemen
CAVALRY																		
R. A.																		
R. E.																		
INFANTRY																		
R. A. M. C.																		
A. O. C.																		
A. V. C.																		

Detail of Wanting to Complete	Brigade Section Pioneers	General-duty Pioneers	Signallers	Instrument Repairers	Motor Cyclists	Motor Cyclist Artificers	Telephonists	Clerks	Machine Gunners	Armament Artificers Fitters	Armament Artificers Range Finders	Armourers	Storemen	Privates	W.O.'s and N.C.O.'s (by ranks) not included in trade columns	TOTAL to agree with wanting to complete Officers	TOTAL to agree with wanting to complete Other Ranks	Horses Riding	Horses Draught	Horses Heavy Draught	Horses Pack
CAVALRY																					
R. A.																					
R. E.																					
INFANTRY														68		4 (1 Major 3 Capts)		1			
R. A. M. C.																					
A. O. C.																					
A. V. C.																					

Remarks:—

R. E. [illegible] Lieut. Col. Signature of Commander.

2nd Bn Royal Dublin Fus. Unit.

10th Inf Bde Formation to which attached.

11/8/16 Date of Despatch.

(B 99511) Wt. W15519/M149. 1,000,000. 1/16. J. P. & Co., Ltd. Forms/B. 213/7.

[P.T.O.

Only additional information regarding "wanting to complete" is to be entered on this side.

1 Second-in-Command Urgently Required.

Perforated Sheet giving detail of personnel and horses wanting to complete, shown on Army Form B. 213.

Number of Report 48

Detail of Wanting to Complete.	Drivers									Farriers				Wheelers						
	R. A.	R. E.	A. S. C.	Car	Lorry	Steam	Gunners	Smith Gunners	Range Takers	Serjeants	Corporals	Shoeing, or Shoeing and Carriage Smiths	Cold Shoers	R. A.	H. T.	M. T.	Saddlers or Harness Makers	Blacksmiths	Bricklayers and Masons	Carpenters and Joiners
CAVALRY																				
R. A.																				
R. E.																				
INFANTRY																				
R. A. M. C.																				
A. O. C.																				
A. V. C.																				

Detail of Wanting to Complete.	Fitters & Turners (R. E.)		Fitters			Electricians			Engine Drivers											
	Wood	Iron	R. A.	Wireless	Plumbers	Ordinary	W. T.	Signalmen	Loco.	Field	Air Line Men	Permanent Line Men	Operators, Telegraph	Cablemen	Brigade Section Pioneers	General-duty Pioneers	Signallers	Instrument Repairers	Motor Cyclists	Motor Cyclist Artificers
CAVALRY																				
R. A.																				
R. E.																				
INFANTRY																				
R. A. M. C.																				
A. O. C.																				
A. V. C.																				

Detail of Wanting to Complete.				Armament Artificers					W.O's. and N.C.O's (by ranks) not included in trade columns.										TOTAL to agree with wanting to complete		Horses			
	Telephonists	Clerks	Machine Gunners	Fitters	Range Finders	Armourers	Storemen	Privates											Officers	Other Ranks	Riding	Draught	Heavy Draught	Pack
CAVALRY																								
R. A.																								
R. E.																								
INFANTRY																				4 Captain and Majors	48			
R. A. M. C.																								
A. O. C.																								
A. V. C.																								

Remarks :—

[illegible] Lt. Col. Signature of Commander.

2nd Bn Royal Dublin Fus. Unit.

10th I.B. Formation to which attached.

15 Aug 1916. Date of Despatch.

(26149.) Wt. W. 10698/4046. 500,000. 10/15. M.R.Co., Ltd. Forms/B. 213/6.

(P.T.O.

Perforated Sheet giving detail of personnel and horses wanting to complete, shown on Army Form B. 213.

Number of Report 47.

Detail of Wanting to Complete.	Drivers. R. A.	Drivers. R. E.	Drivers. A. S. C.	Drivers. Car	Drivers. Lorry	Drivers. Steam	Gunners	Smith Gunners	Range Takers	Farriers Serjeants	Farriers Corporals	Shoeing, or Shoeing and Carriage Smiths	Cold Shoers	Wheelers R. A.	Wheelers H. T.	Wheelers M. T.	Saddlers or Harness Makers	Blacksmiths	Bricklayers and Masons	Carpenters and Joiners
CAVALRY																				
R. A.																				
R. E.																				
INFANTRY																				
R. A. M. C.																				
A. O. C.																				
A. V. C																				

Detail of Wanting to Complete.	Fitters & Turners (R. E.) Wood	Fitters & Turners (R. E.) Iron	Fitters R. A.	Fitters Wireless	Plumbers	Electricians Ordinary	Electricians W. T.	Signalmen	Engine Drivers Loco.	Engine Drivers Field	Air Line Men	Permanent Line Men	Operators, Telegraph	Cablemen	Brigade Section Pioneers	General-duty Pioneers	Signallers	Instrument Repairers	Motor Cyclists	Motor Cyclist Artificers	Telephonists	Clerks	Machine Gunners
CAVALRY																							
R. A.																							
R. E.																							
INFANTRY																							
R. A. M. C.																							
A. O. C.																							
A. V. C																							

Detail of Wanting to Complete.	Armament Artificers Fitters	Armament Artificers Range Finders	Armourers	Storemen	Privates	W.O.'s and N.C.O.'s (by ranks) not included in trade columns.									TOTAL to agree with wanting to complete Officers	TOTAL Other Ranks	Horses Riding	Horses Draught	Horses Heavy Draught	Horses Pack
CAVALRY																				
R. A.																				
R. E.																				
INFANTRY															4 Majors or Capts	30		1		
R. A. M. C.																				
A. O. C.																				
A. V. C																				

Remarks :—

[illegible] Lieut-Col Signature of Commander.

2nd Bn Royal Dublin Fus. Unit.

10th Inf: Bde 4th Div. Formation to which attached.

6/8/16. Date of Despatch.

(26149.) Wt. W. 10698/4046. 500,000. 10/15. M.R.Co. Ltd. Forms/B. 213/6.

Only additional information regarding "wanting to complete" is to be entered on this side.

1 Second-in-Command urgently Required.

To:-

Headquarters,
10th Inf Bde.

Nominal Roll of Officers For Week Ending, 4-8-18.

Commanding Officer,	Lieut. Col. R.G.B.Jeffreys,	2nd Bn.
Adjutant,	Capt. J.D.Glegg,	2nd Bn.
Quarter Master,	Major. J.Burke,	2nd Bn.
Lewis Gun Officer,	Lieut. H.G.Aylmer,	2nd Bn.
Transport Officer,	2 " W.I.Black,	4th Bn.
Signalling Officer,	2 " F.T.A.Power,	2nd Bn.
Other Officers:-	CAPT L.G KETTLEWELL	4th Bn.
	Capt. W.A.Redmond,	3rd Bn.
	Capt. R.M.Patterson,	4th Bn.
	Lieut. L.A.King,	3rd Bn.
	" J.B.Moffat,	2nd Bn.
	" J.A.Noblett,	3rd Bn.
	" S.J.Craddock,	4th Bn.
	2nd " T.F.Handyside,	4th Bn.
	" " A.H.West,	4th Bn.
	" " W.N.Henchy,	3rd Bn.
	" " E.C.B.Dillon,	3rd Bn.
	" " J.B.Sheehan,	3rd Bn.
	" " G.S.T.Fenning,	2nd Bn.
	" " W.G.Scott,	4th Bn,
	" " H.G.Killingley,	2nd Bn.
	" " L.G.Doran,	3rd Bn.
	" " W.Pedlow,	3rd Bn.
	" " C.B.Donovan,	2nd Bn.
	" " W.H.Hynes,	2nd Bn.
	" " B.P.Glancy,	3rd Bn.
	" " H.J.Lemass,	3rd Bn.
	" " P.N.Gordon,	3rd Bn.
	" " A.R.Henry,	3rd Bn.
	" " R.G.Bourke,	10 3rd Bn.
	" " R.F.Nalder,	10 3rd Bn.
	" " H.W.Gibson,	10 3rd Bn.

Officers Datached :-

Lieut. Col.H.M.Cliff, Pine School of Instruction. 4th Divn
Capt. C.St.L.Webb, 10th Bde Transport Officer, 3rd Bn.
~~Lieut. L.G.Kettlewell, Instructor of Drafts, Attached to No. 2. Inf Base Depot,~~ 4th Bn.
Capt. G.F.Napier-Martin, Town Major, Louvencourt. 3rd Bn.

Officers Attached:-

2nd Lieut. R.Mac.I.Stobart, 3rd Bn Wiltshire Regt.

Medical Officer Lieut. A.B.Moffat, R.A.M.C.

Chaplain, Rev.E.Dowling, C.F.

4-8-18.

Lieut. Col.
O.C. 2nd Bn Royal Dublin Fusiliers.

10th Brigade.

4th Division.

2nd BATTALION

ROYAL DUBLIN FUSILIERS

SEPTEMBER 1 9 1 6

2nd Bn Royal Dublin Fusrs

Instructions regarding War Diaries and Intelligence Summaries are contained in F. S. Regs., Part II. and the Staff Manual respectively. Title Pages will be prepared in manuscript.

WAR DIARY
or
INTELLIGENCE SUMMARY
(Erase heading not required.)

Army Form C. 2118

2 R Dublin 4/10

SEPTR 1916

Vol 25

Place	Date	Hour	Summary of Events and Information	Remarks and references to Appendices
TRENCHES HQ OPPOSITE "THE DUMP."	1-9-16		There was heavy shelling by the enemy during the day, one OR being killed and two OR wounded. In the night the Bn was relieved by 3rd Bn AUSTRALIANS, 1st Bde, 1st Division	
ERIE CAMP G.11 C 7.4	2-9-16		Bn marched out via RAILWAY CUTTING + LINE, to ASYLUM YPRES, entraining there, and detraining at BRANDHOEK: Hence by road to ERIE CAMP, half a mile South of YPRES-POPERINGHE ROAD. The camp was moderately kept, parts being very unsanitary.	
	3rd		There was a gas alarm at night, which was afterwards discovered to have been started by the enemy. During the day shells were heard overhead POPERINGHE being shelled for the first time for 7 weeks. 2 officers & 100 O.R left to take over billets etc at 2nd Army School	
POPERINGHE, RUE DE FURNES	4th		Bn left camp at 11 30 a m for POPERINGHE where accomodation was provided in billets which were quite satisfactory, the weather is dull but not rainy	
	5th		A route march took place by Companies towards PROVEN, distance about 9 miles. During the day 12" guns in the vicinity were firing on the Germans	
	6th		Another route march to "M" + "N" Camps where training by Coys was carried on. A part of the Bn was issued with the new Box Respirators, small.	
	7th		Training at M & N Camps ~~2 officers~~ + 50.O.R formed part of a Composite Coy from Bn for training with VIII Corps O.T.C	
	8th		As above: preparations were made for a move on the morrow	
EN ROUTE	9th		Bn left POPERINGHE at 9.0 a m, the men's packs being conveyed in Lorries, route taken was ST JAN TER BIEZEN - WATOU - WINNEZEELE - HAEGDEONE - WEMAERS - CAPPEL and NOORDPEENE. "C" + "D" Coys were billeted in WEMAERS-CAPPEL during the night, with "A" + "B" Coys and Headquarters at NOORDPEENE. Bn arrived at 6 30 p m having covered 17 miles.	
TATINGHEM	10th		Bn marched to TATINGHEM, via ZUYTPEENE - LES TROIS ROIS - ARQUES - ST OMER. A start was made at 9.0 a.m. and destination was reached at 1 30 p m. The men marched splendidly, doing 7 miles in 2¼ hours, and the C.O. expressed his great satisfaction at their performance to the General, and to the men by Bn Routine Orders. The weather was fine and rather warm for marching. Excellent billets were to be had, and everyone quite contented with the prospect of a month's stay in the village. The Bn now came under the jurisdiction of the Second Army Central School of Instruction	
	11th		The day was spent quietly in cleaning up billets.	
	12th		A Composite Coy formed under Capt H G Aylmer + consisting of 4 platoon officers with 220 N.C.Os + men proceeded to 2nd Army School to carry out work detailed for them. The remainder of the Bn worked at the School. 2 officers + 10 N C Os were instructed in Bayonet Fighting at the School daily. Surplus officers attended lectures given daily at the School	
	16th		Orders were received to stand by ready to march off in the afternoon, all parades cancelled.	346c SB+EB

1875 Wt. W593/826 1,000,000 4/15 J.B.C. & A. A.D.S.S./Forms/C. 2118.

Instructions regarding War Diaries and Intelligence Summaries are contained in F. S. Regs., Part II. and the Staff Manual respectively. Title pages will be prepared in manuscript.

WAR DIARY
or
INTELLIGENCE SUMMARY
(Erase heading not required.)

Army Form C. 2118.

Septr 1916

Place	Date	Summary of Events and Information	Remarks and References to Appendices
TATINGHEM.	16th	Orders were received later that the Bn would entrain on the morrow	
EN ROUTE TO	17th	Bn left village at 8.0 p.m. and entrained at ST OMER at 11 p.m. arriving LONGEAU STN at about 9.0 a.m. Breakfast was served when clear of the town and Bn then marched to RAINNEVILLE about 9 miles distant arriving at 1.30 p.m. It rained practically the whole way, the night having been very stormy also.	
RAINNEVILLE.		Billets were very crowded and not very good.	
	18 – 22nd	Coy training carried out in chilly and rainy weather.	
		Bn ordered to move on the morrow.	
	23rd	Coy training in the morning.	
CORDIE.	24th	Bn moved to CORDIE in the morning. A Brigade exercise was carried out on the way. Bn arrived at about 6 p.m. and were accomodated in good billets.	
SAILLY-LE-SEC.	25th	Bn marched out at 9.45 and proceeded to SAILLY-LE-SEC. A Bn exercise was practised en route during which several hostile aeroplanes flew overhead. Bn arrived at about 2.30 p.m. and were billeted in good quarters.	
	26th	There were bathing parades in the SOMME and as the weather is hot the water was much appreciated.	
	27th	Coy parades were held. Orders to move were received but subsequently cancelled. A heavy thunderstorm passed over the village in the evening.	
	28th	Brigade training & operations took place in anticipation of the Bn going into action shortly. In the evening an interesting match took place between 23rd Regt of Dragoons & a team from the Bn. The result was a victory for the French by 3 goals to 1. The Commanding Officer afterwards entertained the Commander to tea.	
DAOURS.	29th	The Bn moved off from the village and proceeded via CORBIE to DAOURS where good billets were obtainable. The village of SAILLY-LE-SEC was evacuated by British troops, the French taking over the sector in front of the village.	
	30th	Bn training carried out to the [illegible] of the village	

[illegible signature] Lieut. Colonel
Comdg. [illegible] Royal Dublin [illegible]

9 26 6 W 257–976 100,000 1/12 H W V 79/3298

2nd Bn Royal Dublin Fusrs

Appendix to War Diary
Month of September 1916.

Date	Remarks
1·9·16	1 other Rank killed-in-action 2 other Ranks wounded-in-action
8·9·16	Capt C. E. Jameson joined the Battalion.
"	2/Lt J. W. Sheehan admitted to hospital (sick)
10·9·16	2/Lt G. S. T. Fenning appt. adjt. to 10th T. M. Battery
15·9·16	12 other Ranks joined the Battalion.
19·9·16	2 " " " " "
22·9·16	Capt J. G. F. Raper-Martin struck off strength (To duties as R.T.O.).
"	10 other Ranks joined the Battalion.
20·9·16	2 Other Ranks " " "
26·9·16	4 " " " " "
28·9·16	4 " " " " "
29·9·16	2/Lt T. F. Handyside admitted to hospital (Sick)
12·9·16	2/Lt G. L. Graham joined the Battalion.

2·10·16.

[signature]
Lieut Colonel
O C 2nd Bn Royal Dublin Fusrs

Unit 2nd Bn Royal Dublin Fusiliers
Place In the Field
Date 2 Sept 1916

FIELD STATE.

Army Form B. 231.

To be rendered in accordance with Field Service Regulations, Part II.

UNIT	FIGHTING STRENGTH — This should not include details attached to unit, or personnel detailed to march with the Train, or any men unfit to go into action with unit											RATION STRENGTH — To include Fighting Strength, Personnel detailed to march with the Train, and all Personnel and animals attached for Rations and Forage										
	Personnel		Horses and Mules		Other Animals		Guns and Ammunition Wagons (stating nature)	Machine Guns	Ambulances	Tool Carts, Technical Carts (stating nature)	Remarks	Personnel	Horses and Mules		Other Animals		Mechanically Propelled Vehicles					Remarks
	Officers	Other Ranks	Riding	Draught and Pack								Total, all Ranks entitled to Rations.	Heavy Horses	Other Horses and Mules			Motor Cars	Motor Bicycles	Lorries. 3 Ton	Lorries. 30 Cwt.	Tractors	
(1)	(2)	(3)	(4)	(5)	(6)	(7)	(8)	(9)	(10)	(11)	(12)	(13)	(14)	(15)	(16)	(17)	(18)	(19)	(20)	(21)	(22)	(23)
Trench Strength	7	701	12	44			Lewis	8				802	9									
10th I Bde T.O. & Transport	3	72										2	1									Attached
4th Div School	1	2																				
Army Schools		2																				
1/7th Brigade	1	14																				
Hospital	3	.																				
T.M. Batty attached		26																				
M.G. & 172 Tunnelling Coy		27																				
Grenade School	1	22																				
Other Details	3	31																				
TOTALS ...	39	897	12	44				8				804	10									

Ammunition with Unit:—

·303 inch; approximate number of rounds per Man 208

·303 inch; " " " per Machine Gun 8300

Gun or Howitzer; approximate number of rounds per Gun or Howitzer

Supplies with Unit:—

Approximate number of days' rations for men of ration strength Two

" " " forage for Animals " "

" " " fuel and lubricants for Mechanically Propelled Vehicles

Signature of Commander R.A. Heffer[?] Lieut Col

Oc 2nd Roy Dub Fusiliers

(90988.) Wt.W. 5216—2140. 900,000 7/15. J. P. & Co. Ltd. Forms B 231 / 3

Unit 2nd Bn Royal Dublin Fusiliers
Place In the Field
Date 24 Sept 1916

FIELD STATE.

Army Form B 231.

To be rendered in accordance with Field Service Regulations, Part II.

UNIT	FIGHTING STRENGTH — This should **not** include details attached to unit, or personnel detailed to march with the Train, or any men unfit to go into action with unit — Personnel: Officers	Personnel: Other Ranks	Horses and Mules: Riding	Horses and Mules: Draught and Pack	Other Animals	Other Animals	Guns and Ammunition Wagons (stating nature)	Machine Guns	Ambulances	Tool Carts, Technical Carts (stating nature)	Remarks	RATION STRENGTH — To include Fighting Strength, Personnel detailed to march with the Train, and all Personnel and animals attached for Rations and Forage — Personnel: Total, all Ranks entitled to Rations.	Horses and Mules: Heavy Horses	Horses and Mules: Other Horses and Mules	Other Animals	Other Animals	Mechanically Propelled Vehicles: Motor Cars	Motor Bicycles.	Lorries. 3 Ton	Lorries. 30 Cwt.	Tractors	Remarks
(1)	(2)	(3)	(4)	(5)	(6)	(7)	(8)	(9)	(10)	(11)	(12)	(13)	(14)	(15)	(16)	(17)	(18)	(19)	(20)	(21)	(22)	(23)
[illegible]	40	547	13	46																		
[illegible] Transport	3	72					[illegible]	8				649	10	49								
[illegible] School	3	10										2	8									A.S.C. attached
[illegible] School	2	104																				
[illegible]		5																				
[illegible]	3	–																				
[illegible]	[illegible]	[illegible]																				
[illegible]	1	[illegible]																				
[illegible] School	[illegible]	[illegible]																				
[illegible]	[illegible]	21																				
[illegible]	–	518																				Att. to VIII Corps
TOTALS ...	37	901	13	46								651	18	49								

Ammunition with Unit:—

·303 inch; approximate number of rounds per Man 208

·303 inch; " " " per Machine Gun 8800

Gun or Howitzer; approximate number of rounds per Gun or Howitzer

Supplies with Unit:—

Approximate number of days' rations for men of ration strength Two

" " " forage for Animals " " Two

" " " fuel and lubricants for Mechanically Propelled Vehicles

[illegible] serving with the Divisional Coy [illegible]

Signature of Commander [illegible] Lieut Col
O.C. 2 Bn Roy Dub Fusiliers

(90988.) Wt. W. 5216—2140. 900,000 7/15. J. P. & Co. Ltd. Forms B 231 / 3

Unit 2nd Royal Dublin Fusiliers
Place In the Field
Date 16th Sept 1916

FIELD STATE.

Army Form B 231.

To be rendered in accordance with Field Service Regulations, Part II.

UNIT	FIGHTING STRENGTH. This should *not* include details attached to unit, or personnel detailed to march with the Train, or any men unfit to go into action with unit — Personnel: Officers	Personnel: Other Ranks	Horses and Mules: Riding	Horses and Mules: Draught and Pack	Other Animals	Other Animals	Guns and Ammunition Wagons (stating nature)	Machine Guns	Ambulances	Tool Carts, Technical Carts (stating nature)	Remarks	RATION STRENGTH. To include Fighting Strength, Personnel detailed to march with the Train, and all Personnel and animals attached for Rations and Forage — Personnel: Total, all Ranks entitled to Rations.	Horses and Mules: Heavy Horses	Horses and Mules: Other Horses and Mules	Other Animals	Other Animals	Mechanically Propelled Vehicles: Motor Cars	Motor Bicycles.	Lorries: 3 Ton	Lorries: 30 Cwt.	Tractors	Remarks
(1)	(2)	(3)	(4)	(5)	(6)	(7)	(8)	(9)	(10)	(11)	(12)	(13)	(14)	(15)	(16)	(17)	(18)	(19)	(20)	(21)	(22)	(23)
TRENCH STRENGTH	22	69[illegible]																				
with BnTO & Transport	3	74					Lewis	8				726	[illegible]	35								
4th Div School	3	4										4	9	1								4 [illegible]
3rd Army School		18																				
10th Brigade	1	13																				
Hospital	3																					
TM Bty attached	1	31																				
[illegible] Tunnelling Coy	1	31																				
Grenade School	1	3																				
Composite Company		50																				
Other Details	2	24																				
TOTALS ...	37	946																				

Ammunition with Unit:—

·303 inch; approximate number of rounds per Man 208

·303 inch; ,, ,, ,, per Machine Gun 8300

Gun or Howitzer; approximate number of rounds per Gun or Howitzer

Men serving with Divisional Reserve Coy 60

Supplies with Unit:—

Approximate number of days' rations for men of ration strength Two

,, ,, ,, forage for Animals ,, ,, Two

,, ,, ,, fuel and lubricants for Mechanically Propelled Vehicles

Signature of Commander R G [illegible] Lieut Col.
OC 2nd Roy Dub Fusrs

(90988.) Wt.W. 5216—2140. 900,000 7/15. J. P. & Co. Ltd. Forms B 231 / 3

Army Form B 231.

FIELD STATE.

Unit 2nd Bn. Royal Dublin Fusiliers.
Place In the Field
Date 24.9.16.

To be rendered in accordance with Field Service Regulations, Part II.

FIGHTING STRENGTH (columns 2–12): This should not include details attached to unit, or personnel detailed to march with the Train, or any men unfit to go into action with unit

RATION STRENGTH (columns 13–23): To include Fighting Strength, Personnel detailed to march with the Train, and all Personnel and animals attached for Rations and Forage

UNIT	Personnel		Horses and Mules		Other Animals		Guns and Ammunition Wagons (stating nature)	Machine Guns	Ambulances	Tool Carts, Technical Carts (stating nature)	Remarks	Personnel	Horses and Mules		Other Animals		Mechanically Propelled Vehicles					Remarks
	Officers	Other Ranks	Riding	Draught and Pack								Total, all Ranks entitled to Rations.	Heavy Horses	Other Horses and Mules			Motor Cars	Motor Bicycles	Lorries, 3 Ton	Lorries, 30 Cwt.	Tractors	
(1)	(2)	(3)	(4)	(5)	(6)	(7)	(8)	(9)	(10)	(11)	(12)	(13)	(14)	(15)	(16)	(17)	(18)	(19)	(20)	(21)	(22)	(23)
Trench Strength	24	773	13	44			Lewis	9				864	9	48								
Transport	3	62											5	5								M.M.P.
3rd Army School		2											5	5 H.D.								A.S.C. Att^d
4th Div. Reinfts.	3	6												1 L.D.								" "
10th Inf. Bde.		14																				
M.G. & T.M.B.	1	26																				
Base & 11th Bde.	2	4																				
Hospital	3																					
Other Details		22																				
TOTALS ...	36	909	13	44								864.										

Ammunition with Unit:—

·303 inch; approximate number of rounds per Man 208

·303 inch; " " " per Machine Gun 8300

Gun or Howitzer; approximate number of rounds per Gun or Howitzer —

Men with 4th Div Res Co^y. 40
Ret^d from " " " 5.

Supplies with Unit:—

Approximate number of days' rations for men of ration strength Two

" " " forage for Animals " " Two.

" " " fuel and lubricants for Mechanically Propelled Vehicles

Signature of Commander [signature]
Lieut. Colonel
Comdg. 2nd Battn. Royal Dublin Fusrs.

(90968.) Wt.W. 5216—2140. 900,000 7/15. J. P. & Co. Ltd. Forms B 231 / 3

Unit 2nd. Bn Royal Dublin Fusiliers

Place In the Field

Date 30th Sept 1916

FIELD STATE.

Army Form B 231.

To be rendered in accordance with Field Service Regulations, Part II.

UNIT	FIGHTING STRENGTH — This should *not* include details attached to unit, or personnel detailed to march with the Train, or any men unfit to go into action with unit											RATION STRENGTH — To include Fighting Strength, Personnel detailed to march with the Train, and all Personnel and animals attached for Rations and Forage										
	Personnel		Horses and Mules		Other Animals							Personnel	Horses and Mules		Other Animals		Mechanically Propelled Vehicles					
	Officers	Other Ranks	Riding	Draught and Pack			Guns and Ammunition Wagons (stating nature)	Machine Guns	Ambulances	Tool Carts, Technical Carts (stating nature)	Remarks	Total, all Ranks entitled to Rations.	Heavy Horses	Other Horses and Mules			Motor Cars	Motor Bicycles.	Lorries. 3 Ton	Lorries. 30 Cwt.	Tractors	Remarks
(1)	(2)	(3)	(4)	(5)	(6)	(7)	(8)	(9)	(10)	(11)	(12)	(13)	(14)	(15)	(16)	(17)	(18)	(19)	(20)	(21)	(22)	(23)
Trench Strength	20	758	13	44								855	9	48								
Transport	3	66											5	1 L.D.								A.S. G[illegible]
3rd Army School		2																				
4th Div & Grenade Sch }	3	13																				
10th Infty Bde }		15																				
M. 4 T. M. B	1	29																				
[illegible] & 11th Bde	2	3																				
Hospital	4	-																				
Other Details	2	28																				
TOTALS ...	35	944	13	14																		

Ammunition with Unit:—

·303 inch; approximate number of rounds per Man 208

·303 inch; " " " per Machine Gun 8300

Gun or Howitzer; approximate number of rounds per Gun or Howitzer —

Men with 4th Div Res Coy 28

Supplies with Unit:—

Approximate number of days' rations for men of ration strength Two.

" " " forage for Animals " " Two.

" " " fuel and lubricants for Mechanically Propelled Vehicles

Signature of Commander R G [illegible] Lieut Col

(90988.) Wt.W. 5216—2140. 900,000 7/15. J. P. & Co. Ltd. Forms B 231/3

To be made up to and for Sunday in each week.

No. of Report 50

FIELD RETURN.

Army Form B. 213.

(To be furnished by all arms, services, and departments (except A.S.C. units) to the A. G.'s Office at the Base in accordance with Field Service Regulations, Part II.)

RETURN showing numbers (*a*) Effective strength of Unit. (*b*) Rationed by Unit. 2nd Bn Royal Dublin Fusiliers at In the Field 2nd Sept 1916. Date.

Detail	Personnel: Officers	Personnel: Other ranks	Personnel: Natives	Animals: Horses: Riding	Horses: Draught	Horses: Heavy Draught	Horses: Pack	Mules: Large	Mules: Small	Camels	Oxen	Guns, carriages and limbers, showing description	Ammunition wagons and limbers	Machine guns	Aircraft, showing description	Horsed: 4 wheeled	Horsed: 2 wheeled	Mechanical: Motor Cars.	Tractors	Lorries, showing description	Trucks, showing description	Trailers	Motor Bicycles	Bicycles	Remarks
Effective Strength of Unit	39	935		12	26	9	9						Lewis Gun	8										9	
Details, *by Arms* attached to unit as in War Establishment:—																									
R.A.M.C.	1	5																							
A.O.C.		1																			24				
Total	40	941		11	26	9	9																	9	
War Establishment	30	995		13	26	9	9																	9	
Wanting to complete (Detail of Personnel and Horses below)		2	54																						majors [illegible]
Surplus	8																								Subalterns
*Attached (not to include the details shown above)	1			1																					Chaplain R.C.
Civilians:— Employed with the Unit						1																			
Accompanying the Unit		2																							A.S.C. Attached
Total Rationed...	29[illegible]	[illegible]		12	26	10	9																		

Remarks (details):

Detail	Off.	O.R.
Detached [illegible]		2
2nd Army School		
[illegible]	1	2
10th Bde	1	1
[illegible] Res Coy		4
M. G. [illegible]		3
T. M. B[illegible]		26
Tunnel Coy.		14
Survey / [illegible]		2
[illegible]	2	7
Base & [illegible]		6
[illegible]		3
A O C & [illegible]		4
[illegible] Coy		1
[illegible]		2
Hospital	3	
[illegible]	1	2
[illegible] other Details	2	
	6	
	17	168

* In the case of field ambulances, hospitals or depots, the number of patients are to be included here, the names being shown in A. F. A. 36.

[illegible] Lieut Col Signature of Commander.

2/9/16 Date of Despatch.

For information of the A.G.'s Office at the Base.

Officers and men who have become casuals, been transferred or joined since last report.

Place In the Field Date 2nd Sept 1916

Regtl. Number	Rank	Name	Corps	Nature of casualty, or name of unit from or to which transferred	Date of being struck off or coming on the ration return	Remarks*
	Capt	W.A. Redmond	2nd Roy Dub Fus	To Hospital	28-8-16	
	Lieut	L.C. Byrne	2nd Roy Dub Fus	Rejoined	27-8-16	
25893	Pte	Dunne	2nd Roy Dub Fus	To Base	30-8-16	
	A	draft of 31 O.R.	joined Bn.	30th 8 16		
5629	Pte	Shea P	2nd Roy Dub Fus	Kld in A	1-9-16	

* State whether absence is of a permanent or temporary nature, adding, in the case of casuals from wounds or disease, any available information for communication to the relatives.

To be made up to and for Sunday in each week.

No. of Report 51

Army Form B. 213.

FIELD RETURN.

(To be furnished by all arms, services, and departments (except A.S.C. units) to the A. G.'s Office at the Base in accordance with Field Service Regulations, Part II.)

RETURN showing numbers (*a*) Effective strength of Unit. (*b*) Rationed by Unit. 2nd Bn Royal Dublin Fusiliers at In the Field 9th Sept 1916 Date.

DETAIL	Personnel: Officers	Personnel: Other ranks	Personnel: Natives	Animals: Horses: Riding	Horses: Draught	Horses: Heavy Draught	Horses: Pack	Mules: Large	Mules: Small	Camels	Oxen	Guns, carriages and limbers, showing description	Ammunition wagons and limbers	Machine guns	Aircraft, showing description	Horsed: 4 wheeled	Horsed: 2 wheeled	Mechanical: Motor Cars	Tractors	Lorries, showing description	Trucks, showing description	Trailers	Motor Bicycles	Bicycles	REMARKS
Effective Strength of Unit	37	942		13	27	10	9						Lewis Gun	8										9	[illegible]
Details, *by Arms* attached to unit as in War Establishment:—																									
R A M C		5																							
A O C		1																							
Total	[38]	948		13	27	10	9																	9	
War Establishment	30	995		13	26	9	9																	9	
Wanting to complete (Detail of Personnel and Horses below)	2	[53]																							[illegible]
Surplus	8				1	1																			
*Attached (not to include the details shown above)	1																								Chaplain R.C.
Civilians:— Employed with the Unit																									A.S.C. attached
Accompanying the Unit		2																							
TOTAL RATIONED...	[illegible]	[illegible]		15	27	18	9																		

* In the case of field ambulances, hospitals or depots, the number of patients are to be included here, the names being shown in A. F. A. 36.

[illegible signature] Lieut Col Signature of Commander.

8th Sept 1916 Date of Despatch.

For information of the A.G.'s Office at the Base.

Officers and men who have become casuals, been transferred or joined since last report.

Place In the Field Date 8th Sept 1916

Regtl. Number	Rank	Name	Corps	Nature of casualty, or name of unit from or to which transferred	Date of being struck off or coming on the ration return	Remarks*
	Capt	C.E. JAMESON	2nd Roy Dub Fus	Joined	5th Sept 1916	
	2/Lt	J.B. SHEEHAN	2nd Roy Dub Fus	To Hosp	6th Sept 1916	
[illegible]	Pte	McGowan M	2nd Roy Dub Fus	W in A	31-8-16	
[illegible]	"	Byrne J	" "	W in A	1-9-16	
7926	"	Regan C	" "	W in A	1-9-16	
11392	Pte	Ryan P	2nd Roy Dub Fus	Discharged from Base		
17294	Sgt	Catley T	2nd Roy Dub Fus	Instructor in Training Depot	2-9-16	
5903	CQMS	Partridge	Performed the duties of Coy QrMr [illegible]		A Coy from [illegible]	
2812	Sgt	Duffy (Com Barry)				
[illegible]	CQMS	[illegible]			B Coy	
7750	CQMS	[illegible]			C Coy	
[illegible]	CQMS	[illegible]			D Coy	
7122	LCpl	Curran W	Performed the duties of Bn Chiropodist for the month of August			

* State whether absence is of a permanent or temporary nature, adding, in the case of casuals from wounds or disease, any available information for communication to the relatives.

To be made up to and for Sunday in each week.

No. of Report 52

FIELD RETURN.

Army Form B. 213.

(To be furnished by all arms, services, and departments (except A.S.C. units) to the A. G.'s Office at the Base in accordance with Field Service Regulations, Part II.)

RETURN showing numbers (*a*) Effective strength of Unit. (*b*) Rationed by Unit. 2nd Bn Royal Dublin Fusrs [?] at [illegible] 12th Sept 1916 [?] Date.

DETAIL	Personnel: Officers	Other ranks	Natives	Animals: Horses: Riding	Draught	Heavy Draught	Pack	Mules: Large	Small	Camels	Oxen	Guns, carriages, and limbers and transport vehicles: Guns, carriages and limbers, showing description	Ammunition wagons and limbers	Machine guns	Aircraft, showing description	Horsed: 4 wheeled	2 wheeled	Mechanical: Motor Cars	Tractors	Lorries, showing description	Trucks, showing description	Trailers	Motor Bicycles	Bicycles	REMARKS
Effective Strength of Unit		[illegible]		13																					[illegible]
Details, *by Arms* attached to unit as in War Establishment:—																									
Total	[illegible]	[illegible]																							
War Establishment	3[illegible]	[illegible]		13	[illegible]	9	9																		
Wanting to complete (Detail of Personnel and Horses below)		50																							
Surplus	7																								
*Attached (not to include the details shown above)																									
Civilians:— Employed with the Unit / Accompanying the Unit																									A.S.C. attached
TOTAL RATIONED...	25	724	2	13	27	18	9																		

* In the case of field ambulances, hospitals or depots, the number of patients are to be included here, the names being shown in A. F. A. 36.

R. G. [illegible] Lieut Col Signature of Commander.

16th Sept 1916 Date of Despatch.

For information of the A.G.'s Office at the Base.

Officers and men who have become casuals, been transferred or joined since last report.

Place ____________ Date ____________

Regtl. Number	Rank	Name	Corps	Nature of casualty, or name of unit from or to which transferred	Date of being struck off or coming on the ration return	Remarks*

* State whether absence is of a permanent or temporary nature, adding, in the case of casuals from wounds or disease, any available information for communication to the relatives.

To be made up to and for Sunday in each week.

No. of Report 53.

FIELD RETURN.

Army Form B. 213.

(To be furnished by all arms, services, and departments (except A.S.C. units) to the A. G.'s Office at the Base in accordance with Field Service Regulations, Part II.)

RETURN showing numbers (a) Effective strength of Unit. (b) Rationed by Unit. 2nd Bn Royal Dublin Fus at In the Field 24th Sept 1916 Date.

Detail	Personnel: Officers	Personnel: Other ranks	Personnel: Natives	Animals: Horses: Riding	Animals: Horses: Draught	Animals: Horses: Heavy Draught	Animals: Horses: Pack	Animals: Mules: Large	Animals: Mules: Small	Animals: Camels	Animals: Oxen	Guns, carriages and limbers, showing description	Ammunition wagons and limbers	Machine guns	Aircraft, showing description	Horsed: 4 wheeled	Horsed: 2 wheeled	Mechanical: Motor Cars	Mechanical: Tractors	Mechanical: Lorries, showing description	Mechanical: Trucks, showing description	Mechanical: Trailers	Motor Bicycles	Bicycles
Effective Strength of Unit	37/36	949		11	26	9	9						Lewis	9										9
Details, by Arms attached to unit as in War Establishment:—																								
R.A.M.C. Att'd	1	5		1																				
Total	38/37	954		12	26	9	9							9										9
War Establishment	30	995		13	26	9	9							9										9
Wanting to complete (Detail of Personnel and Horses below)	3	41																						
Surplus	10																							
*Attached (not to include the details shown above)	1			1																				
Civilians:— Employed with the Unit / Accompanying the Unit		2		5	1	5																		
TOTAL RATIONED...	29	840		18	27	14	9																	

REMARKS

Det'ls R'nder	Off's	O.R.
3rd Army School		2
4th Div:	2	5
Grenade	1	1
10th Inf Bde		14
M.G.		13
T.M.	1	15
Hospital.	3	
Base	1	3
11th Bde	1	1
Other details		22
4th Div Res Cy		40
Total	9	116

Wanting to complete: Majors or Capt's

Surplus: Subalterns.

Attached: Chaplain R.C.

M.M.P.

A.S.C.

* In the case of field ambulances, hospitals or depots, the number of patients are to be included here, the names being shown in A. F. A. 36.

[signature] Lieut. Colonel, Comdg. 2nd Battn. Royal Dublin Fus. Signature of Commander.

24/9/16. Date of Despatch.

For information of the A.G.'s Office at the Base.

Officers and men who have become casuals, been transferred or joined since last report.

Place In the Field   Date 24.9.16.

Regtl. Number	Rank	Name	Corps	Nature of casualty, or name of unit from or to which transferred	Date of being struck off or coming on the ration return	Remarks*
	Capt	J.G.F. Napier Martin	Struck off	Strength as R.T.O.	22-9-16	Auth'y 4th Div. G/248. d 22-9-16
18335	L/C.	Plunkett W.	"D"		20.9.16	
8645	Pte	Craddock M.	"C"		" "	
24558	L/C.	Crowley	A	25503 Pte Byrne	"B" Coy joined	22-9-16
15232	Pte	Dicker	A	26506 " O'Rourke	"B" Coy joined	22-9-16
25871	"	Burke	A	26344 " Kennedy	"B" Coy joined	22-9-16
15588	"	Brady	"C"	25122 " Stapleton	"D" Coy "	" "
18540	"	McAndrew	"C"	25956 " Stanton	"D" Coy "	" "
To 23223	Pte	Deegan M.	+ 22043 Pte Delaney	"D" Coy	Joined	19-9-16.
7896	Pte	Wright	"B" Coy	Rejoined Bn from	20-9-16	
8342	"	Dawes	"A" "	4th Divn Res. Coy	"	
17685	"	Stewart	"A" "	"	" "	
18257	"	Ward	"D" "	"	" "	
17474	"	Murray	"C" "	"	" "	

* State whether absence is of a permanent or temporary nature, adding, in the case of casuals from wounds or disease, any available information for communication to the relatives.

To be made up to and for Sunday in each week.

No. of Report [illegible]

FIELD RETURN.

Army Form B. 21.

(To be furnished by all arms, services, and departments (except A.S.C. units) to the A. G.'s Office at the Base in accordance with Field Service Regulations, Part II.)

RETURN showing numbers (*a*) Effective strength of Unit. (*b*) Rationed by Unit. [illegible] at In the Field 30th Sept 1916 Date.

DETAIL	Personnel: Officers	Personnel: Other ranks	Personnel: Natives	Animals: Horses: Riding	Horses: Draught	Horses: Heavy Draught	Horses: Pack	Mules: Large	Mules: Small	Camels	Oxen	Guns, carriages and limbers, showing description	Ammunition wagons and limbers	Machine guns	Aircraft, showing description	Horsed: 4 wheeled	Horsed: 2 wheeled	Mechanical: Motor Cars	Tractors	Lorries, showing description	Trucks, showing description	Trailers	Motor Bicycles	Bicycles	REMARKS
Effective Strength of Unit	5	[illegible]		12	26	9	9						[illegible]	8										9	[illegible]
Details, *by Arms* attached to unit as in War Establishment:—																									
R.A.M.C. [illegible]	1	5																							
A.S.C. [illegible]																									
Total	6	[illegible]		12	26	9	9							8										9	
War Establishment	[illegible]	[illegible]		12	26	9	9							8										9	
Wanting to complete (Detail of Personnel and Horses below)	3	59																							[illegible]
Surplus	9																								[illegible]
*Attached (not to include the details shown above)	1			1																					[illegible] R.C.
Civilians:— Employed with the Unit / Accompanying the Unit		2			1	5																			A.S.C.
TOTAL RATIONED...	[illegible]	[illegible]		13	27	14	9																		

* In the case of field ambulances, hospitals or depots, the number of patients are to be included here, the names being shown in A. F. A. 36.

[illegible signature] Lt Col Signature of Commander.

30th Sept 1916 Date of Despatch.

For information of the A.G.'s Office at the Base.

Officers and men who have become casuals, been transferred or joined since last report.

Place In the Field [illegible] Date [illegible]

Regtl. Number	Rank	Name	Corps	Nature of casualty, or name of unit from or to which transferred	Date of being struck off or coming on the ration return	Remarks*
	2/Lt	[illegible]	2nd Roy Dub Fusr	To Hospital [illegible]		
	2/Lt	[illegible] Graham	2nd Roy Dub Fusr	[illegible]	28-9-16	
[illegible]	Pte	Stephens C	2nd Roy Dub Fusr	Suspension of Sentence [illegible]	[illegible]	[illegible]
				Dated [illegible] Quashed [illegible]		[illegible]
[illegible]	"	[illegible]	2nd Roy Dub Fusr	Suspension of Sentence [illegible]		[illegible]
				Dated [illegible] Quashed [illegible]		[illegible]
[illegible]	"	Allen J	2nd Roy Dub Fusr	Suspension of Sentence [illegible]		[illegible]
				Dated 20/9/16 Quashed [illegible]		[illegible]
[illegible]	"	Clarke E	2nd Roy Dub Fusr	Suspension of Sentence [illegible]		[illegible]
				Dated 20/9/16 Quashed [illegible]		[illegible]
	A	Draft of [illegible] O.R. joined Bn on		26-9-16		
	A	Draft of [illegible] O.R. joined Bn on		28-9-16		
[illegible]	[illegible]	[illegible]	Performed the duties of Coy [illegible]		for A Coy	for month of Sept
[illegible]	"	[illegible]	"		B Coy	"
7760	"	[illegible]	"		C Coy	"
[illegible]	"	[illegible]	"		D Coy	"
7122	L/Cpl	[illegible]	Performed the duties of Bn [illegible]			

* State whether absence is of a permanent or temporary nature, adding, in the case of casuals from wounds or disease, any available information for communication to the relatives.

Perforated Sheet giving detail of personnel and horses wanting to complete, shown on Army Form B. 213.

Number of Report 54

Detail of Wanting to Complete	Drivers R. A.	Drivers R. E.	Drivers A. S. C.	Drivers Car	Drivers Lorry	Drivers Steam	Gunners	Smith Gunners	Range Takers	Farriers Serjeants	Farriers Corporals	Shoeing, or Shoeing and Carriage Smiths	Cold Shoers	Wheelers R. A.	Wheelers H. T.	Wheelers M. T.	Saddlers or Harness Makers	Blacksmiths	Bricklayers and Masons	Carpenters and Joiners	Fitters & Turners (R. E.) Wood	Fitters & Turners (R. E.) Iron	Fitters R. A.	Fitters Wireless	Plumbers	Electricians Ordinary	Electricians W. T.	Signalmen	Engine Drivers Loco.	Engine Drivers Field	Air Line Men	Permanent Line Men	Operators, Telegraph	Cablemen	Brigade Section Pioneers	General-duty Pioneers	Signallers	Instrument Repairers	Motor Cyclists	Motor Cyclist Artificers	Telephonists	Clerks	Machine Gunners	Armament Artificers Fitters	Armament Artificers Range Finders	Armourers	Storemen	Privates	W.O's. and N.C.O's. (by ranks) not included in trade columns	Sgt. Shoemaker	Drummers					TOTAL to agree with wanting to complete Officers	TOTAL Other Ranks	Horses Riding	Horses Draught	Horses Heavy Draught	Horses Pack
CAVALRY																																																													
R. A.																																																													
R. E.																																																													
INFANTRY																																					4											18		1	6					3					
R. A. M. C.																																																													
A. O. C.																																																													
A. V. C.																																																													

Remarks:—

[signature] Lieut. Col. Signature of Commander.

2nd Bn Royal Dublin Fusiliers Unit.

10th Infy Bde Formation to which attached.

30th September 1916. Date of Despatch.

(B 99511.) Wt. W15519/M149. 1,000,000. 1/16. J. P. & Co., Ltd. Forms/B 213/7.

[P.T.O.

Only additional information regarding "wanting to complete" is to be entered on this side.

1 Sgt. Shoemaker to replace Sgt. due for discharge [illegible]
16 Trained Drummers
4 Trained Signallers

Perforated Sheet giving detail of personnel and horses wanting to complete, shown on Army Form B. 213.

Number of Report 53.

Detail of Wanting to Complete	Drivers R.A.	Drivers R.E.	Drivers A.S.C.	Drivers Car	Drivers Lorry	Drivers Steam	Gunners	Smith Gunners	Range Takers	Farriers Serjeants	Farriers Corporals	Shoeing, or Shoeing and Carriage Smiths	Cold Shoers	Wheelers R.A.	Wheelers H.T.	Wheelers M.T.	Saddlers or Harness Makers	Blacksmiths
CAVALRY																		
R.A.																		
R.E.																		
INFANTRY																		
R.A.M.C.																		
A.O.C.																		
A.V.C.																		

Detail of Wanting to Complete	Bricklayers and Masons	Carpenters and Joiners	Fitters & Turners (R.E.) Wood	Fitters & Turners (R.E.) Iron	Fitters R.A.	Fitters Wireless	Plumbers	Electricians Ordinary	Electricians W.T.	Signalmen	Engine Drivers Loco.	Engine Drivers Field	Air Line Men	Permanent Line Men	Operators, Telegraph	Cablemen	Brigade Section Pioneers	General-duty Pioneers	Signallers
CAVALRY																			
R.A.																			
R.E.																			
INFANTRY																			4
R.A.M.C.																			
A.O.C.																			
A.V.C.																			

Detail of Wanting to Complete	Instrument Repairers	Motor Cyclists	Motor Cyclist Artificers	Telephonists	Clerks	Machine Gunners	Armament Artificers Fitters	Armament Artificers Range Finders	Armourers	Storemen	Privates	W.O.'s and N.C.O.'s (by ranks) not included in trade columns: Sgt. Shoemaker	W.O.'s and N.C.O.'s: Drummers	TOTAL to agree with wanting to complete: Officers	TOTAL: Other Ranks	Horses Riding	Horses Draught	Horses Heavy Draught	Horses Pack
CAVALRY																			
R.A.																			
R.E.																			
INFANTRY											20	1	16	3 Capts: or Majors	41				
R.A.M.C.																			
A.O.C.																			
A.V.C.																			

Remarks:—

[illegible] Lieut. Colonel, Comdg. 2nd Battn. Royal Dublin Fusrs. Signature of Commander.

Unit.

10th Bde, 4th Divn. Formation to which attached.

24/9/16 Date of Despatch.

(B 99511.) Wt. W15519/M149. 1,000,000. 1/16. J. P. & Co., Ltd. Forms/B 213/7.

[P.T.O.

Perforated Sheet giving detail of personnel and horses wanting to complete, shown on Army Form B. 213.

Number of Report [illegible]

Detail of Wanting to Complete	Drivers R.A.	Drivers R.E.	Drivers A.S.C.	Drivers Car	Drivers Lorry	Drivers Steam	Gunners	Smith Gunners	Range Takers	Farriers Serjeants	Farriers Corporals	Shoeing or Shoeing and Carriage Smiths	Cold Shoers	Wheelers R.A.	Wheelers H.T.	Wheelers M.T.	Saddlers or Harness Makers	Blacksmiths	Bricklayers and Masons	Carpenters and Joiners	Fitters & Turners (R.E.) Wood	Fitters & Turners (R.E.) Iron	Fitters R.A.	Fitters Wireless	Plumbers	Electricians Ordinary	Electricians W.T.	Signalmen	Engine Drivers Loco.	Engine Drivers Field	Air Line Men	Permanent Line Men	Operators, Telegraph	Cableman	Brigade Section Pioneers	General-duty Pioneers	Signallers	Instrument Repairers	Motor Cyclists	Motor Cyclist Artificers	Telephonists	Clerks	Machine Gunners	Armament Artificers Fitters	Armament Artificers Range Finders	Armourers	Storemen	Privates	W.O's and N.C.O's (by ranks) not included in trade columns					TOTAL to agree with wanting to complete Officers	TOTAL to agree with wanting to complete Other Ranks	Horses Riding	Horses Draught	Horses Heavy Draught	Horses Pack
CAVALRY																																																											
R. A.																																																											
R. E.																																																											
INFANTRY																																																											
R. A. M. C.																																																											
A. O. C.																																																											
A. V. C.																																																											

Remarks:—

[illegible] Signature of Commander.

Unit.

Formation to which attached.

[illegible] 1916 Date of Despatch.

(B 99511.) Wt. W15519/M149. 1,000,000. 1/16. J. P. & Co., Ltd. Forms/B 213/7.

[P.T.O.

Only additional information regarding "wanting to complete" is to be entered on this side.

Perforated Sheet giving detail of personnel and horses wanting to complete, shown on Army Form B. 213.

Number of Report 38

Detail of Wanting to Complete	Drivers R.A.	Drivers R.E.	Drivers A.S.C.	Drivers Car	Drivers Lorry	Drivers Steam	Gunners	Smith Gunners	Range Takers	Farriers Serjeants	Farriers Corporals	Shoeing, or Shoeing and Carriage Smiths	Cold Shoers	Wheelers R.A.	Wheelers H.T.	Wheelers M.T.	Saddlers or Harness Makers	Blacksmiths	Bricklayers and Masons	Carpenters and Joiners	Fitters & Turners (R.E.) Wood	Fitters & Turners (R.E.) Iron	Fitters R.A.	Fitters Wireless	Plumbers	Electricians Ordinary	Electricians W.T.	Signalmen	Engine Drivers Loco.	Engine Drivers Field	Air Line Men	Permanent Line Men	Operators, Telegraph	Cablemen	Brigade Section Pioneers	General-duty Pioneers	Signallers	Instrument Repairers	Motor Cyclists	Motor Cyclist Artificers	Telephonists	Clerks	Machine Gunners	Armament Artificers Fitters	Armament Artificers Range Finders	Armourers	Storemen	Privates	W.O.'s and N.C.O.'s (by ranks) not included in trade columns	TOTAL to agree with wanting to complete Officers	TOTAL to agree with wanting to complete Other Ranks	Horses Riding	Horses Draught	Horses Heavy Draught	Horses Pack
CAVALRY																																																47		2 Majors or Capts					
R.A.																																																							
R.E.																																																			57				
INFANTRY																																																							
R.A.M.C.																																																							
A.O.C.																																																							
A.V.C.																																																							

Remarks :—

R. B. Peppers Lieut Col Signature of Commander.

O.C. 2nd Bn Royal Dublin Fusiliers Unit.

10th Inf Bde Formation to which attached.

8th Sept 1916 Date of Despatch.

(B 99511.) Wt. W15519/M149. 1,000,000. 1/16. J. P. & Co., Ltd. Forms/B 213/7.

P.T.O.

Only additional information regarding "wanting to complete" is to be entered on this side.

1 Sergt Shoemaker to replace Sgt Hayes due for discharge November

6 Trained Signallers urgently required

12 Trained Grenadiers required

10 Drummers Required (urgently)

Perforated Sheet giving detail of personnel and horses wanting to complete, shown on Army Form B. 213.

Number of Report 51.

Detail of Wanting to Complete	Drivers: R.A.	Drivers: R.E.	Drivers: A.S.C.	Drivers: Car	Drivers: Lorry	Drivers: Steam	Gunners	Smith Gunners	Range Takers	Farriers: Serjeants	Farriers: Corporals	Shoeing, or Shoeing and Carriage Smiths	Cold Shoers	Wheelers: R.A.	Wheelers: H.T.	Wheelers: M.T.
CAVALRY															
R.A.															
R.E.															
INFANTRY															
R.A.M.C.															
A.O.C.															
A.V.C.															

Detail of Wanting to Complete	Saddlers or Harness Makers	Blacksmiths	Bricklayers and Masons	Carpenters and Joiners	Fitters & Turners (R.E.): Wood	Fitters & Turners (R.E.): Iron	Fitters: R.A.	Fitters: Wireless	Plumbers	Electricians: Ordinary	Electricians: W.T.	Signalmen	Engine Drivers: Loco.	Engine Drivers: Field	Air Line Men	Permanent Line Men
CAVALRY																
R.A.																
R.E.																
INFANTRY																
R.A.M.C.																
A.O.C.																
A.V.C.																

Detail of Wanting to Complete	Operators, Telegraph	Cablemen	Brigade Section Pioneers	General-duty Pioneers	Signallers	Instrument Repairers	Motor Cyclists	Motor Cyclist Artificers	Telephonists	Clerks	Machine Gunners	Armament Artificers: Fitters	Armament Artificers: Range Finders	Armourers	Storemen	Privates
CAVALRY																
R.A.																
R.E.																
INFANTRY																54
R.A.M.C.																
A.O.C.																
A.V.C.																

Detail of Wanting to Complete	W.O.'s and N.C.O.'s (by ranks) not included in trade columns											TOTAL to agree with wanting to complete: Officers	TOTAL to agree with wanting to complete: Other Ranks	Horses: Riding	Horses: Draught	Horses: Heavy Draught	Horses: Pack
CAVALRY																	
R.A.																	
R.E.																	
INFANTRY												2 Majr & Capts	54	1			
R.A.M.C.																	
A.O.C.																	
A.V.C.																	

Remarks:—

R G Dagger Lieut.-Col Signature of Commander.

3rd Bn Royal Dublin Fus. Unit.

10th Inf: Bde Formation to which attached.

3rd Sept 1916. Date of Despatch.

(B 99511.) Wt. W15519/M149. 1,000,000. 1/16. J. P. & Co., Ltd. Forms/B 213/7.

[illegible].O.

Only additional information regarding "wanting to complete" is to be entered on this side.

1 Second in Command urgently required

1 Sergt Shoemaker to replace Sgt due for discharge November

1 Rider for C.O. to suit Officer 5ft 13in. Weight 12½ Stone

6 Trained Signallers urgently required

12 Trained Grenadiers required

10th Brigade.

4th Division

Battalion transferred to 48th Bde 16th Division
15th Nov.1916.

2nd BATTALION

ROYAL DUBLIN FUSILIERS

OCTOBER 1 9 1 6

Instructions regarding War Diaries and Intelligence Summaries are contained in F. S. Regs., Part II. and the Staff Manual respectively. Title Pages will be prepared in manuscript.

WAR DIARY
or
INTELLIGENCE SUMMARY
(Erase heading not required.)

Army Form C. 2118.

October 1916 — 2nd Bn Royal Dublin Fus. — 10th Inf. Bde

Place	Date October	Hour	Summary of Events and Information	Remarks and references to Appendices
DAOURS	1st		The clock was put back one hour at 1 a.m. on the morning of the 1st, so that the time will be normal GREENWICH time for the Winter.	
	5th		The weather was very bad. Both Brigade and Divisional programmes were arranged but often postponed or abandoned and training was carried out under difficulties.	
	6		Coy training was carried out in the morning on the training ground N. of DAOURS. In the afternoon Coys were shown how to make mine dug-outs by the R.E. Orders were recd for the Bn to move on the morrow.	
	7		Bn left DAOURS at 9.45 a.m. Coys marching at 200 yards interval, and a distance of 1000 yards between the different Regiments of the Bde. Route DAOURS - CORBIE - MERICOURT - VILLE-SUR-ANCRE to MEAULTE. The Bn halted for dinners at MERICOURT during which time it rained heavily. The Bn left at 2.45 and reached MEAULTE at about 5.0 p.m. The billets were poor most of the houses being in a broken down condition.	
	8		Bn moved off at 9.45 a.m. to MANSEL CAMP which is situated near CARNOY, on the way we crossed the regained British & German lines: every place is now very desolate owing to the previous bombardments. The camp is of tents, and - owing to the recent heavy rains - in a very muddy condition.	
	9		Bn moved off at 7.0 a.m. at intervals of 200 yards to a place just East of TRONES WOOD remaining there during the day. The first line of Transport remained near CARNOY. The Bn relieved 1st KENSINGTON Regt at about 7.0 p.m. and took up a position in support at T.9.d. The SEAFORTH HGHLDRS were in reserve, with 1st R. WARWICKSHIRE Regt & 1st R IRISH FUSRS on the Right & Left of the front line respectively.	
	10		The night was fairly quiet. The front & support lines were shelled all day very heavily with 5.9 & 8" guns. The French 32nd Regt are on our immediate right. The task set us is to take the BROWN LINE which is a jumping off place for the attack on the LE TRANSLOY LINE.	
	11		Normal night but the Germans put 5.9" shells into the front & support lines all night. Our own guns bombard night & day. The 1st R.I.F. & 1st R.W.R. are going to carry out an attack on the enemy front line on the morrow. We are sending up two Coys A+B to occupy our front line when the two Regts have moved off. The French are attacking on our right. The 56th Divn have had two attacks on this line but have been driven back owing to the GUN PITS and a STRONG POINT in the centre of our line (T.5.a).	
	12		Report on operations carried out on 12th October 1916 by Lieut-Col R. G. B. JEFFREYS, O.C. 2nd R. DUB. FUS. "On October 12th 1916 the 10th Brigade were ordered to attack the line DEWDROP, GUN PITS, + HAZY Trench. Bn was distributed as follows:- 1 Coy FLUFF Trench, 3 Coys T.9.d. The Bns attacking were 1st WARWICKS on right, 1st R. IRISH FUS on left. 2/R. DUB FUS supported WARWICKS. 2/SEAFORTHS RESERVE. At 2.5 p.m. WARWICKS + R. IRISH FUS advanced to attack. At 2.25 p.m. "A" Coy 2/R.D.F moved to GERMAN Trench vacated by 1st R. WAR REGT. "B" Coy moved up to FLUFFY TRENCH. From information received that WARWICKS were in need of support I ordered "A" Coy up. They got up without many casualties. They eventually pushed forward + assisted in new	

1875 Wt. W593/826 1,000,000 4/15 J.B.C. & A. A.D.S.S./Forms/C. 2118.

Instructions regarding War Diaries and Intelligence Summaries are contained in F. S. Regs., Part II. and the Staff Manual respectively. Title Pages will be prepared in manuscript.

WAR DIARY
or
INTELLIGENCE SUMMARY
(Erase heading not required.)

II.

Army Form C. 2118

2nd Bn Royal Dublin F

Place	Date	Hour	Summary of Events and Information	Remarks and references to Appendices
	October 16		trench (now called ANTELOPE). They met with a certain amount of resistance. "B" Coy reinforced the 1st R IRISH FUS but were not heavily engaged with the enemy. Information was received from O.C. WARWICKS that STRONG POINT was still in possession of enemy & I ordered O.C "A" to attack the position from S.W. My message however never reached its destination. I later got the order from the Brigade to find out if DEWDROP & HAZY trench were occupied by the enemy & endeavoured to do so but communication was impossible. My Bn was eventually withdrawn from the front line that night. Casualties 1 officer wounded O.R. 58. Lieut GAFFNEY was in command of "A" Coy and Capt BYRNE "B" Coy.	
FRONTLINE TRENCHES	13		Heavy shelling all day. The Brigadier-General visited Bn H.Q. during the day. At 6 p.m. the Bn commenced to take over the line from 1st R. WARWICK REGT. Relief was completed at midnight with only 3 casualties. The SEAFORTHS are on the left, R IRISH FUS in support and R. WARWICK REGT in Reserve. 2/Lieut E. C. B. DILLON was unfortunately killed by a 77 m.m on the LES BOEUFS - MORVAL Ridge.	
	14		During the night the SEAFORTH HIGHLDRS and 50 of our own men were ordered to take the GUN PITS & STRONG POINT by a bayonet charge. The enemy did not discover the attack until 7 minutes after ZERO (hour of attack) & then opened a very strong M.G. & rifle fire. His barrage came down under half a minute and it was almost impossible to get through it. Some of the SEAFORTHS did get into the GUN PITS but as they were so few they were driven out by an immediate bombing attack.	
	15		Fairly quiet day. Our heavies bombarded GUN PITS, FROSTY TRENCH etc & sent over thousands of shells. Very cold day.	
	16		The night was quiet. At evening "Stand-to" the enemy put down a very heavy barrage of 5.9 & 9.2 shells; the reason was not known. E. LANCASHIRE Regt relieved R. WARWICKSHIRE Regt & RIFLE Bde from Roy. IRISH FUS.	
	17		Very cold night; temp. was down to 35°F. The enemy fired a few shells round Battn H.Q. during the day. The G.O.C. - GENRL LAMBTON came to Bn H.Q. in the morning. Relief commenced at 6 p.m. and it rained hard until midnight.	
A3 C4.0	18		Relief completed at about 12.30 a.m. but many men did not arrive until 8.0 a.m. in the morning. Bn H.Q. were in two huts, the remainder in old German dug-outs & therefore not very comfortable in such wet weather.	
	19-21		Weather still wet.	
	22		Orders were received to proceed to the trenches on the morrow & the Bn attached to 11th Inf. Bde for operations. Battn moved off at 10 minute intervals & relieved 11th Bde in the trenches at 6.30 orders having been changed to that effect.	
			Report on part taken by 2nd Royal Dublin Fusiliers in Action on 23rd Oct. 1916. by Lt Col. R.G.B. Jeffreys On 22nd Oct 1916, prior to Action on 23rd inst at Conference held by G.O.C. 11th Brigade, the disposition and plan of attack were explained. On returning to my Camp I held a Conference of all Officers of my battalion and everything was thoroughly explained to all. Owing to the limited time it was not possible to issue written Orders. Immediately after my Conference (3 p.m.) Company Commanders went to the line to look at the ground they had to attack over. At 4.30. p.m. the battalion marched at 15 minutes between Companies, up to Assembly trenches. At 6.30 a.m. 23rd Oct. I received report that all were in position and ready to advance at 7 a.m. Battn: Head Quarters were in SUNKEN ROAD T. 10. a. Sheet 57c S.W 1.20,000.	

1875 Wt. W593/826 1,000,000 4/15 J.B.C. & A. A.D.S.S./Forms/C. 2118.

Appendix Contd.

Date	Remarks
23-10-16	36. other Ranks Missing in Action.
28-10-16	2. " " joined the Battalion
27-10-16	The following officers joined the Battalion:-
	2nd Lieuts. F. Holmes, H.R. Montgomery, E.J. Jordan
	D.J. Hughes, A.J. Yates, D. O'Shea.
19-10-16	Major R.H. L.C. Robinson joined the Battalion
12-10-16	2nd Lieut. R.G. Rourke wounded in action 2-10-16

3/12/16

Lieut. Colonel

O.C. 2nd Bn. Royal Dublin Fusrs.

Army Form C. [illegible]8

WAR DIARY
or
INTELLIGENCE SUMMARY
(Erase heading not required.)

Instructions regarding War Diaries and Intelligence Summaries are contained in F. S. Regs., Part II. and the Staff Manual respectively. Title Pages will be prepared in manuscript.

2nd Bn Royal Dublin Fusrs

Place	Date	Hour	Summary of Events and Information	Remarks and references to Appendices
	October 1916			
GUN PITS	23rd		The objective allotted to my Bn was on line from N 35. A 9 3 to T 5 b 3 6 + my assembly trenches were BURNABY, TOGGY, MUGGY and trench joining up TOGGY and ANDREWS POST (hereinafter called NEW TRENCH) My battalion was disposed as under:- Leading Companies. "D" Coy (Lieut MOFFAT), on right in NEW TRENCH. "C" Coy (CAPT PATTERSON on left in South end of BURNABY TRENCH + north end of TOGGY TRENCH Support Coys:- "A" Coy (Lieut GAFFNEY) in left of German Trench. "B" Coy (Lt BYRNE) in South End of TOGGY TRENCH, supporting D + C Coys respectively. At 2.30 p.m. the Bn went over the parapet in 4 waves, and doubled up to our own Artillery barrage. The Coys on the Right being some distance in rear of those on the left + had a considerable distance to double to get into Line. However the Battn got forward in time to escape the enemy's barrage. There were only 20 ft distance between waves on arriving at our own barrage. No opposition was met within about 30 ft of GUN PITS, when a heavy machine gun + rifle fire was met + compelled our leading lines to lie down. They however crawled forward + bombed the GUN PITS and eventually got into them, where very heavy hand to hand fighting ensued, and it was the survival of the fittest. The GUN PITS were strongly held and had 4 machine guns (three were destroyed) and 1 is now in the possession of my Bn. One Coy "C" went right thro' the Pits and on to the STRONG POINT, which was greatly damaged + knocked about by shell fire: little opposition was here met with, + this Coy went on + established a line about 200 ft beyond GUN PITS. Two Coys "A" + "B" remaining in GUN PITS + surrounding shell holes cleared up, which apparently was thoroughly well done. "A" Coy soon went up to line: "D" Coy remained to make certain + then went on to front line leaving 20 men to garrison these pits. "D" Coy on right got somewhat disconnected and a Platoon on the right got into touch with RIFLE BRIGADE on the right, the remaining three platoons going for GUN PITS + more or less changing their direction to left, leaving a gap of about 100 yards. This was caused, I think, by no definite line of trenches being observed + they were attracted by the GUN PITS + the fire from them. Consequently the congestion was rather great here, + to a great extent the cause of heavy casualties. However the majority of the casualties were caused	

Instructions regarding War Diaries and Intelligence Summaries are contained in F. S. Regs., Part II. and the Staff Manual respectively. Title Pages will be prepared in manuscript.

WAR DIARY
or
INTELLIGENCE SUMMARY
(Erase heading not required.)

Army Form C. 2118

October 1916 — 2nd Bn Royal Dublin Fusrs

Place	Date	Hour	Summary of Events and Information	Remarks and references to Appendices
GUN PITS	23rd		in the hand to hand fighting in the PITS & by M G fire just before getting into them. The whole of the GUN PITS, STRONG POINT & shell holes were held and third lines in front of the PITS dug & joined up. The first line newly dug, the second line through the enemys STRONG POINT, & the 3rd a new line in rear of this. The line joining these lines was dug as a defensive flank trench, and for protection from a M G which was [illegible] a lot of trouble from South of DEWDROP Trench. These lines were also joined up into GUN PITS. Trenches when handing over on relief were about 5 ft deep. The men dug with the greatest energy although the weather conditions were unfavourable for such work. [illegible] of DEWDROP Tr had been taken my battalion could have advanced with safety but [illegible] both my flanks being unprotected it was thought advisable to remain where we were as ammunition and bombs were running out, and the men were done up and I doubt whether they would have withstood a determined counterattack with both flanks exposed; and the danger was if counter attacked they might have been driven back right beyond the GUN PITS and I considered it best to make certain of these GUN PITS. The GUN PITS were knocked about by shells, but the dug outs were intact. There were 4 machine guns, 3 were damaged but one was taken and is now in the possession of my battalion. The 1st R WARWICKSHIRE REGT gave my battalion the greatest assistance and most effective support, the consolidation of the position being largely due to their assistance. At the final stage both battalions were fighting side by side and held the positions gained in this manner. No attempt was made to reorganize battalions till they were relieved on night of 24th October [illegible] rear of the line. The two battalions spent the night in digging.	

1875 Wt. W593/826 1.000,000 4/15 J.B.C. & A. A.D.S.S./Forms/C. 2118.

Army Form C. 2118

WAR DIARY
or
INTELLIGENCE SUMMARY
(Erase heading not required.)

Instructions regarding War Diaries and Intelligence Summaries are contained in F. S. Regs., Part II. and the Staff Manual respectively. Title Pages will be prepared in manuscript.

2nd Bn. Royal Dublin Fus.

Place	Date October 1916	Hour	Summary of Events and Information	Remarks and references to Appendices
GUNPITS	23		An attempt was made to get ammunition & bombs to the new lines on 23rd but was unsuccessful. I attach summary kept during operations. The men had a hard time of it & underwent severe trials, but throughout were cheerful and confident. (Sd) R G B JEFFREYS, Lieut-Col Comdg 2nd Bn Royal Dublin Fusrs. 25-10-16	
	24.		Fairly quiet day. Front line was fortunately not very heavily shelled. Orders for relief by 20th Royal Welsh - who are in 55th Divn received. Relief commenced 6.30 p.m.	
MANSEL CAMP.	25		Relief complete at 2.30 a.m. Battn marched to TRONES WOOD and had hot tea. At 6.0 a.m. marched off to MANSEL CAMP which was taken over from 9th H L I. Men were in a terrible mess but quite cheerful: accomodation was in tents.	
	26		Wet day. Orders received to move.	
CORBIE.	27		Entrained at CARNOY at 12.0 noon, arrived CORBIE 4.0 p.m. The Bn was accomodated in same billets as last time. The Bn now under orders B.G.C. 10th Inf: Bde	
	28		Battn reorganized: Battn paraded at 11.30 a.m. when B.G.C. 10th Inf: Bde thanked the Battn for work done in the attack on the GUNPITS. Major General Hon: W. LAMBTON also thank the Bn for the work on 23rd, and also conveyed the thanks of the EARL of CAVAN Comdg XIV Corps. Orders recd to move on the 30th to ARRAINES, & thence by road to HUPPY.	
	29		Fine day: reorganization of Battn carried on. First line of Transport was brigaded and marched by road to HUPPY. Our line halted at S. Sauveur for the night.	
	30.		Entrained at CORBIE at 12.35 p.m. & arrived at ARRAINES at 4.30 marched to HUPPY 12 miles, and arrived at 9.5 p.m. Fairly good billets but scattered.	
	31.		Fine day, kit inspections.	

R G B Jeffreys
Lieut. Colonel,
Comdg. 2nd Battn. Royal Dublin Fusrs.

1875 Wt. W593/826 1,000,000 4/15 J.B.C. & A. A.D.S.S./Forms/C. 2118.

2nd Bn Royal Dublin Fusiliers

Appendix to War Diary
Month of October 1916

Date	Remarks
1-10-16	2. Other Ranks joined the Battalion.
8-10-16	Temp. Captain R.H. Patterson rejoined the Bn. from Hospital.
6-10-16	2/Lt T.F. [illegible], transferred to England (sick).
10-10-16	Capt. [illegible] Wounded in Action.
12-10-16	2nd Lieut P.N. Green Wounded in Action.
12-10-16	8. Other Ranks Killed in Action.
	54 " " Wounded in Action
	4. " " Missing in Action.
13-10-16	2nd Lieut E.C.B. Dillon. Killed in Action
	2 Other Ranks " " "
	16. " " Wounded in Action.
14-10-16	1. Other Rank. Killed in Action.
	3. Other Ranks Wounded in Action.
	22. " " Joined the Battalion.
15-10-16	1 Other Rank Killed in Action.
	2. Other Ranks Wounded in Action
16-10-16	9. " " Killed in Action.
	14. " " Wounded in Action.
23-10-16	2nd Lieuts L.J. Doran, H.G. [illegible], H.J. [illegible], Killed in Action
	Lieut. J. [illegible] Wounded in Action.
	2nd Lieuts B.P. Glancy, R.F. [illegible], [illegible], H.D. Gibson
	Wounded in Action
	14. Other Ranks Killed in Action.
	124. " " Wounded in Action.

To be made up to and for Sunday in each week.

No. of Report ....

FIELD RETURN.

Army Form B. 213.

(To be furnished by all arms, services, and departments (except A.S.C. units) to the A. G.'s Office at the Base in accordance with Field Service Regulations, Part II.)

RETURN showing numbers (*a*) Effective strength of Unit. (*b*) Rationed by Unit. .... at .... Date.

Detail	Personnel: Officers	Personnel: Other ranks	Personnel: Natives	Animals: Horses: Riding	Animals: Horses: Draught	Animals: Horses: Heavy Draught	Animals: Horses: Pack	Animals: Mules: Large	Animals: Mules: Small	Animals: Camels	Animals: Oxen	Guns, carriages and limbers, showing description	Ammunition wagons and limbers	Machine guns	Aircraft, showing description	Horsed: 4 wheeled	Horsed: 2 wheeled	Mechanical: Motor Cars	Mechanical: Tractors	Mechanical: Lorries, showing description	Mechanical: Trucks, showing description	Mechanical: Trailers	Motor Bicycles	Bicycles	Remarks
Effective Strength of Unit																									
Details, *by Arms* attached to unit as in War Establishment:—																									
Total																									
War Establishment																									
Wanting to complete (Detail of Personnel and Horses below)																									
Surplus																									
*Attached (not to include the details shown above)																									
Civilians:— Employed with the Unit																									
Accompanying the Unit																									
Total Rationed...																									

* In the case of field ambulances, hospitals or depots, the number of patients are to be included here, the names being shown in A. F. A. 36.

.... Signature of Commander.

.... Date of Despatch.

For information of the A.G.'s Office at the Base.

Officers and men who have become casuals, been transferred or joined since last report.

Place In the Field Date 7 – 10 – 16

Regtl. Number	Rank	Name	Corps	Nature of casualty, or name of unit from or to which transferred	Date of being struck off or coming on the ration return	Remarks*
	Tempy Captain	R. M. Patterson	2nd Roy Dub Fusrs	Rejoined from [illegible]	[illegible] 16	
	Tempy Captain	S. J. Craddock	2nd Roy Dub Fusrs	Admitted to Hospl	3 – 10 – 16	
	2	O. Ranks joined	the Bn on the 1st 10 – 16			
24549	Pte	Kelly J	4th Bn Roy Dub Fusrs			
15414	"	Pidgeon J	4th Bn Roy Dub Fusrs			
23444	Pte	O'Hara J	2nd Bn Roy Dub Fusrs	Committed to Prison 4/10 Sentenced to 2 years H.L. 18th August 1916		

* State whether absence is of a permanent or temporary nature, adding, in the case of casuals from wounds or disease, any available information for communication to the relatives.

Only additional information regarding "wanting to complete" is to be entered on this side.

1 Sgt. Shoemaker required to replace Sgt. [illegible] for discharge November

6 Drummers required to complete

6 Signallers required

Perforated Sheet giving detail of personnel and horses wanting to complete, shown on Army Form B. 213.

Number of Report ________

Detail of Wanting to Complete	Drivers: R.A.	Drivers: R.E.	Drivers: A.S.C.	Drivers: Car	Drivers: Lorry	Drivers: Steam	Gunners	Smith Gunners	Range Takers	Farriers: Serjeants	Farriers: Corporals	Shoeing or Shoeing and Carriage Smiths	Cold Shoers	Wheelers: R.A.	Wheelers: H.T.	Wheelers: M.T.	Saddlers or Harness Makers	Blacksmiths	Bricklayers and Masons	Carpenters and Joiners	Fitters & Turners (R.E.): Wood	Fitters & Turners (R.E.): Iron	Fitters: R.A.	Fitters: Wireless	Plumbers	Electricians: Ordinary	Electricians: W.T.	Signalmen	Engine Drivers: Loco.	Engine Drivers: Field	Air Line Men	Permanent Line Men	Operators, Telegraph	Cablemen	Brigade Section Pioneers	General-duty Pioneers	Signallers	Instrument Repairers	Motor Cyclists	Motor Cyclist Artificers	Telephonists	Clerks	Machine Gunners	Armament Artificers: Fitters	Armament Artificers: Range Finders	Armourers	Storemen	Privates	W.O.'s and N.C.O.'s (by ranks not included in trade columns)						TOTAL to agree with wanting to complete: Officers	TOTAL: Other Ranks	Horses: Riding	Horses: Draught	Horses: Heavy Draught	Horses: Pack
CAVALRY																																																							2 Majors or Captains					
R.A.																																																											
R.E.																																																											
INFANTRY																																																15	1	46	1									
R.A.M.C.																																																											
A.O.C.*																																																											
A.V.C.																																																											

Remarks:—

[illegible] Signature of Commander.

[illegible] Unit.

[illegible] Formation to which attached.

6-10-16 Date of Despatch.

(B 99511.) Wt. W15519/M149. 1,000,000. 1/16. J. P. & Co., Ltd. Forms/B 213/7.

[P.T.O.

To be made up to and for Sunday in each week.

No. of Report 56

FIELD RETURN.

Army Form B. 213.

(To be furnished by all arms, services, and departments (except A.S.C. units) to the A. G.'s Office at the Base in accordance with Field Service Regulations, Part II.)

RETURN showing numbers (*a*) Effective strength of Unit. (*b*) Rationed by Unit. 2nd Bn Roy: Dublin Fus.s at In the field 14th Oct 1916. Date.

Detail	Personnel: Officers	Personnel: Other ranks	Personnel: Natives	Animals: Horses: Riding	Animals: Horses: Draught	Animals: Horses: Heavy Draught	Animals: Horses: Pack	Animals: Mules: Large	Animals: Mules: Small	Animals: Camels	Animals: Oxen	Guns, carriages and limbers, showing description	Ammunition wagons and limbers	Machine guns	Aircraft, showing description	Horsed: 4 wheeled	Horsed: 2 wheeled	Mechanical: Motor Cars	Mechanical: Tractors	Mechanical: Lorries, showing description	Mechanical: Trucks, showing description	Mechanical: Trailers	Motor Bicycles	Bicycles
Effective Strength of Unit	30	929		12	26	9	9						Lewis	8										
Details, *by Arms* attached to unit as in War Establishment:—																								
R.A.M.C.	1	5																						
A.O.C.		1																						
Total	31	935		12	26	9	9							8										
War Establishment	30	995		13	26	9	9							8										
Wanting to complete (Detail of Personnel and Horses below)	0	60		1	-	-	-																	
Surplus																								
*Attached (not to include the details shown above)		8																						
Civilians:— Employed with the Unit		1			1	3																		
Accompanying the Unit	1																							
Total Rationed...	19	835		12	27	12	9																	

Remarks

Details not away.

3rd Army School 4th Div	3	7
Grenade		2
10th Bde	1	18
4th Div. Res. Co		28
M.G. Coy	1	17
T.M.B.	1	10
10th Bde H.Q.	1	1
L.G. School	1	3
Hospital	3	
Base	1	3
Other details	1	18
	13	109

R.A.M.C.
A.S.C.
L.D. and H. Draught ...
Chaplain R.C.

* In the case of field ambulances, hospitals or depots, the number of patients are to be included here, the names being shown in A. F. A. 36.

R.G. Griffiths Lieut. Colonel. Signature of Commander.

14/10/16. Date of Despatch.

To be made up to and for Sunday in each week.

No. of Report 57

FIELD RETURN.

Army Form B. 213.

(To be furnished by all arms, services, and departments (except A.S.C. units) to the A. G.'s Office at the Base in accordance with Field Service Regulations, Part II.)

RETURN showing numbers (*a*) Effective strength of Unit. (*b*) Rationed by Unit. [illegible] at [illegible] 22-10-16 Date.

Detail	Personnel: Officers	Personnel: Other ranks	Personnel: Natives	Animals: Horses: Riding	Horses: Draught	Horses: Heavy Draught	Horses: Pack	Mules: Large	Mules: Small	Camels	Oxen	Guns, carriages and limbers, showing description	Ammunition wagons and limbers	Machine guns	Aircraft, showing description	Horsed: 4 wheeled	Horsed: 2 wheeled	Mechanical: Motor Cars	Mechanical: Tractors	Lorries, showing description	Trucks, showing description	Trailers	Motor Bicycles	Bicycles	Remarks
Effective Strength of Unit	29	849		12	26	9	9						Lewis	8											
Details, *by Arms* attached to unit as in War Establishment:—																									
R.A.M.C.	1	13																							
A.O.C.		1																							
Total	30	863		13	26	9	9							8											
War Establishment	30	[illegible]	[illegible]	13	26	[illegible]	[illegible]							8											
Wanting to complete (Detail of Personnel and Horses below)	5	132																							Majors or Capts
Surplus																									
*Attached (not to include the details shown above)	[illegible]				1	3																			4th A.S.C.
Civilians:— Employed with the Unit																									
Accompanying the Unit																									R.C. Chaplain
TOTAL RATIONED...	21	763		13	27	12	9																		

Details at Army School etc.	Off.	O.R.
3rd Army School		2
4th [illegible]		1
4th Div.	4	7
Brigade	1	2
10th Bde. H.Q.	1	19
Res. Coy.		20
M.G. Coy.	1	16
T.M.B.	1	9
Sick Absent		10
Hospital	2	
Other details		20
	10	106

* In the case of field ambulances, hospitals or depots, the number of patients are to be included here, the names being shown in A. F. A. 36.

[illegible] Lieut (A) Signature of Commander.

22-10-16 Date of Despatch.

For information of the A.G.'s Office at the Base.

Officers and men who have become casuals, been transferred or joined since last report.

Place In the field Date 14-10-16

Regtl. Number	Rank	Name	Corps	Nature of casualty, or name of unit from or to which transferred	Date of being struck off or coming on the ration return	Remarks*
	2/Lieut	E.C.B. Dillon		K. in A.	13-10-16	
	Capt	R. McT. Stobart		W. in A.	10-10-16	
	2/Lt	R.A. Bowker			12-10-16	
		P.N. Gordon			12-10-16	
	Lieut	J.A. Nesbitt	To 4th Div School of Instruct.		7-10-16	
	2/Lt	W. Callow				
		W.H. Hynes				
		G.L. Graham	To L.G. School	ETAPLES	7-10-16	
		Draft of Sergt Brown + 4 O.R.		Joined Bn.	11-10-16	
			32		14-10-16	

* State whether absence is of a permanent or temporary nature, adding, in the case of casuals from wounds or disease, any available information for communication to the relatives.

To be made up to and for Sunday in each week.

No. of Report 59

FIELD RETURN.

Army Form B. 213.

(To be furnished by all arms, services, and departments (except A.S.C. units) to the A. G.'s Office at the Base in accordance with Field Service Regulations, Part II.

RETURN showing numbers (a) Effective strength of Unit. (b) Rationed by Unit. 2nd Bn Royal Dublin Fusrs at In the Field. 29-10-16. Date.

Detail	Personnel: Officers	Personnel: Other ranks	Personnel: Natives	Horses: Riding	Horses: Draught	Horses: Heavy Draught	Horses: Pack	Mules: Large	Mules: Small	Camels	Oxen	Guns, carriages and limbers, showing description	Ammunition wagons and limbers	Machine guns	Aircraft, showing description	Horsed: 4 wheeled	Horsed: 2 wheeled	Mechanical: Motor Cars	Mechanical: Tractors	Mechanical: Lorries, showing description	Mechanical: Trucks, showing description	Mechanical: Trailers	Motor Bicycles	Bicycles
Effective Strength of Unit	26	665		12	26	9	9						Lewis	8										9
Details, by Arms attached to unit as in War Establishment:—																								
R.A.M.C.	1	5		1																				
A.O.C.		1																						
Total	27	671		13	26	9	9							8										
War Establishment	30	995		13	26	9	9							8										9
Wanting to complete (Detail of Personnel and Horses below)	3	324			–	–	–																	9
Surplus																								
*Attached (not to include the details shown above)	1																							
Civilians:— Employed with the Unit		2																						
Accompanying the Unit				1	5																			
Total Rationed...	18	555		27	14																			

Remarks: Detd. Rd. Away	Offrs.	O.R.
4th Army Schl.		3
4th Div	4	6
T.M.B.	1	8
4th D Res. Col.		23
M.G. Coy.	1	15
10th Bde H.Q.		19
A.P.M. Corbie		4
Leave & Course	1	13
Base	1	3
Hospital	1	21
11th Bde Details	1	1
	10	116

Remarks (continued): Copies & Maps; Chaplain R.C.; A.S.C. Attached; Attached.

* In the case of field ambulances, hospitals or depots, the number of patients are to be included here, the names being shown in A. F. A. 36.

Signature of Commander.

29-10-16. Date of Despatch.

For information of the A.G.'s Office at the Base.

Officers and men who have become casuals, been transferred or joined since last report.

Place

Date

Regtl. Number	Rank	Name	Corps	Nature of casualty, or name of unit from or to which transferred	Date of being struck off or coming on the ration return	Remarks*

* State whether absence is of a permanent or temporary nature, adding, in the case of casuals from wounds or disease, any available information for communication to the relatives.

For information of the A.G.'s Office at the Base.

Officers and men who have become casuals, been transferred or join'ed since last report.

Place In the Field Date 29-10-1916

Regtl. Number	Rank	Name	Corps	Nature of casualty, or name of unit from or to which transferred	Date of being struck off or coming on the ration return	Remarks*
	2/Lt	L. J. Doran ~~E. B. Dillon~~	K-in-A		23-10-16	
	–	H. J. Lewers	– – –		– –	
	–	H. G. Killingley	– –		– –	
	–	B. P. Glacey	W^d – –		– –	
	–	W. H. Hynes	– – –		– –	
	–	H. W. Gibson	– – –		– –	
	–	R. F. Holder	– – –			
	Lt.	J. Gaffney				
	Major	R. H. S. C. Robinson	3rd Bn R.D.F.	joined Bn	27-10-16	
	2/Lt.	D. I. Inglis	–	– –	– –	
	–	J. E. Jordan	–	– –	– –	
	–	M. R. Montgomery	–	– –	– –	
	–	A. Holmes	–	–	– –	
	–	A. J. Yates	–	–	– –	
	–	H. O'Shea	–	– –	– –	
18369	Pte	Clarke	Rejoined from prison		27-10-16.	
		(on Remission A.G.G.H.Q., D/121 d. 21-10-1916).				
16831	Pte	White.	2nd R.D.F.	rejoined from V Corps &	25-10-16.	
		I.O.M. 27 Ordnance Workshop				

* State whether absence is of a permanent or temporary nature, adding, in the case of casuals from wounds or disease, any available information for communication to the relatives.

Only additional information regarding "wanting to complete" is to be entered on this side.

Only additional information regarding "wanting to complete" is to be entered on this side.

Perforated Sheet giving detail of personnel and horses wanting to complete, shown on Army Form B. 213.

Number of Report 59

Detail of Wanting to Complete				
CAVALRY				
R.A.				
R.E.				
INFANTRY				
R.A.M.C.	8	365	Cooks & Majors.	3324
A.O.C.				
A.V.C.				

Sergt Shoemaker

Remarks:—

R.L.[illegible] Lieut. Col. Signature of Commander.

2nd Bn Royal Dublin Fus. Unit.

4th Div., 10th Inf. Bde. Formation to which attached.

29-10-16. Date of Despatch.

[P.T.O.

(B 99019) Wt W15190/M149. 1,000,000. 1/16. J. P. & Co. Ltd. Forms/B 213/7.

Only additional information regarding "wanting to complete" is to be entered on this side.

Perforated Sheet giving detail of personnel and horses wanting to complete, shown on Army Form B. 213.

Number of Report 57

Detail of Wanting to Complete	Drivers R.A.	Drivers R.E.	Drivers A.S.C.	Drivers Car	Drivers Lorry	Drivers Steam	Gunners	Smith Gunners	Range Takers	Farriers Serjeants	Farriers Corporals	Shoeing or Shoeing and Carriage Smiths	Cold Shoers	Wheelers R.A.	Wheelers H.T.	Wheelers M.T.	Saddlers or Harness Makers	Blacksmiths	Bricklayers and Masons	Carpenters and Joiners	Fitters & Turners (R.E.) Wood	Fitters & Turners (R.E.) Iron	Fitters R.A.	Fitters Wireless	Plumbers	Electricians Ordinary	Electricians W.T.	Signalmen	Engine Drivers Loco	Engine Drivers Field
CAVALRY																													
R.A.																													
R.E.																													
INFANTRY																													
R.A.M.C.																													
A.O.C.																													
A.V.C.																													

Detail of Wanting to Complete	Air Line Men	Permanent Line Men	Operators, Telegraph	Cablemen	Brigade Section Pioneers	General duty Pioneers	Signallers	Instrument Repairers	Motor Cyclists	Motor Cyclist Artificers	Telephonists	Clerks	Machine Gunners	Armament Artificers Fitters	Armament Artificers Range Finders	Armourers	Storemen	Privates	W.O.'s and N.C.O.'s (by ranks) not included in trade columns: Sergt. Shoemaker	TOTAL to agree with wanting to complete: Officers (Including 1 Capt.)	TOTAL Other Ranks	Horses Riding	Horses Draught	Horses Heavy Draught	Horses Pack
CAVALRY																									
R.A.																									
R.E.																									
INFANTRY																		131	1	5	132				
R.A.M.C.																									
A.O.C.																									
A.V.C.																									

Remarks:—

Lieut Col ....Signature of Commander.

2nd Bn Royal Dublin Fusrs ....Unit.

10th I.Bde 4th Divn ....Formation to which attached.

22-10-16. ....Date of Despatch.

(B 9961.) Wt. W15519/M149. 1,000,000. 1/16. J. P. & Co., Ltd. Forms/B 213/7.

[P.T.O.

Perforated Sheet giving detail of personnel and horses wanting to complete, shown on Army Form B. 213.

Number of Report 56.

Detail of Wanting to Complete	Drivers						Gunners	Smith Gunners	Range Takers	Farriers		Shoeing, or Shoeing and Carriage Smiths	Cold Shoers	Wheelers			Saddlers or Harness Makers	Blacksmiths	Bricklayers and Masons	Carpenters and Joiners	Fitters & Turners (R.E.)		Fitters		Plumbers
	R.A.	R.E.	A.S.C.	Car	Lorry	Steam				Serjeants	Corporals			R.A.	H.T.	M.T.					Wood	Iron	R.A.	Wireless	
CAVALRY																									
R.A.																									
R.E.																									
INFANTRY																									
R.A.M.C.																									
A.O.C.																									
A.V.C.																									

Detail of Wanting to Complete	Electricians		Signalmen	Engine Drivers		Air Line Men	Permanent Line Men	Operators, Telegraph	Cablemen	Brigade Section Pioneers	General-duty Pioneers	Signallers	Instrument Repairers	Motor Cyclists	Motor Cyclist Artificers	Telephonists	Clerks	Machine Gunners	Armament Artificers		Armourers	Storemen	Privates
	Ordinary	W.T.		Loco.	Field														Fitters	Range Finders			
CAVALRY																							
R.A.																							
R.E.																							
INFANTRY												6											
R.A.M.C.																							
A.O.C.																							
A.V.C.																							

Detail of Wanting to Complete	W.O.'s and N.C.O.'s (by ranks) not included in trade columns									TOTAL to agree with wanting to complete		Horses			
	Serjt Shoemaker						Drummers			Officers	Other Ranks	Riding	Draught	Heavy Draught	Pack
CAVALRY															
R.A.															
R.E.															
INFANTRY	1						6			-	47				
R.A.M.C.															
A.O.C.															
A.V.C.															

Remarks:—

[signature] Lieut. Col. Signature of Commander.

2nd Bn Royal Dublin Fus. Unit.

4th Div. 10th Inf. Bde Formation to which attached.

14th Oct 1916. Date of Despatch.

(B 99511) Wt. W15519/M149. 1,000,000. 1/16. J. P. & Co., Ltd. Forms/B. 213/7.

[P.T.O.

www.ingramcontent.com/pod-product-compliance
Lightning Source LLC
Chambersburg PA
CBHW080859230426
43663CB00013B/2582
* 9 7 8 1 4 7 4 5 0 5 1 7 8 *